PRINCESS

VIJAYARAJE SCINDIA
with MANOHAR MALGONKAR

PRINCESS

The Autobiography of
the Dowager Maharani of Gwalior

CENTURY PUBLISHING

LONDON

Back cover photograph/The palace at Gwalior, 1882
Copyright © Vijayaraje Scindia and Manohar Malgonkar

First published in Great Britain in 1985
by Century Hutchinson Ltd,
Brookmount House,
62–65 Chandos Place,
Covent Garden, London WC2N 4NW

British Library Cataloguing in Publication Data

Scindia, Vijayaraje
Princess: the autobiography of the dowager
Maharani of Gwalior.
1. Scindia—Vijayaraje   2. India—Kings
and rulers—Biography
I. Title   II. Malgonkar, Manohar
954.04′092′4   DS481.S3/

ISBN 0 7126 1035 9

Typeset by Deltatype, Ellesmere Port
Printed in Great Britain by
St Edmundsbury Press, Bury St Edmunds, Suffolk
Bound by Butler & Tanner Ltd, Frome, Somerset

Contents

PART I

IN THE SHADOW OF NEPAL

CHAPTER ONE
Grandfather Khadga

I WAS BORN in a place called Sagar, a small district town in the folds of the Vindhya mountains of Madhya Pradesh in India. Madhya Pradesh means 'the Central State'. In the days of the British this part of India was known as 'the Central Provinces'. My home town might justifiably claim to be the very navel of India. And yet, the world I grew up in was not of India; it was more like a segment of Nepal transplanted to the heartland of the Indian subcontinent: a couple of hundred acres of sparsely forested hillside overlooking the lake of Sagar, where the British had permitted my maternal grandfather to put down his roots.

Khadga Samsher Jung Bahadur Rana was marked by destiny to play a major role in the history of his country, Nepal. As it was, he turned out to be one of its more awkward rejects, being only in his mid-thirties when he was forced to flee Nepal and to seek asylum in what was then the Raj. The British, ever indulgent to a scion of the Ranas of Nepal in distress, readily obliged. All they asked for was that he should not live in any of their provinces that bordered Nepal and that he should refrain from consorting with the dozen or so other Ranas who were also political refugees in India.

My grandfather eventually chose Sagar because the hills and the jungles reminded him of his native land. Here he built a huge mansion and created around himself a make-believe Nepal. Behind the house the two horseshoes of servants' quarters were crammed with retainers brought from Nepal. The language of the household was Gurkhali, the language of Nepal. Although the gods in the family shrine were the same gods that the Indians worshipped, the forms of our prayers, our rituals and our festivals were those of Nepal. Even as he was building the house, the people of Sagar had taken to calling it 'the Nepal Palace', and that was the name that stuck.

*　　*　　*

My only memory of my grandfather is of when he was about to be taken to Benaras to die. As I was later to learn, he was the sort of man who, rather than letting events overtake him, strove to shape them to fit into his plans; if he found that he could not alter their course he preferred to meet them halfway and on ground of his own choosing. Now he had decided to meet death halfway, and in Benaras, which, after all, was the proper place for Hindus to die with their feet immersed in the sacred waters of the River Ganges and the prayers of the priests ringing in their ears: 'Wasansi jeernani yatha vihaya . . . even as we cast off old clothes, so does the immortal soul abandon a worn out body.'

It is strange that I should remember the event at all, for I could not have been much more than two years old. But the magnitude of the crisis that had gripped our household must have made an impression on my consciousness. I remember that, as I stood in the doorway of his bedroom, my hands were fumbling with the wooden catch which kept the door open. He had been transferred from his bed into one of those reclining cane-bottomed chairs with extendable arms, which were designed to prop your feet up and were as much a feature of the Raj as solar topees or punkhas. He was bundled up in a soft quilted cover, for it was one of those crisply cold mornings of the Central Indian winter. As I watched, fascinated but detached, four servants filed in, lifted the chair and carried it deftly away. One was my own man-servant whom my grandmother had allotted to me in addition to my three personal maids.

I turned away from the vast, empty room, with its faint smell of hookah tobacco and cough drops, and scampered onto the balcony which overlooked the front porch. One of the servants held me up so that I could see what was going on. Below me, drawn up near the front steps, was what must have been one of the very first motor cars in Sagar. Around the canvas-topped maroon tourer, with its bulb horn and gleaming brass lamps, stood my uncles, their wives and children, relations by marriage, dependants and servants.

For a long time, or so it seemed, nothing happened. They must, of course, have been waiting for the precise moment worked out by the family priests as being the most propitious for such a departure. When that moment came, my grandfather was lifted tenderly out of his chair and placed on the rear seat of the car beside my grandmother. As the car began to move, those who were gathered round it bowed, their hands folded in a last farewell to a man who, for so many years, had formed the very centre of their world. They were still bent, as though trying to hide their tears from my grandmother's notice, when the car gathered speed and disappeared among the trees beyond the tennis court.

*　　*　　*

This picture of my grandfather as an inert bundle being taken away to be transformed into a corpse could hardly be less fair to his memory. Khadga Samsher was above all a Rana of Nepal. He revelled in the dominance of his sex; he was a soldier and a hunter, a strutting egocentric who, reputedly, felt more at home in the saddle than the chair, attired in the gaudy uniform of an officer of the Nepalese army.

He could not have been quite thirty years old when he had contrived to make himself the army's Commander-in-Chief. The coup had been both swift and bloody. My grandfather was known to have committed at least one murder: he killed his uncle, Rana Ranadip, the ruling Maharaja of Nepal. Two other members of the Rana family, Jagat Jung and his son Judha Pratap, were also killed that night, but whether by my grandfather or by his brother (and fellow conspirator), Bir Samsher, was never conclusively established.

My grandmother, fiercely loyal to her husband, could never bring herself to think of these events as even remotely reprehensible. 'A confrontation between two rival factions,' was how she put it. 'A brave man seeking out and killing those enemies who were plotting to do away with him. By the grace of God, your grandfather came out the winner in that struggle. The entire army was on his side, the army and the people of

Nepal too. Otherwise the plot would never have succeeded, would it? His was the right cause.'

Right or wrong, what my grandfather did on that night nearly a hundred years ago provides a glimpse of the snake-pit of intrigue and venom that the court of Nepal had become in the last quarter of the nineteenth century.

*   *   *

In those days the king of Nepal was, if anything, even more of a figurehead than the 'constitutional' monarch of today. The real power was wielded by the Maharaja of Nepal, who was also the Prime Minister. It was he who was the absolute ruler of the country and who, by an unalterable decree called a *sanad*, had been invested with the power to 'appoint and dismiss all government servants, declare war, make peace and sign treaties with foreign powers, make new laws and repeal old ones'.

The supreme office of the Maharaja had been made hereditary, the exclusive preserve of one family, the Ranas. Unusually, the succession did not pass to the eldest son, but 'to the oldest surviving male member of the generation ... priority of birth being the principal consideration between brother and cousin'.

This preposterous system of succession had been devised by Maharaja Jung Bahadur, a man who is generally regarded as a sort of colossus of the Rana clan and indeed of Nepal itself. In 1841 he seized power by a military coup and then ruled his land with a whip hand for the next thirty-six years. He managed to divest the king of all power and banished him to a limbo or, as he chose to describe it, 'a pinnacle of power from which he should never descend to demean himself with the humdrum affairs of administration'. Jung Bahadur fathered more than a dozen sons, of whom at least ten were alive at the time of his death in 1877. Before he had himself transported to the banks of the Bagmati River in preparation for its advent, however, he passed on the reins of office to his youngest brother, Ranadip. Ranadip's successor, of course, would be whoever happened to be the most senior in the next generation of the clan.

But the next generation was not prepared to sit back and

await its turn. There were at least a score of Rana siblings who believed that they had a fair chance of becoming the Maharaja of Nepal. The most impatient among them was Jung Bahadur's eldest son, Jagat Jung. A headstrong and crafty man who held the rank of Major-General, he had always taken it for granted that he would succeed his father, and he had strong allies among the senior courtiers. His two principal rivals were the sons of Jung Bahadur's brother, Dhir Samsher, Bir Samsher and his younger brother Khadga Samsher, my maternal grandfather.

Jagat Jung was the first to act. He hatched a plot to exterminate Rana Ranadip. But the plot was discovered and Jagat Jung was banished to India. Twenty-one co-conspirators were ceremonially beheaded. Several years later, however, in 1884, a curt announcement from the Thapatali Palace declared that Ranadip had granted a full pardon to his cousin. Jagat Jung returned to Katmandu, and soon afterwards he was reinstated in the role of succession.

While, to most outsiders, this appeared to be no more than an act of misplaced magnanimity, the courtiers of Nepal were quick to read the signs. Jagat Jung, in another bid to make himself master of Nepal, had somehow managed to enlist the Maharaja himself on his side. It was apparent that a new alignment of forces had taken place, and its targets were the two young men whose names were also high up in the list of succession, Bir Samsher and Khadga Samsher.

In his book, *Nepal the Home of the Gods*, Sardar Ikbal Ali Shah described the situation almost in the very words that my grandmother used in describing it to me:

> Gradually (Jagat Jung) assumed a position which spelt ill for Bir Samsher and his brother . . . the enmity between the two branches of the family was such that their very lives were endangered. The time came when they had seriously to consider a situation which had already passed beyond the intolerable, and they had to decide whether they should quietly await the death which was being prepared for them, or take action.

My grandmother, and others who knew the Samsher brothers well, believed that, left to himself, Bir would have done nothing: 'He just did not have the gumption. And even if he had, how could he have gained entry into the Maharaja's private chambers?' my grandmother would ask.

'How could Grandfather?'

'For him it was easy. He was the English reader to the Court; he opened all English letters and had them translated. All he had to say was that he had an urgent message to deliver.'

So Bir Samsher was persuaded that unless they acted boldly they would both be put to death. 'All you need to do is to stand beside me,' Khadga is said to have told him, 'I'll do whatever is to be done.'

The twenty-second of December 1885 was a cold but bright day, my grandmother remembered: 'Overnight the mountains had crept closer. Your grandfather had spent the morning at his brother's house. Towards evening, he came home and told me that he was about to go on a mission from which he might not return.' He waited for night to fall before setting out again, putting on his favourite 'British Warm' with deep pockets. He called for his brother and together they went to the Prime Minister's palace.

According to my grandmother, whose account was, I am sure, more authentic than the history books', her husband brushed past the guards at the door, saying that he had an important letter from the British Resident which needed immediate action. The brothers were admitted into the bedchamber where Maharaja Ranadip was having his legs massaged by a bevy of maidservants. He sat up in bed and asked: '*Ke ho?* (What is it?)'.

'*Yeh!*' Khadga told him as he pulled out his revolver and fired two shots into him at pointblank range.

That night their cousin, Jagat Jung, and his son were also murdered. Which brother was responsible was never revealed, but in our house in Sagar it was always taken for granted that my grandfather committed all three murders.

*   *   *

The very next day Bir Samsher became the Maharaja of Nepal and promptly appointed my grandfather as the Commander-in-Chief of Nepal's army. Both the court and the army hierarchy seemed to accept the new men at the top without demur. As for my grandfather, he had achieved the goal of his life: to be the chief soldier in a land that venerated the profession of arms. He loved uniforms, parades and martial music. It was his ambition to modernize Nepal's army along British lines, and he set about doing so with the single-minded zeal of a schoolboy playing with toy soldiers.

'After all, if he had really wanted to make himself the Maharaja, he could have so easily done so at the time of the coup or soon after, couldn't he?' my grandmother would argue. 'As the Commander-in-Chief he was the most powerful man in Nepal and his officers and men used to adore him.'

I myself have never questioned this. Khadga was now number two in the line of succession and the Maharaja, whom he had, so to speak, frog-marched into that position, was his meek and easy-going brother.

That was just the rub. Bir Samsher was a man without a will of his own; like his predecessors in office, he had a domineering wife with whom he was hopelessly infatuated. My grandmother, who knew her and did not like her, thought her bold, crude and cunning. 'In the court she would openly taunt her husband that he was nothing but a puppet ruler; that all Nepal knew that a leaf could not stir without Khadga Samsher's orders. Oh, it did not take her long to poison his mind, to make it appear that his brother was secretly plotting to take over. Was not his absorption in the army itself proof of such designs?'

Was it? Nepal's historians also seem to think that it was. On the other hand, my grandfather's reactions should absolve him from suspicion of any sinister designs. His was the reaction of a man taken wholly by surprise, not of a plotter who could not have failed to take the most elementary precautions against discovery and the inevitable retribution. The schoolboy had been caught playing truant and gamely accepted his chastisement.

A few months after his appointment, out of the blue, he was served with a 'Red Flag Order'. A messenger came from the palace, bearing a letter and a red flag and accompanied by a heavy military escort. The letter had to be opened in front of the messenger and instantly acted upon. Khadga's Order told him that he had been removed from his post of Commander-in-Chief and banished to Palpa, the westernmost province of Nepal. Palpa was at least two hundred miles from the Katmandu valley, and the only road to it was a mule track.

Without hesitation he gave up his office and repaired to Palpa, where he lived for the next two years, an exuberant, restless man of action, consigned to a limbo and watched over by teams of informers. Whether the Maharaja was shamed by the dignity and decorum of his brother's conduct, or regretted his harshness towards the man who, after all, had made him the Maharaja of Nepal, two years later he relented. In the autumn of 1887 he appointed Khadga Governor of the Palpa province.

If this was something of a comedown from being head of Nepal's army, at least it showed that he was back in favour. Since the Maharaja himself had served as Governor of Palpa a few years earlier, surely it would not be long before he was restored to his rightful position as heir apparent?

Meanwhile, there were compensations. As the Governor, he would have a small garrison under his command and could once again play at soldiers to his heart's content. He pounced on this force, which could have been hardly more than a battalion in strength. He drilled them, smartened up their uniforms, assembled a band for them and put them through manoeuvres. The ever-watchful informers took note and made reports. In Katmandu, a week's distance away by fast runners acting in relays, these reports sparked old fears. Khadga was up to his tricks again. All this hectic military activity could have only one purpose: mutiny.

Such was the official view, and it was almost inevitable that it should be reflected in the history books of the times, which were sponsored by the reigning maharajas.

Within days, over the dizzy mountain tracks fanning out from the capital, came another dreaded Red Flag Order. My grandfather was banished from Nepal and his name was removed from the list of succession. A number of others who were said to have been implicated in the plot were put to death.

If Khadga had really organized a mutiny, surely, with enough troops under his command to overcome the escort that had accompanied the Red Flag messenger, he could have defied the order? But this time, too, he obeyed with alacrity and that very day, or the next, headed for India.

Far from turning his back on Nepal, he was convinced that

his exile was no more than a phase and that he would be back again as Maharaja of Nepal after his brother's death. That he was to be the Maharaja was something pre-ordained, written by the moving finger of Pashupatinath, Katmandu's presiding deity. For Rana Khadga Samsher had in his possession the Gajmani.

The Gajmani was not a pearl; it looked like a pearl, with both the sheen and the translucence of nacre but it was, in fact, an oval-shaped piece of bone the size of a pigeon's egg. It had been found embedded in the forehead of Nepal's legendary eighteenth-century elephant, Gajaraj, who was said to have been twelve feet tall. Today you can see his enormous skull in the Royal Museum at Katmandu, with a hole the size of a cricket ball right in the middle of the forehead where the stone had been hacked out.

This great unnatural pearl the Ranas believed was some sort of a diabolical talisman, which could bring either good or bad luck, make its possessor rich and powerful or cause his ruin. Khadga Samsher never doubted that it would bring him anything but good luck; indeed, that it would make him the master of Nepal. But how he came to acquire the Gajmani is his own secret; if he told it to my grandmother, she for her part never revealed it. It had been one of Jung Bahadur's most prized possessions before he had passed it on to his eldest son, Jagat Jung. Had my grandfather, when he (or his brother) murdered Jagat Jung, taken it from the shrine where it was kept as an object of daily worship? The fact that he had chosen to take it out with him in his saddlebag as he fled to India shows how much store he had set by it.

After he left, it took my grandmother months of agonizing entreaties to her brother-in-law to be given permission to follow her husband into exile. As soon as it was given she lost little time in making tracks for India, taking with her her children, dependants and servants. Her husband had, in the meantime, bought an estate outside Dehra Dun in the Himalayan foothills, not more than a day's march from Nepal's borders. Thither my grandmother travelled over the fern-filled goat tracks crawling with leeches, in a mile-long caravan of mules and palanquins carried by a hundred or so bearers. In the upholstery of these palanquins she somehow managed to secrete much more of the family's gold, jewellery and other valuables than her permit entitled her to take out of the country. Practical above all, she had confined her selection strictly to whatever was most valuable.

For my grandfather Dehra Dun should have been a sort of paradise. The jungles surrounding it were teeming with game, and here he could indulge his passion for hunting to his heart's content. What was more, Dehra Dun also sheltered two other Rana families who had been expelled from Nepal as a consequence of earlier struggles for power. Here my grand-parents could talk about the past, compare notes and exchange gossip in their own language, even share their dreams.

But it took them years to settle down. The spell of Nepal held them, and they believed it was their destiny to return. Any day now, another Red Flag Order would come, this time recalling my grandfather to take his rightful place in the Rana hierarchy.

It was not until a new century had dawned and, almost coinciding with it, drastic changes occurred in Nepal, that my grandparents freed themselves from the spell of Nepal. Maharaja Bir Samsher died, and his place was taken by Khadga's younger brother Deva Samsher. It was a measure of my grandfather's acceptance of his lot that he sent an exuberant message to the new Maharaja, praising him and wishing him well.

Deva Samsher, however, was fated not to rule long. Within a couple of months of his accession, Nepal saw something of a repeat performance of my grandfather's coup. Yet another of his numerous younger brothers, Chandra Samsher, forced Deva to abdicate at the point of a gun, and made himself Maharaja.

Deva, an educated man who spoke English well and was enamoured of Western society, chose the hill resort of Mussoorie, famous for its cosmopolitan gaiety and licence. But Mussoorie is barely a dozen miles from Dehra Dun, and what was to prevent that arch-intriguer, Khadga Samsher, from enlisting his brother's help in hatching yet another of his infernal plots to become the Maharaja of Nepal?

Khadga had to be shifted to somewhere well away from

Benaras or Dehra Dun, where the Ranas in exile had tended to congregate. Chandra Samsher therefore sent emissaries to Calcutta to wait upon the Viceroy. Lord Curzon was at the time hatching his own plot to bring off an invasion of Nepal's northern neighbour, Tibet. He was more than anxious to maintain amicable relations with whoever was in power in Nepal, and readily cooperated.

So, in the winter of 1902, another peremptory message was brought to Khadga Samsher, this time not by a Red Flag messenger but by a polished civil servant of the Raj, who carried with him a polite but firm request from the Indian Government to remove himself more towards the centre of the subcontinent. He was assured that the administrators of the Raj would give him all possible help in choosing his place of residence.

Having been uprooted from Dehra Dun, my grandparents eventually settled down in Sagar, where they lived happily for the next twenty years. Here they made a new beginning, raised their children and made friends. Thanks largely to the risks my grandmother had run in bringing the extra trinkets out of Nepal, they were in a position to lead a low-key princely life. Until that day in November 1921, when another sort of Red Flag Order arrived; this time from death itself. And, as on the two previous occasions, my grandfather hastened to obey.

*   *   *

I shall finish the story of the Gajmani here. After my grandfather had become reconciled to the fact that he would never see Nepal again, he had the stone set into a brooch in the shape of a peacock with a fanned-out tail, the stone forming the chest and the tail made by emeralds and diamonds. My grandmother wore it on festive occasions. On my grandfather's death, the precious stones were shared out among his sons, the Gajmani itself being left to the eldest, my uncle Hem Samsher. He died at an early age and his daughter, Khem Kuwar, inherited it. After her husband's retirement from the army he became the manager of an apple orchard I had acquired in the Himalayas. He died while still in his fifties, and I remember Khem coming to me in tears and almost literally throwing the stone in my lap. She believed the Gajmani had brought her and her father nothing but bad luck. Being superstitious myself, I did not want to keep a fetish of such unpredictable properties. I therefore offered it to my husband's Bombay jeweller, Nanubhai, who – since it had no intrinsic value – bought it for the equivalent of £150. In 1967, on a visit to Nepal as a guest of King Mahendra, I saw the elephant's skull in the museum. Thinking it best that the Gajmani should return to where it originally came from, I bought it back from Nanubhai, who was glad to sell it to me for exactly the price he had paid for it. I then sent the Gajmani as a present to King Mahendra. Judging by the eminence he has acquired in Nepal's affairs, I can only surmise that it has served His Majesty well.

CHAPTER TWO

I Become a Ward

THE RANAS WERE originally Rajputs from India who had
invaded Nepal and eventually become its rulers. They were
also orthodox Hindus who, for nearly two centuries, had lived
among a people who were, for the most part, Buddhists.
Inevitably, to their own special stock of superstitions, taboos
and prejudices, they had added those of the people of Nepal.

My maternal grandmother was, of course, steeped in this
culture. And yet she must have possessed a streak of rugged
independence because, as soon as she became settled in her
new environment, she began to shed some of the more
oppressive restraints of the old. For her models she had the
wives of the British officials of Sagar — the same gossipy
women whom a young British subaltern named Winston
Churchill had dismissed as 'nasty vulgar creatures'. To her
they must have seemed exquisitely self-assured and emanci-
pated.

It was my grandfather who ruled the household; indeed, he
was regarded as something of a tyrant by his sons and
daughters, my uncles and aunts. And yet he made a valiant
effort to fit his family into the new social order in which he
found himself. He encouraged his wife to go riding along the
shaded cantonment roads, side-saddle and dressed, like
Sagar's memsahibs, in green or plum-coloured velvet habits.
She also was given piano lessons and taught to sing English
songs. I remember her at her piano in the upstairs reception
room, the afternoon sunlight slanting through the open
windows and making the carpets glint. She was thumping out
a tune with fierce concentration and singing in a slightly

trembly voice, which may well have been in imitation of some memsahibs's:

'Darling, I am growing old, silver threads among the gold.'

Of course, she did not have golden hair; it was jet black. But then she had no idea what the words of the song meant; she knew no English, even though she had taught herself to sign her name in it.

The Ranas scoffed at book learning. Until the last quarter of the nineteenth century, there was not a single school in the whole of their kingdom. The male offspring, such as my grandfather, were given a rudimentary education and, on the whole, taught to speak English by family tutors recruited from Bengal. But such education as there was was a male privilege, and the general attitude towards literacy was one of disapproval mixed with contempt, as bearing the taint of such non-martial classes of Nepalese society as priests or shopkeepers. The very thought of educating a Rana girl would have sent shockwaves through the clan councils. Who would ever marry such an oddity when, as it was, they were finding it necessary to send scouts ever deeper into India to look for bridegrooms of the requisite lineage and to agree to extortionate dowries!

That my mother should have received any education at all in the teeth of such prejudice must be ascribed to the influence of the memsahibs of Sagar upon my grandmother. To her they represented both glamour and emancipation. She was resolved not to let her daughter grow up with the handicaps she herself had suffered. My grandfather, for all his reputation for sternness, must have given in with good grace, only stipulating that their daughter should not be sent to the local school, for that too would have been an outrage against his idea of decorum. So my grandmother employed a set of private tutors at home. My mother became the very first Nepalese girl to pass the matriculation examination. This achievement was duly acknowledged by her uncle, Chandra Samsher, Maharaja of Nepal, by the grant of a special prize of Rs 1000, a sum which in those days represented princely munificence.

Over the years the two brothers had patched up their differences, or at least had come to terms with the realities of their situations. Khadga sent reassurances to his brother that he never had any thought of ousting him from his position. Chandra, for his part, could afford to be magnanimous. In 1909, during an official visit made by Chandra Semsher to Calcutta, then capital of India, he invited his brother to a meeting. After they had embraced each other, Khadga explained that he wanted nothing more than to be allowed to live out his days in Sagar as a country gentleman. He wished his brother well in all that he was doing to modernize Nepal. Chandra then bestowed on Khadga the title of His Highness and Raja and, what must have been even more welcome, settled on him a generous pension.

*   *   *

My mother was keen to continue her studies in college. She was a strong-willed person, and also happened to be her father's favourite. She wore down her parents' opposition and secured admission to the Isabella Thoburn Women's College in Lucknow. Since there was no question of a Rana living in a women's hostel which was open to all castes, creeds and social backgrounds, a pleasant bungalow was rented for her near the college, staffed with Sagar servants.

Colleges in India open after the summer vacation in mid-June. Barely had my mother settled into her new routine when Lucknow was deluged by one of the worst floods in its history. The normally placid River Gomati broke its banks and raced through the low-lying areas. Its waters entered my mother's bungalow and swept away most of her belongings; she herself had to be carried pick-a-back by one of her servants to safety. She returned to Sagar in something of a daze. Her parents took the floods as an unmistakable warning from the gods against an outrageous violation of the proprieties. Then, with renewed fervour, they set about doing what their daughter's absurd passion for studies had prevented: finding a husband for her.

*   *   *

The year was 1917. The First World War was entering its fourth and darkest year. There must have been more than a dozen Rana families living in exile in various parts of India. Most of them were still very rich, and nearly all had numerous daughters. Because of their severed connections from the land of their birth, the daughters had to be found husbands from among the Rana connections in India, and these were restricted to the few Rajput clans from which they themselves had sprung. The most desirable grooms, of course, were the sons of Rajput princes or of rich landowners. They proved not to be particularly difficult to snare: Rana girls were proverbially good looking, with dark, dancing almond-shaped eyes and glowing petal-smooth complexions; and the Ranas were well known to be generous with dowries.

But it was this class which formed the entrenched rearguard of feudal privileges, in particular of multiple marriages for men and of the seclusion in purdah for women. There were even said to be a few who secretly regretted the banning of *sati*, the practice of widow-burning. Any Rajput prince who did not possess half a dozen legal wives and at least as many concubines would have been regarded by his peers as something of an eccentric or, worse, too impoverished to afford a properly-stocked harem or even, the ultimate insult, lacking in manly vigour. On the other hand, if any one of their wives or concubines were to allow herself to be seen in public she would have been at once branded as a shameless hussy who had violated the hallowed traditions of her class.

My grandparents seem to have been determined not to consign their educated daughter to living in some sealed-off apartment in a prince's palace. Instead, they would find her a husband from a respectable family, capable of earning a decent living – someone, in fact, who came closest to the official élite of Sagar.

As was customary among the Rana families in exile, the search was entrusted to middlemen from the priestly caste. Before long they turned up with the name of a young man who exactly answered my grandmother's requirements. Thakur Mahendra Singh came from a respectable Rajput family with a lineage uncontaminated by misalliances. Tall, handsome and in good health, he was also something of a physical fitness faddist: a wrestler and the possessor of a splendid torso of rippling muscles. He was a university graduate and held a job as Deputy Collector in one of the highest paid government services.

It is not easy in the permissive social climate of today to come to terms with the prevailing attitudes of the first quarter of this century. If my grandparents had broken a minor taboo of their Rana past, their daughter displayed a mystifyingly primitive response. Once they had shown her a photograph of her chosen husband-to-be, she not only approved but also, almost in imitation of the heroine of some mythological romance, at once considered herself irrevocably affianced to him.

Cheered by her acceptance, they proceeded to seal the engagement with the proper exchange of gifts, and the preparations for the wedding were set in motion. It was then that they discovered that the young man was already married, with a wife still living and in excellent health. My grandfather was furious. Then and there he would have broken off the negotiations had he not found that his daughter was wholly against such a step. She revealed that she had already accepted Mahendra Singh as her husband and that, as a properly brought up Hindu girl, she would never tolerate the thought of replacing his image with another's. If she could not marry him, she would remain unmarried all her life. Even my grandfather's much-feared temper was of no avail against her obduracy.

So my grandparents gave in. The horoscopes of the bride and bridegroom were scanned by astrologers and pronounced to be complementary, and the marriage took place. But either the horoscopes had been carelessly read or there had been collusion to conceal the fact that they were wholly unmatched. The stars that governed their lives were so locked in hostile positions that any union was bound to be short-lived. It was my mother, able to read Sanskrit script, who made this shocking discovery. But by then it was too late: she was already married and with child.

My mother's careful reading of the two horoscopes turned up the further prediction that she would give birth to a daughter and within a few days of that event would die. So convinced was she of the inevitability of these prophesies that, when she went to Sagar for her delivery, she took her jewellery, as well as other portable valuables such as gold and silver goblets and plate, with her. These were to be left to her unborn daughter, a nest-egg to take care of her upbringing and dowry.

Her confinement took place in the annexe of one of the several bungalows in the cantonment which my grandfather owned. This was where I was born on 12 October 1919. Nine days later my mother died.

After this there followed one of those family conflicts which have tended to blight my life. Luckily this time I was too young to know what was happening. My father wanted to take me to his house to be brought up, but my grandfather feared that my stepmother would ill-treat me and refused to part with me. Although my father went to court, he did not bargain for my grandfather's gamesmanship. He made out a case that my father was only interested in laying his hands on the jewellery and other valuables that my mother had left to me. Made to look like someone capable of robbing his own infant daughter, my father wisely capitulated. The case was settled by a consent decree. My grandparents could keep me with them until I was seven years old, provided they laid no claim to my legacy. After that I would have to go and live in my father's house. A crisis had been averted; and who could say what would happen at the end of seven years!

That was how, long before I was aware of it, I became a ward of my grandparents. Two years later my grandfather died. It was my grandmother who brought me up.

CHAPTER THREE

My Grandmother

TEN MILES FROM Sagar, where the road crosses the River Bewas, is a hamlet called Chitora. Of the village itself, you see nothing as you pass. What catches your eye is a modest stone shrine with steps leading down to the water level. Just behind it is a yellow-painted shed, which, a signboard tells you, is a *dharamsala* or free camping place for travellers. Both the shrine and the *dharamsala* were built by my grandfather as a memorial to my mother, who was cremated beside the river.

The Bewas is a small river, almost like a fishing stream, but here it broadens out into dark green pools. The slopes on either side are still sparsely wooded, and somehow the shrine and the yellow shed are exactly right in their setting. The place has changed little in the sixty odd years since my mother's death, and I can imagine no better memorial to her.

The names of Rana children were chosen by the stars rather than by their parents, for names had to be matched with the horoscopes. I was given Lekha Divyeshwari, but I don't remember anyone ever calling me by that name. My grandmother called me Nani, which was what I should have called her, for 'Nani', in most Indian languages, means grandmother. In Gurkhali it also means 'pupil of the eye'. I grew up calling my grandmother Muan, which means mother. It is difficult to imagine what else I could have called this woman who, for all my growing years, was not only like a real mother to me, but also the very centre of the world, the unflagging source of everything craved for, love, affection and warmth, and someone to run to when hungry, frightened or just feeling neglected. Her name was Dhankumari Devi.

Muan was an altogether remarkable woman, strong and sparkling with vitality. It was almost by a process of natural selection that, after my grandfather's death, she became the head of the family, even though such a thing was almost unheard of in a joint Hindu family such as ours, in which there was at least one grown-up son who was capable of taking over as the *karta* or manager. In fact, there were three sons, all of them married and the fathers of children. Unlike my grandmother, they had gone through school, even if without any special distinction. Nevertheless, they accepted her as the head of the family and, I feel sure, had no reason to regret their choice.

She served them well, managing her funds and estates in such a way as to enable all of us to live in the same style as my grandfather Khadga had adopted. There was always at least one car, in addition to a couple of horse carriages and a couple of riding horses. Seasonal tea and dinner parties and tennis afternoons for the local civil and military officers were soon resumed, and the Colonel of the Cavalry Regiment and the Deputy Commissioner of Sagar never failed to pay their courtesy calls. My uncles had their own cars and went out on hunting and fishing expeditions whenever the fancy took them, and ordered their suits and jackets from bespoke tailors in Bombay and Calcutta.

I don't believe my grandmother ever dismissed a servant even though, as in my grandfather's time, there seemed to be far too many of them. The quarters behind the house were filled to overflowing. Besides the teams of maids and men-servants allotted to each member of the family, there were also general house servants such as cooks (different ones for the vegetarians and for the meat-and-fish eaters, and each of them had to have a helper), bearers, table-boys, water-carriers, sweepers, maids, *syces* or grooms and watchmen, to say nothing of a couple of *darzis* or house tailors and *masalchis* or lamplighters, a masseur or two, a chauffeur and a mechanic for the car, a carpenter and a bevy of *pujaris* or priests. There was a sort of witch-doctor, and a 'Doctor-babu', a half-baked 'compounder' of Western medicine, and between them they catered for our medical needs. Then there were perhaps a dozen others who had no specific duties except to remain on call. They were more like poor relations than servants, with ties of loyalty, of shared adversity and even, I suspect, of blood, for the Rana menfolk, as a class, were not known for celibacy. Multiple wives, concubines and impromptu affairs with comely maidservants were more the rule than the exception, and their progeny invariably attached themselves to the main household.

*   *   *

The earliest sounds I remember must have been those of prayer. I awoke to the chanting of *slokas* or hymns and to the clanging of bells emanating from the family shrine. My grandmother would have already finished her bath and be deep into her *puja* in her private shrine, her head bent before the array of shining idols of gods and goddesses. As she grew older, her *pujas* became more protracted and her penitential fasts more frequent. And since, as a child, I spent most of my waking hours almost stuck to my grandmother, I learnt to recite devotional songs almost as my own children, placed in charge of nurses or governesses, learnt nursery rhymes. I set up my own shrine in a room next to my bedroom and harried my maids to bring fresh flowers for my *pujas*. I had mastered their ritual long before I learned the alphabet. Every so often I would grandly announce that I was going to join my grandmother in observing some holy festival as a day of fasting. But then this was no special hardship. Children were always allowed to eat as much as they liked of the 'permitted' preparations that are a special feature of Indian fasts, and some of them are really delicious.

My grandmother, no doubt anxious about my fate when her seven-year guardianship ended, pampered me outrageously. I merely had to go into a fit of sulks or, in an emergency, bring on a flood of tears to make her give in to my whim. In the face of such flagrant favouritism, it is surprising that my cousins, who also grew up in the Sagar house, remained friendly with me. But then they could depend on me to wheedle out a special treat for us all, such as an impromptu picnic or a visit to the cinema. I would often go on strike on behalf of my cousin Prem, who was my favourite, threatening that I would not accept a new doll unless Muan bought one exactly like it for her too, or demanding that she should prevail upon Prem's parents to let her accompany us on a shopping spree to Bombay or Calcutta. Grandmother always gave in, or so it seemed.

Alas, it was not all dolls and picnics; the coin had its reverse side. As her favourite, I became the natural target of my grandmother's native remedies, on which she herself had been brought up. I remember with horror one such remedy for which you did not even have to fall ill. Muan was convinced that, for a girl's hair to grow thick, soft and lustrous, it was essential to have her head periodically shaved. I was twice subjected to this ordeal, the first time when I was five years old, and then again a couple of years later, both times, I am ashamed to say, having to be won over with extravagant bribes. The lost hair itself was simulated by a gorgeous black headdress made of silk netting and liberally festooned with spangles, a proud creation of the family *darzi* working under my grandmother's instructions.

I remember the first time well. When I ventured out in my imitation hair and fancy new clothes to match, I discovered that I caused among my cousins more shock than envy. They ragged me mercilessly for being a *mudoli mau*, an old lady with a shaven head. On the second occasion I stuck out for an even more outrageous bribe: a shopping expedition to Calcutta, accompanied by my cousin Prem. My grandmother probably had every intention of having my head shaved at least once more but, either because of the tantrums I threw or, more likely, the businesslike reminders from my father that the time had come to send me back to him, she must have dropped the idea.

*   *   *

On my seventh birthday, the fight over my custody was resumed at the precise point at which it had been left off. My father fired the first broadside, politely reminding my grandmother of the arrangement that had been agreed upon between them seven years earlier. He demanded that his daughter should be sent to live in his house, and that the money, jewellery and plate that his late wife had bequeathed their daughter should be sent under proper escort.

My poor grandmother must have realized that she did not have a leg to stand on. What she had in abundance, however, was her Rana obduracy and feminine guile. This time she decided to ooze sweet reasonableness, and try and keep me with my father's consent and blessings.

My father, after all, was not a rich man and he already had a large family to look after. My grandmother was able to convince him that he would be blessed with many more children who would have to be educated, found jobs and married. Why should he take on an additional troublesome child who had grown up in another house and was happy there? If, as she surmized, my father was anxious about my mother's legacy, why then she was quite willing to hand it over, confident that it would be held in trust for me.

Like all litigants, each suspected the other's motives. My grandmother, always somewhat jaundiced against my father, was sure that all he was interested in was the money and the jewellery, and that his anxiety to gain custody over me was merely a pretext. My father, for his part, must have felt similarly apprehensive. I am happy to say that they were both wrong. Whatever flaws of character or eccentricities either of them possessed, they were scrupulously honest. My father held my nest-egg in trust for me. Years later, when my marriage was arranged and I went to seek his blessings, he brought out my mother's battered tin boxes. Each box had a list of its contents. When he began to check through the items and compare them with their descriptions from the yellowed lists, my eyes pricked with tears.

*   *   *

So my grandmother won an easy victory, and this time she had made sure that she had me for keeps. As for me, I was touched that my father should have wanted me to live with him at all, and that realization suddenly brought him closer to me. Henceforward, even though I continued to live in Sagar, I felt I had someone else to turn to in case of need, at least for advice and moral support.

It was about this time that my schooling began, which does not mean that I was sent to school. Sagar did not, in those days, have a school exclusively for girls, but even if it had, I doubt if I would have been sent there. My grandmother was brought up in a society which regarded schools as plebeian institutions; the Ranas did not even send their boys to schools. So I was educated at home, in a room set aside for the purpose and duly blessed by the priests – nothing ever began in our house without a *puja* to placate the evil spirits and to seek the aid of the benign ones. I was instructed in Hindi, English, geography, history and maths. Muan, who never tired of recounting her daughter's prowess in passing the matriculation examination, had set the same goal for me.

Whatever I learned of these subjects, the credit must go to my tutors; I don't believe I made a good docile pupil. To me lessons were an imposition, to be borne with fortitude; homework was a chore that could be neglected with impunity, knowing that I would not be punished, or at times judiciously turned into an excuse for demanding special treats.

But of religion, I could never have enough. My grandmother was my inspiration and model. I imitated her rituals and learnt her prayers by heart, and while I was unable, being a child, to observe all the fasts that she did, I gave up eating meat, fish or eggs during the period known as *chaturmas*, which roughly covers the four months from July to October.

I listened avidly to the stories from the *puranas* that the priests tended to telescope and reduce in the course of their worship. Again and again I pestered my grandmother to tell me about the gods and the goddesses with multiple heads and hands, the elephant-god, the monkey-god and the lion-god and their incredible victories over the forces of evil. Then there were the terrifying creatures of the nether world with wings, claws and horns, many-headed serpents and cunning agents of the devil who could transform themselves at will into playful animals or seductive maidens.

Upon this ornate canvas danced one figure by himself. A little dark god, with the normal number of limbs, Krishna was somehow more than merely celestial. Gentle, loving and full of pranks, he was also powerful enough to destroy serpents or lift an entire mountain to hold it as an umbrella over his herd of cows to protect it from rain. In his mature years he was so enlightened that he propounded the Gita, which my grandmother was convinced was not only the core of our religion, but also the essence of human wisdom.

Not that I had the vaguest notion of what the Gita was about, nor was I much concerned with wisdom, content to regard Muan as an inexhaustible storehouse of it. But the Krishna who played the flute, tended his cows, stole butter from irate housewives and slew dragons, became my private god.

As I grew up, so my god grew up and became a man. The child Krishna blossomed into Gopal Krishna, the dream-lover of all the milkmaids in the neighbourhood. I discovered the *bhajans* or songs composed in his honour by Meerabai, a fifteenth-century Rajput princess who became an ardent worshipper. As I recited these devotional, and romantic, songs, I would imagine myself to be that princess wooing her god as some secret lover, and tears would roll down my cheeks with the intensity and ecstasy of my emotions.

The rest of our large household had little truck with holiness; the Ranas held this to be a special preserve of their womenfolk. My uncles lived in a self-consciously male world of their own, and never seemed to be content unless on horseback or in the jungles pursuing some animal or other to its death. But, oddly enough, I was fully at home in their world too – more so, in fact, than any of their own daughters. And it was with their sons that I raced on bicycles in dizzy circles round the tennis court, played gulli-danda (a primitive form of cricket) and went on children's picnics into the woods behind the house.

As a family, we were inveterate campers. When we were in some *dak*-bungalow deep in the jungle or under canvas, there were always plenty of servants to look after our needs, and the food which we ate sitting around log fires was no different from what we ate at home. In these camps I used to practise target shooting with a .22 rifle, but I never took to hunting. I had grown up in a tightly-knit family to whom hunting was infinitely more than a pastime of the rich; it was a cult, an obligation inseparable from being a member of the *kshatriya* or warrior clan. On certain days, such as Sankranti, 14 January, it was imperative for the menfolk to go out hunting and to kill something for the pot; on the Dussera, celebrated either in September or October, every self-respecting Gurkha male was obliged ceremonially to 'blood' his *kukri* or all-purpose knife by severing the heads of dozens of goats or, for some especially favoured individual, fattened buffalo.

As part of an insular tribe, to whom the act of killing was no more than an assertion of manliness, the shooting of wild animals for food or sport did not upset me. Nonetheless, I fended off all my uncles' efforts to get me to share their passion for hunting. My cousins and I preferred to spend our time in camp playing our own mysterious games. It was in a pool in the Dhasan river that I learned to swim. My grandmother strongly disapproved. Did I want to drown myself? Did I want one of my legs chopped off by a lurking crocodile? Yet, on the next trip to Bombay, she bought me an expensive swimming costume.

CHAPTER FOUR

My First Proposal

OUR HOUSE CROUCHED on a spur of the hills overlooking the cantonment. It was separated from the civil station by a belt of trees hiding the lake that gives Sagar – which means 'the sea' – its name. On winter mornings we saw the lake in a blanket of silver mist rising above the trees. An orchard of mangoes, guavas and custard apple trees surrounded the house, but its real pride was a solitary and profuse mulberry tree.

Our compound must have been vast. As children we had no idea how far it extended into the hills at the back; we just took it for granted that everything within range of our walks was ours – or at least our grandmother's. There was no human habitation behind the house, and the jungle beyond the orchard was friendly, sparse and open. It harboured no dangerous animals, only hares, partridges and an occasional jackal.

*   *   *

My grandmother was a restless person, an indefatigable traveller and a compulsive visitor of exhibitions. These were the great events of the era between the two World Wars. If there was one within range (which meant within about 500 miles) she would find some excuse to make the trip – the need for a new car, curtains or furnishing material or for a visit to the doctor. I invariably accompanied her on these jaunts.

In December 1929 my youngest uncle, Kunjar Samsher, who was training to be an air pilot in Delhi, came home for a holiday. He mentioned that Delhi was to have an exhibition of aeroplanes and a flying display early in the new year. That was enough for Muan. 'Oh, I should love to see it,' she announced. 'In fact, we'll all go.'

My grandmother had developed her own style of travelling. The journey was made in a large seven-seater car, usually a Buick, with a lorry for the servants and luggage following behind. The luggage included a fair-sized tent because she wanted to be able to set up camp wherever she pleased and not be bound to hotels or *dak*-bungalows. Apart from the two drivers, she took a mechanic, her own two maids, a male cook, a female cook and a couple of extra servants. Each member of the family was also accompanied by a maid or manservant. Wherever she went, she had to have her own establishment, preferably a bungalow or in Bombay or Calcutta a spacious flat in a quiet district. Since such accommodation had to be hired for at least a couple of months, our city visits were always fairly protracted.

So now she despatched my uncle and his wife in advance to hire a bungalow in Delhi. Her eldest son, Hem Samsher, and his wife accompanied us in the Buick, and I had prevailed on my grandmother to let my favourite cousin, Prem, come with us. We set out from Sagar at the crack of dawn and towards the afternoon we stopped for refreshments and for stretching our legs in King George's Park (now Mahatma Gandhi Park) in Gwalior.

The scale of the surroundings must have been too vast to have made any particular impression on me – I was ten years old at the time – even though I have since thought how our dust-grimed car and its travel-weary passengers must have resembled a detail on a giant Bruegel canvas. This part of Gwalior has the sort of grandeur that the Mughals sought to create in Delhi and Agra, but with less success since neither city has the natural advantage of a rearing hill fort. Here is a setting that calls out for a panoramic display of pomp, rank upon rank of marching soldiers, a charge by plumed lancers or a parade of caparisoned elephants. Blocking off one side and providing a backdrop of stupefying dimensions is the fort itself; opposite lies the white colonnaded expanse of Jaivilas Palace. In between is the stage, a mile or more of immaculate lawns, formal gardens, noble stands of trees and marble pavilions.

Anyhow, on this winter afternoon, when the edges of our ears tingled with pain and felt like wood, there were no elephants, no cavalry; indeed, not even many people out in the park.

We had stopped beside a tiger-house, and it drew me like a magnet. As I stood staring in awe at a big tiger sprawled in front of his cave, I became aware of a stir among the park attendants and the few strollers. Next I heard the clatter of horses' hooves, and all turned to gaze at a boy on a white horse and a girl on a black horse, both of which seemed far too big for them. Close behind rode a man in a turban. They passed by, chatting amongst themselves, and were presently swallowed up by the shrubbery near the enormous gates of the palace.

'Jivajirao Maharaj!' an attendant explained in hushed excitement: 'And his sister, Kamalaraje.'

So this boy was the Scindia – master of the Gwalior palace, the fort, the park and the tiger. Surely, there should have been some sign from the sky, a flash of lightning to mark the tableau on my memory. But if a star skipped in its course, it did so unseen in the thin January sunlight. In fact, there was nothing to tell me that I had been offered a glimpse of my future.

It was getting late, and we had to hurry if we did not want to find ourselves after nightfall in the area of the dreaded Chambal dacoits. Uncle Hem hustled us back into the Buick, and soon we were skirting the rock-fort on our way to Delhi. My thoughts were of the tiger sprawled lazily on the bare rock and of the wonders that the imperial city held in store, not of the boy and the girl on their magnificent horses.

*   *   *

New Delhi was not yet fully built. It was just parts of a town flung about on an arid landscape, bare and unlived-in. We travelled vast distances over dusty roads to see great monuments of pink sandstone, but many were still cluttered by piles of building material. We goggled from the permitted distance at the chopped-off dome of the Viceroy's palace. We decided that the city's vaunted shopping centre, Connaught Place, was not to be compared with our favourite Chowringhee of Calcutta, and we daily consumed enormous teas at Davico's or

Wenger's, the haunts, we were assured, of Delhi's society.

At the exhibition we had come to see, the men trying to sell the various types of aeroplanes treated my grandmother as though she were a potential customer. In retrospect this does not seem so fatuous, since the aeroplanes cost little more than the more expensive cars. We watched the frail gaudily-coloured flying machines being put through their paces, like horses at a rodeo, soaring into the air, flying upside down, circling with their engines shut off and writing messages in the sky with coloured smoke. After six hectic weeks we motored back to Sagar and to routine.

This visit to Delhi, which the Raj had built to proclaim its invincible presence, coincided with what was to prove a watershed in the lives of most Indians of my generation. It was while we were still there that the nationalist leaders declared 26 January 1930 as our 'Independence Day', and launched a campaign of 'Civil Disobedience'.

The first shot in this campaign was fired a few weeks later when Mahatma Gandhi set out on his march to the seaside village of Dandi on the west coast. There, in open defiance of the law, he made a spoonful of salt by boiling sea water in a pan.

To the guardians of the Empire this was nothing short of an act of war against the King Emperor, as the British monarch was invariably referred to in India. For this crime Gandhi was clapped into jail for a four-year term. In the wake of his arrest more than a hundred thousand people rushed to break the law in one way or another. That spoonful of salt had set up a tidal wave that would eventually sweep away the Raj.

To grow up in that era was to be caught up in the tide, to learn to use such words as 'nationalism' and 'patriotism', to be roused to a pitch of frenzy by slogans, to look for heroes to praise and for villains to curse or, for someone brought up as I was, to seek redress in prayer.

*   *   *

My uncles, who were born in Nepal but had lived in India all their lives, never suffered from what I later learned to call a crisis of identity. They, and even their children, regarded themselves as citizens of Nepal. They professed disinterest in the freedom struggle; the problems of their adopted land were not their problems. Nepal was independent; the British had twice attempted to conquer it, but the Gurkhas had thrown them back. Their country had its own king, its own Maharaja; it was not ruled by an alien power beyond the seas. What pride they took in that fact.

Since children customarily took on the citizenship of their fathers, I was unarguably Indian: a cuckoo in the Nepalese nest, a *gulam* or slave in this conquered land. The distinction must have always been there, unspoken, but it had emerged in the course of some family argument. Thus, to the normal confusion of growing up, was added the difficulty of reconciling the pride of my Nepalese connections with the shame of being born an Indian.

My grandmother's unabashed preference for me over her sons' children produced an additional complex. Sensitive to jibes that I was spoilt by my grandmother because I had no home of my own, I was also at an age when one tended to overreact. I suffered agonies and slid into paroxysms of self-pity. In these dark moods I would convince myself that I was destined to suffer such humiliations because my mother had died and left me among strangers. There were times when I worked myself into states of acute depression, imagining that I saw visions of my mother calling out to me from some remote place in the firmament. Once I made myself ill enough to take to my bed; I was so convinced that I was going to die that I solemnly began to say my goodbyes to my uncles and cousins.

Luckily, my grandmother had an exorcist in the form of the resident witch-doctor. Biray was a wizened little man with a face like the inside of a walnut, and he wore a single earring. He brought with him a *sigri* or small charcoal stove with a ready-made fire and squatted down on a board placed near my bed. He mumbled prayers as he blew on the fire to set up a blaze, and then he began heating an evil-looking branding knife. I could have sworn that its edge became red hot. I stared at him as he picked up the knife. I was unable to utter a whimper, caught between paralysis and hypnosis. Braced for the ordeal, I waited to be branded, for the jolt of pain, the sizzling sound of the knife, the smell of burning flesh. Biray took my left hand in his and applied the knife below the crook of the elbow. It was barely warm.

'The spirit has left the girl,' he told my grandmother. And so it had, or at least my illness had.

* * *

Like the other children of the household, I could speak Hindi as fluently as Gurkhali, but I had very little contact with Hindi literature. The history we learned was that contained in the little green and red oilcloth-covered Macmillan or Longman textbooks, showing how heroically the men of the East India Company had conquered India and what prosperity their rule had brought. I don't remember at what age I began to be aware of an urge to learn Hindi, but by the time I was fifteen I had persuaded my grandmother to appoint a Hindi teacher for me.

Rameshwar Prasad Srivastava, Master-saab as I called him, turned out to have that rare mixture of erudition, common sense and humour. He was trim, dark and neatly dressed, carried himself with quiet dignity and spoke with a voice that was perfect for reciting poetry aloud. He handled books with reverence and read them with me (with a slight inclination of the head) as though he too was reading them for the first time. Together we plunged into the core of Hindi literature and, almost without it being explained, I learnt to distinguish between flamboyance and elegance, verbiage and scholarship.

Master-saab hunted out history books, in Hindi as well as in English, and through them I began to learn about the pre-British past of my country. I discovered that we had had a vigorous civilization which, under the shadow of the empire, had curled up and withered; great literature, painting, music, sculpture, scholarship and, above all, a religion based on the bedrock of a philosophy which had withstood the convulsions of history for thousands of years.

To be introduced to this heritage was like breaking the seals to Aladdin's cave. What Master-saab taught me led me to realize the privilege of having been born an Indian, the inheritor of a great tradition.

A sure sign of a resurgent India was the emergence of its own heroes. For a century or more, we had been disciplined into adopting Britain's heroes as our own: Horatio Nelson, Gordon of Khartoum and even the conquerors of our own land, such as Robert Clive, Arthur Wellesley or Henry Lawrence. Now at last we had a crop of Indian men and women with the hallmarks of authentic heroes.

Believing in the power of prayer, a plea for India's liberation from bondage became incorporated in my daily *puja*. A picture of Mother India, festooned in chains, found a place of honour in my prayer alcove, right next to the idol of my private god, Gopal Krishna.

*   *   *

Towards the end of 1935, Lucknow was to hold an exhibition, and it would have been unlike Grandmother if she had kept away. A wedding of a distant relative in nearby Kanpur gave her the necessary excuse and we set off in her caravan. From a bungalow in Kanpur, hired for the winter, we commuted to Lucknow for the exhibition, sometimes staying with relatives for a day or two.

Then I discovered that my father too had come to Lucknow, ostensibly to show the exhibition to his new wife, whom I now met for the first time. My stepmother was only six years older than me, and I took to her instantly. We have remained close friends ever since.

All these years I had seen little of my father. I had never even gone to stay with him. Whenever his work brought him to Sagar, he always paid me a visit, bringing a small present, such as a box of sweets, or a piece of silk for a blouse. These visits were both infrequent – certainly not more than two or three in a year – and brief. Nonetheless, they had the effect of drawing me closer to him. I loved him and venerated him more than any other man, and nothing heard in my grandmother's house would ever alter my affection and regard for him.

My father, then in his mid-forties, was an impressive figure. Tall, handsome and superbly built, he carried himself with a self-assurance that must have come from his position as Deputy Collector in the Provincial Civil Service. Although his friends found him polite and easygoing, he had a reputation for being a brusque and outspoken official, never open to bribery. His superiors, however, seem to have found his integrity and adherence to principles a shade too rigid: he was subjected to frequent transfers and must have been the only officer of his cadre to retire – after more than thirty years of service – in the same rank and position as he had started.

At the Lucknow exhibition I appointed myself as a sort of guide to my stepmother, who was unaccustomed to big cities and bewildered by the scale and grandeur of everything about her. As we were going through a Government Information Centre, which contained large maps and charts showing how the country was governed, and I was showing off my knowledge with my usual exuberance, I noticed that a young man, with a pear-shaped face and in immaculate Western attire, had attached himself to our party and was listening with undisguised interest to everything I had to say. I took him to be an official connected with the exhibition, since he seemed to know my father well. He trailed along with us for the best part of an afternoon, but I was not introduced to him and I don't recall that he addressed a single word to either my stepmother or myself.

A day or two later, in Kanpur, I received a seven-page letter from this young man pouring his heart out to me and proposing marriage. It seemed that he had already spoken to my father, but that my father had declined to press his proposal. Although I was not aware of it then, the proposal must have put my father in an acutely embarrassing position for Mr Singh – as I shall call him – was a member of the Indian Civil Service.

The Raj had its own caste system, more inflexible than that of the Hindus. The members of the ICS, mostly recruited from the British upper middle class but with a few handpicked Indians grudgingly let in, were the country's elite and were generally known as, and by the peasants literally believed to be, 'heaven-born'. To my father, merely a provincial civil servant, Mr Singh must have represented a rare prize as a son-in-law. But the proposal was flawed, because Mr Singh's horoscope was dominated by Mangal or Mars. In spite of its name, which means 'auspicious' or 'festive', Mangal is an unlucky star. For a man to have it in his horoscope means that his wife will die young and vice versa for a woman. The only solution, of course, is for a Mangal to marry a Mangal; but I have no Mangal in my horoscope.

I did not reply to the letter; to have done so would have been a transgression of the rules of behaviour. I don't think I was put off so much by the Mangal as by the age difference: he was thirty and I was barely sixteen. Besides, what little I had seen of Mr Singh had not bowled me over. I tore up the letter, and Mr Singh's proposal was never mentioned again.

Years later, Mr Singh became the centre of one of the most sensational and sordid trials of the time. A maidservant in the Singh household died in mysterious circumstances and Mr Singh was accused of having murdered her. After a protracted trial he was declared to be 'not guilty', and indeed there was a suspicion that he might have been the victim of a frame-up. But the publicity surrounding the trial of such a senior civil servant so upset Mr Singh's wife that she committed suicide. A little later Mr Singh too took his own life. I have often wondered whether it was not the Mangal at work.

CHAPTER FIVE

Going to College

IN 1937 I made my first-ever visit to my father's house. He was stationed in Jhansi then, only 140 miles from Sagar – seven hours by train. I took my own maid with me, and my grandmother provided an escort of two of her most trusted retainers, who were charged to look after me and bring me back. My father looked as pleased as Punch to have me visit him, and I began to look upon him as a guide and mentor to whom I could turn whenever I needed advice or help. I was welcomed as though I were a long-lost daughter by his new wife, whom, almost in the same spirit, I took to calling Mummiji or 'Respected Mother'.

My father was still keen on getting me married off without delay. A week or so later he took me to Banda, 120 miles away, to stay with an old friend of his, an affluent *zamindar* or hereditary landowner, called Virendra Singh Chowdhari. He told me that it had been arranged between them that I should marry Mr Chowdhari's eldest son, and now it was only up to us to give our consent to the match.

After we had been in the Chowdhari house for a few days, the reason for our visit must have become common knowledge in the neighbourhood. One afternoon the daughter of one of the neighbours, whom I had often seen in the house, came to see me. Almost in a teasing vein, she made tender enquiries as to whether I had any objection to marrying Mr Chowdhari's son. I told her, in all honesty, that I would be happy to marry him, upon which she suddenly fainted. This caused quite a bit of panic in the Chowdhari house and they had to send for a doctor to revive her. When I realised that she was violently in love with the young man, I then and there made up my mind that it would be heartless to break up her romance. So when, a day or two later, my consent was formally sought, I pretended that I was not interested in the proposal. I am happy to say that Mr Chowdhari's son did, that very summer, marry the infatuated girl and that their marriage turned out to be an unqualified success.

This stay in the Chowdhari house was, however, to give my life a totally new direction. It was my first experience of living among people with a broader culture than my own, for the family was known for its progressive views. If I was mildly shocked by their heresies, I was also impressed by their unwillingness to conform. By their lights, even my father stood revealed as an obscurantist, someone who had too readily absorbed the official attitudes and outlook of the Raj. Here neither Rana taboos nor the Raj's rules were held to be sacred; all dogma, all institutions, new-fangled or traditional, were treated with irreverence.

*   *   *

Mr Chowdhari, a well-known proponent of women's emancipation, was all for my continuing my education. Being an ardent follower and devotee of that high-priestess of theosophy, Mrs Annie Besant, he persuaded my father that the women's college founded by her in Benaras was the right place for me.

So, by the time we returned to Jhansi, it was settled. Since it was all but certain that my grandmother would object to such a plan on principle, we decided that I should stay on with my father until the colleges opened, and go straight to Benaras from there. Now everything depended on my passing the matriculation examination.

I did pass. My father busied himself with getting the necessary forms and I was admitted to the Besant Women's College. It was important that neither my maid nor my two menservants should get wind of what was afoot. On my last day in Jhansi I sent my maid off on an errand which would keep her away for several hours and busied myself stuffing my most fashionable clothes into an enormous black trunk. On the day-long train journey to Benaras, I was accompanied by one of my father's step-brothers.

It was only after he had seen us off at the railway station and returned home that my father judged it safe to explain to my servants that I had gone to Benaras to join a college and that they were free to return to Sagar. They had formed their own impressions of what had really happened. Aware that there had been talk of my marrying a rich *zamindar*'s son, they were convinced that this was precisely what had been accomplished, and that my father had secretly sent me off to my husband's house. They went wailing to my grandmother with such garbled accounts that she made up her mind that I had been sold by my father for a high price. She had already called in her lawyers to file a suit against him for abduction when she received my letter from college, full of apologies and explanations.

I had written as soon as I possibly could, exonerating both the servants and my father. I said soothing things about how comfortable I was in my hostel room and how good the food was, but that I missed her more than I could say.

It was a long letter, and my eyes brimmed with tears as I wrote it. The bravado and excitement that had gripped me at the thought of going off on my own into the world had been replaced by an awareness of guilt, of having betrayed someone who had brought me up and had been so unfailingly kind and understanding.

*   *   *

It was perhaps just as well that, in those early college days, I did not have much leisure to feel sorry for myself. There were adjustments to make which I had not foreseen.

For the first time in my life I was entirely on my own, without some member of the family to run to and, worse still, without a servant to do my bidding. The hostel attached to the college was much smaller than our Sagar house, and in it I had to share a room. My black trunk suddenly began to look monstrously large, and when I began to unpack some of my belongings I noticed that my room-mate could hardly keep her eyes away from them. At first I thought that it was my modest array of idols that had aroused her interest, but soon discovered that it was my clothes that held her rivetted. I felt a little embarrassed by her stares, but thought no more of it at the time and went to bed.

The next morning I went to class dressed in one of my silk saris and wearing my everyday jewellery, which included a rather showy nose-ring made of a diamond solitaire. More and more of my fellow students turned their heads to glance at me, whispering among themselves. Surely, something was wrong. Slowly it dawned on me that nearly all of them were wearing plain cotton saris and no jewellery.

It took me a couple of days to realize that even the Besant College, for all its preoccupation with liberalism, was stiff with its own orthodoxies. Here most of the students were followers of the theosophical movement, committed to vegetarianism, and practitioners of the cult of Plain Living and High Thinking.

Whether or not there was high thinking among my college-mates, I was made overwhelmingly conscious of their zest for plain living. But then plain living had a much more powerful and persuasive prophet than Annie Besant: none other than the Mahatma himself. It had become a weapon in his non-violent war against the British. At his bidding, millions of people had made bonfires of their fanciest garments and begun to dress themselves like peasants.

Millions, but not me. I had always been too fond of fine clothes and jewellery to give up wearing them. Here in the Besant Women's College I was converted by the urge to conform. I did not want to be marked as an outcast in a colony of plain livers. Feeling a little like a thief hiding stolen goods, I took off my nose-ring and put it away. From then on I resolved to boycott all foreign-made goods, even though it would mean never wearing the lovely French and Italian saris and accessories that I had so assiduously collected over the years. At the very first opportunity I went into the bazaar and bought myself half a dozen cotton saris and material to make blouses. That night, I sat up in my room till the early hours of the morning laboriously hand-stitching a blouse.

That first trip to the bazaar brought home to me how scrupulously the staff of the college themselves practised the cult of plain living, and also how the cult had brought in its wake its own snobberies. Whenever one of the girls wanted to go into town, she had to get a member of staff to go with her. They came readily enough, but what was awkward for us was that they insisted on paying their share of the fare. There were neither buses nor taxis, so we had to take a *tonga* or, an even more plebeian vehicle, the *jhatka*. Since it was unseemly for a Besant College girl to sit in the front seat with the driver, the *tonga* could, with the chaperone, take only two or, if they were very thin, three girls. In the *jhatka*, which had no seats but only a platform on which you had to squat, anything up to half-a-dozen could be squeezed in. It became a point of honour with us to prefer the *jhatka* to the *tonga*. That way, the share of the staff member who went with us came to much less.

*   *   *

In conformity with its dedication to plain living, our hostel catered only for vegetarians. Since I was used to giving up eating meat, fish and eggs for four months every year during the period of *chaturmas*, this was no great deprivation to me. And if I sorely missed the number and variety of dishes that regularly appeared at my grandmother's table, even during the months of self-imposed vegetarianism, I don't think I complained about the plainness and monotony of hostel food half as much as some of the flag-bearers of plain living.

The first friend in college I made was a girl from the far south, who was a stranger to this part of India. Although she spoke English well, she knew not a word of Hindi. Being much more at home in English than the other hostel girls, it was perhaps natural that she should be drawn to me. I began to teach her Hindi, and by the end of term she was quite fluent in it. I made friends with half-a-dozen other girls as well; we formed a group of our own, doing things together, sharing common interests, gossip and a few secrets. One of the girls was married and I remember how we would listen avidly to her stories of the wonder and romance of wedded life, how we all waited with vicarious anticipation for the fat weekly letter that her husband never failed to write, how she would carry it away to read in private, her face flushed and her eyes shining, and how, for days afterwards, we would pester her to tell us what it contained.

*   *   *

Benaras is a holy place, the Mecca and the Rome and the Jerusalem of Hinduism. The mother of rivers, the Ganges, sweeps past its phalanx of temples in a majestic arc. Pilgrims flock to it in their millions, and thousands come here merely to die, as my grandfather had done.

But to the inmates of our hostel, the Ganges was no more than an awesome presence to be glimpsed only when we went to the bazaar in chaperoned groups for our shopping, or were allowed out to see an approved film at one or other of the city's cinemas. We led a sheltered life, superintended by a portly and stern-faced spinster from Maharashtra, whom we called Mohan Tai. A self-righteous prickly woman, she took pride in running a tight ship. Her eyes, magnified and distorted by thick lenses, would flash fire at the slightest infringement of her barrage of rules. We all stood in awe of her and concocted impracticable plans for defying her authority, but we must have secretly admired her too.

I remember one incident when Mohan Tai refused to let us go and see a film which was being shown in one of the local cinemas. It was called *Mukti* and it was made by a company called New Theatres. Their earlier pictures had been immensely popular and their songs had caught the fancy of young and old alike. But in this latest offering Tai had detected a nude statuette which was shown in one of the scenes. I remember getting into a heated argument with Tai about the merits of these earlier films and how a film company with such a reputation could not possibly produce a film that would corrupt the morals of young girls. It was to no avail. Tai did not even tell us about the nude statuette, but lost her temper and ordered us back to our rooms. We were furious and talked at length of retaliation. I spent half the night tossing in bed, trying to devise a plan to redress what I was convinced was a great injustice. The next morning I tried to talk the other girls into going on a hunger strike. Alas, my suggestion was not received with much enthusiasm. We were at an age when meals were all but indispensable. The 'injustice' simmered for a week or so and then died.

The term progressed. The skies darkened with clouds and the monsoon broke loose on cue. The half-moon of the river filled out to become a vast brown lake, its waters swirling through the lower-level temples. Then as abruptly as they had come, the rains went, the skies cleared and the Ganges lost its bloated look and became sedate and serene once again. The temple spires glistened in the sun. I was no longer an outsider, but part of the life of the hostel and the college.

I look back on my two years in Benaras with fondness. I revelled in the extra-curricular aspects of hostel and college life and took part in musical programmes and in plays. In my second year I graduated to being an organizer of these activities. I took extra lessons in music and art. It was only towards the end of the last term that I got down to serious study, keeping awake at nights to make up for earlier neglect. Then came the examinations and the sudden wrench of parting from friends.

My father had meanwhile been transferred to Mirzapur, almost next door to Benaras. It was to his house that I went for my summer holidays. The house was in turmoil because one of my father's brothers was getting married in the village of their birth, Gangni. I went along with them, on a trip that turned out to be an exercise in search of my roots.

Gangni is not far from Agra. Remote and forlorn, the village was only approachable by a dusty cart-track. The house in which my father was born was no different from the dwellings of the other villagers, stunted and built of mud-bricks with uneven wall surfaces which were painted with crude good-luck signs on both sides of the front door and, at the back, were encrusted with drying cowpats for the winter fuel.

I was not conscious of any sense of let-down; two years among the plain-livers had changed more than my way of dressing. Rather, I was filled with a sense of awe and pride that someone who had been born in such a house, in such a village, should have struggled against caste and clan prejudices, have risen in the world entirely through his own efforts and ability, and been sought as a son-in-law by a man who had so nearly become the Maharaja of Nepal.

In June came the results. All the girls in our group had passed. I was determined to continue my studies, and this time my grandmother made no objection. I managed to get admission to the same Isabella Thoburn Women's College in Lucknow that my mother had so briefly attended. Here I found to my great pleasure that I was sharing a room in the hostel with one of our group from Benaras.

The College was a venerable institution, the most prestigious in the entire province. Life seemed to be far less restricted and preoccupied with plain living than in the Benaras college. I at once felt at home, made new friends and plunged into a variety of social activities. I was looking forward to the next two years and to getting my Bachelor of Arts degree with pleasurable anticipation.

But it was not to be. I did not know it then, but both my father and my grandmother were busy as beavers, each trying to outdo the other in finding a suitable husband for me.

CHAPTER SIX
Marriage Talks

THE RANAS, IN spite of having been removed from their Indian roots for well over four centuries, still considered themselves to be more Rajput than the Rajputs themselves. Like so many transplanted communities, they had become insular and inbred. Fencing themselves off from their environment for fear of contamination, their lives were governed by the racial taboos of the time of their emigration.

In the sphere of their marital alliances, these taboos were all but inflexible. Rana sons and daughters could not marry outside the *kshatriya* or warrior caste. Wealth, looks, education and the compatibility of the planetary influences were among a host of secondary considerations in which compromises were permissible. But it was caste that reigned supreme.

*   *   *

Girls from families such as mine married the man of their parents' choice. They were not supposed to have any personal views on the subject or, if they did, to express them.

My own thoughts about the sort of person I would eventually like to marry would have shocked both my grandmother and my father, as they vied with each other to find a husband for me before the other succeeded. My ideas, romantically vague as they were, centred round some as yet unidentified figure in the forefront of the freedom struggle. The freedom fighter of my youth was nothing like today's violent revolutionary. He was a starry-eyed idealist who offered himself rather than others as a sacrifice. His uniform was the peasants' garb, a knee-length shirt worn over either *dhoti* or pyjamas made of hand-spun cotton, and a white cotton cap. It was his proud boast that he was equipped with neither arms nor armour; his greatest strength was his vulnerability to physical assault. The picture he evoked was of a moth drawn into a raging fire. His principal 'weapon' was a maddeningly obtuse philosophical concept called *ahimsa*, meaning 'non-violence'. His campaign was *satyagraha*, meaning literally 'protest for truth', and somewhat clumsily translated into English as 'civil disobedience'. It took the form of breaking the laws of the Raj systematically, openly (with a good deal of fanfare) and, above all, peacefully, so that those who administered the laws would have no alternative but to clap him into jail.

At first the imperialists had laughed; to them the Indian freedom fighter was a figure of fun. But as civil disobedience began to show results, the British rulers betrayed their misgivings in nervous ticks, in groans and curses. The empire, which Rudyard Kipling had depicted as a hallowed institution, was being shown up for what it was, a system of keeping a nation enslaved. The curry-Colonels of the Raj reacted with mounting severity. They caned mobs, fired blanks, made horseback charges, took hostages, imposed crippling collective fines and filled the country's jails to overflowing.

Gandhi had astutely banked on the temperament of the typical British administrator. 'I never allowed anyone to shout "Mahatma Gandhi" without giving him six on the bottom with a stick,' boasted one senior police officer. Such men, who could be depended on to foam at the mouth on cue, hastened the retreat of the imperialists. The participants in the civil disobedience movement absorbed the punishment and went to jail, still shouting Gandhi's name, in their millions.

I myself was guiltily aware of not being wholly reconciled to the Mahatma's preachings. Non-violence went against the grain of my *kshatriya* background and instincts; it had a negative masochistic connotation. How could any red-blooded man see women and children being caned and clubbed by the police without being aroused to hit back? Subhas Chandra Bose, who had already shown himself to be the stormy petrel of the freedom movement, was more like my ideal of a freedom fighter.

Like the vast majority of the men and women of my generation, I was inexorably drawn into the wave. I had already stopped wearing imported saris, even though the saris I preferred were made not in England but in France or Italy. Those who made the rules did not know the difference, but in any case it was the done thing to wear only Indian-made things. This had been a major sacrifice. But sacrifice was in the air; it was, in some undefined way, inseparable from the national struggle. It showed that you belonged. The more you gave up, the more patriotic you were. So I conformed. Unlike others from my background, I turned away from Western society and embraced Hindu mores of behaviour. I avoided clubs, tea-dances and cocktail parties. I disapproved of the drinking of alcohol, a practice I associated with the white rulers, and took to a wholly vegetarian diet.

*   *   *

It was in my first term at the Lucknow College that my father came up with another proposal for my hand. Lieutenant Chauhan, one of the last of the King's Commissioned Officers of the Indian Army, came from a *jahgirdar* family and thus belonged to the landed aristocracy. The *jahgirdars* were hereditary noblemen whose titles to their estates had been recognized by the British.

To his surprise, my father found that he had a staunch ally in my grandmother's household. My uncle, Hem Samsher, had run away as a young man and enlisted as a private in a Gurkha regiment. It had taken all my grandfather's influence among the British officials to secure his release. But the hardships of life in the ranks had not cured my uncle's infatuation with the profession, and he was convinced that the ideal husband had been found for his niece.

Lieutenant Chauhan had been posted to Sagar. Uncle Hem went to see him and was instantly won over. After my grandmother's consent had been secured, there was an exchange of horoscopes, which were found to be complementary. The next step was an exchange of photographs, so that the two people most concerned could give their approval. Along with the picture of the officer in his dashing uniform came a glowing letter from my cousin Khem, no doubt written at her father's bidding. She told me that even though, as a military officer, Lieutenant Chauhan lived among hard-drinkers, he neither touched alcohol nor smoked – an appeal, no doubt, to my new-found enthusiasm for plain living. It made it much easier for me, however, to make up my mind. I said yes, and apparently so did Lieutenant Chauhan. A date for the wedding was decided for the coming year: 8 May 1940.

And so it was settled. The stars beamed brightly and there was little to do except shop around at leisure for the hundreds of things that a girl thinks she needs in preparation for her marriage; a pleasurable exercise that provided the spur for yet another of my grandmother's expeditions.

*   *   *

Meanwhile, almost unnoticed by us, something had happened in the outside world. A new war had started. In India we were not aware of any sense of urgency or alarm; the war was kept at the proper distance and the Raj went on at its own unhurried pace. My grandmother, Uncle Hem, his wife, their daughter and I set off in the usual caravan to Calcutta.

The city had never looked more festive, more gay. Society had gathered for the annual 'season', which lasted for three weeks when the Viceroy happened to be in residence: the polo, the races, the flower show and the dog show filled the papers, consigning the war to the back pages. For the Viceroy's Cup, the scarlet-robed bodyguards led the procession down the green turf. Firpo's, the stamping ground of the city's high society, glittered with parties. Although I was not a participant in these gaieties of the Raj and its social élite, it was impossible to be in Calcutta without being aware of them. You only had to go for a drive along Chowringhee and pass a dozen Rolls Royces flying the flags of our Maharajas to feel that you were somehow a part of the pageant.

We stayed for three months in Calcutta. In early March we set off on the five-day journey back to Sagar. The first overnight halt was made in the travellers' bungalow in Patna. That night my cousin Khem complained of a severe pain in her stomach and was rushed to the Government Hospital, where it was discovered that she had a ruptured appendix. An emergency operation was performed, and for nearly a month her life hung in the balance. Two months later, on 8 May – the day of my proposed wedding – poor Khem, still in hospital, was pronounced to be out of danger. We were unable to leave Patna until the middle of June, when she was at last considered fit to resume the journey.

In the meantime, Lieutenant Chauhan's battalion had received orders for overseas service. He wrote to my father suggesting that our engagement should be treated as cancelled. He had no intention of leaving his newly-married wife for the war with the possibility of her widowhood. Nor did he wish the marriage to be held over until the end of the war, which would, he thought, probably continue for several years.

I have always been thankful to this man whom I never saw except in a photograph for his selfless and sensible gesture. Rather than keep things suspended, as most people in his position might have done, he had made a decision which was in the best traditions of his calling.

*   *   *

I had left college to get married and was now back in Sagar. I was in my twenty-first year, five feet five inches tall, painfully thin and weighing no more than ninety pounds. My grandmother tried her best to feed me up, but when after three months she found that I had not even put on an extra ounce, she gave up. 'It's all due to your vegetarianism,' she would tell me with a despairing shake of her head.

Later that same year my favourite and youngest uncle, Kunjar Samsher, and his wife, whom I called Mamiji, were going to Calcutta for a holiday and suggested that I should go with them. It was only when, on the eve of our departure, I heard my grandmother giving Mamiji elaborate instructions to make sure, whenever they took me out, that I wore long-sleeved blouses to hide my skinny arms, that I realized that Uncle Kunjar had now taken it upon himself to find a husband for me, with my grandmother's approval. On the train to Calcutta my uncle told me that the man he had in mind was Rajkumar Durjay Kishor Dev Varma, younger brother of the Maharaja of Tripura. No wonder my grandmother had been won over. Tripura, up until the Japanese entry into the war, was a fantasy domain, part Shangri-la and part Never-Never Land. It was separated from the rest of India by two of Asia's mightiest rivers and therefore almost inaccessible. It was a land of bewildering paradoxes, savage and civilized, ancient and modern, of tribal animism and of an enlightened secularism, of witchcraft and of science, of tantric voodoo and of scholarship. It was also a paradise doomed, but, of course, no one could have foreseen it at the time.

Tripura was ruled by a dynasty of great antiquity known as the Manikyas; the ruling Manikya, eldest brother of Durjay, was the 180th of his line. His principality covered a sparsely populated area of more than 4,000 square miles wedged intricately between India and Burma, a rich tract washed by fast-flowing rivers, with fertile plains rising through densely forested slopes to rugged mountains.

In the forest lived wild elephants, tigers, leopards, sambhars, cheetahs and other game; in the hills were the tribes which had lived their own kind of lives since medieval times. Tripura's capital, Agartala, with a population of under 40,000, was like some sleepy, sun-warmed holiday resort. In the middle, surrounded by wooded parkland, was the Vijayanta Palace, a rambling complex of domed pavilions joined together by colonnaded passages running through lawns and enclosing ornamental pools. It was a structure designed more as a showcase for the priceless objects that the Manikyas had collected over the centuries than as a residence – indeed, the palace had no living accommodation at all. The Maharaja and his family lived in several annexes, using the palace principally for state occasions and for entertaining their guests. Among the exhibits in the palace was the ivory and gold throne which the Tripura rulers were said to have used for their coronations for more than four thousand years.

Whether or not the Manikyas were, as they claimed, the oldest princely dynasty of India, they were certainly among the most enlightened; well known as patrons of the arts, and of music and learning. It was the father of the then Maharaja, Bir Chandra, who, himself a painter of note, had 'discovered' Rabindranath Tagore, India's most revered literary prophet of modern times, and who had given help and encouragement to the country's equally illustrious scientist, Jagdish Chandra

Bose. The Manikyas were educated at public schools of the British pattern and were well-travelled. They excelled in outdoor games, were connoisseurs of European art and music and they prided themselves on being highly Westernized. They were bright and fun and fully at home in the social whirl of Calcutta, where they maintained a splendid town house. They entertained lavishly and took their guests to hunt wild buffalo and tiger in their preserves. While the guests danced the rhumba or the tango on the polished teakwood floor of the dance pavilion of the Vijayanta Palace, the tribal drums picked up the beat in the surrounding forest.

You will not recognize in the Tripura of today the land I have described. Now the capital has become a camp for refugees from Bangladesh, a huddle of unsightly shanties pulsating with humanity at its most degraded. The woods have been cut down for fuel, the fountains are dry and the ornamental pools serve as refuse bins. Only the great white palace remains, exposed and neglected, its plaster cracking, its paintwork peeling and its marble halls dimmed with dust. Sparrows nest among its chandeliers and flocks of pigeons inhabit the domes.

If Tripura was remote from the rest of India, I knew that its ruling dynasty had always had close links with the Ranas of Nepal. At least one of Tripura's Maharanis had come from the Rana family, and it was an established custom over much of the century that the Dewan, or Principal Minister, of Tripura had to be a Rana.

There are influences in life that no one can explain. Did I in some earlier life-cycle owe some kind of obligation to Tripura – some promise made in a moment of pride or abberation and lightly forgotten? For Tripura, in spite of its transformation from a holiday resort into a hive of refugees, has continued to hover hauntingly close to my own life, reminding me, or so it seems in retrospect, of obligations owed. I did not marry Durjay Kishor Dev Varma. In families such as ours, marriages were not made by the intending couples, but by their relatives and astrologers. Equally, engagements were broken by others. Durjay and I went about our separate ways without so much as a backward glance. But I have a feeling that the house of the Manikyas had never quite forgotten whatever it was that I owed. It bided its time; a dynasty that is five thousand years old does not count time in ordinary ways. And when that time came, it exercised its spell once again. It was like going back in time, reliving a past experience. For I gave my eldest daughter in marriage to the Maharaja of Tripura. She died young, unhappy and, I suspect, estranged from me. Was that in fulfilment of something that I had escaped from paying, by passing on my debt to my daughter? I have always wondered.

*　　*　　*

A short time before, Tripura had flashed into newspaper headlines and had caused all of us at the Lucknow hostel to sit up and take notice. The activities of the Indian princes had always provided our newspapers with a steady flow of gossip. They were our playboys and eccentrics; they were wealthy, romantic, wicked and unpredictable; they drove fast cars, fell off horses and crashed their private aeroplanes; they played flashy cricket and superb polo and gambled away improbable sums. Tripura broke into the news sedately enough.

It was announced that the Maharaja's sister, Kamal Prabha, was to be married to the Maharaja of Gwalior. A few days later, we were told that the whole city of Gwalior was being given a face-lift for the coming festivities. Simultaneously, there began to appear reports of a powerful lobby opposed to the marriage. The Maharaja of Gwalior was a Maratha, and his mother and his courtiers did not want him to marry someone outside the Maratha community. That was when we began to follow the developments with growing interest. Soon we learnt that some of the well-known diehard Maratha princes had come in on the side of the Gwalior courtiers, and that they had even made representations to the Viceroy to dissuade the Maharaja from proceeding with the marriage. Following a period of tantalizing silence, there came the abrupt announcement from the Gwalior camp that the marriage had been cancelled.

So the reactionaries had won. As girls, we were solidly ranged on the side of the bride, and properly indignant on her behalf. The Maharaja of Gwalior, had he appeared on our campus at that time, would have been coldly received.

*   *   *

The meeting between Durjay Kishor Dev and myself had been arranged to take place on neutral ground, so that it should have the appearance of a chance encounter. So we met at Firpo's, which was then as much of a Calcutta landmark as the Ochterlony monument. My uncle and aunt, an elderly friend and I were already seated at our reserved table, waiting for Durjay and his party. It was nearly six in the evening, and most of the tables in the large room were already taken. Men, Indian and English, in well-cut business suits and accompanied by women in flowered dresses or saris, sipped tea and nibbled at Firpo's famous cakes; others ordered their ritual sundowners. Their talk and laughter made a gentle buzz. As I was taking in the scene, I noticed that people were waving at a newcomer. It was Durjay, dark, slim and looking oddly military, who sailed past his friends with signals of recognition before making his way to our table. Instantly I was struck by the fact that this was his element.

I may have gone to college and spoken in public debates on the issues of the day, but now I was required to be the demure bride-to-be. I played the part diligently, keeping my eyes lowered most of the time, answering questions primly and not volunteering a remark. Uncle Kunjar ordered tea. Durjay at once earned a point from me when, on being asked whether he would not prefer a drink, he politely declined. He was almost as quiet and self-effacing as myself, and I think we both came away from the encounter believing that we had approved of one another. The critical first interview was successfully completed; now the less pertinent questions of dowry, place and date of the wedding, lists of gifts to relatives and sizes of wedding parties could be negotiated at length. Our horoscopes must have already passed an initial scanning, otherwise it is unlikely that we would have met at all.

CHAPTER SEVEN
The Dictates of Destiny

BY NO STRETCH of imagination could I have fitted Durjay
Kishor Dev into the home-spun garb of the freedom fighter of
my dreams. But my instincts and upbringing would not have
permitted me to resist the processes that my grandmother or
father had set in motion. It was as though they represented
destiny itself, and I have always been a strong believer in the
dictates of destiny. All I was expected to do was to wait and
prepare myself to make a home in remote Tripura – unless,
God forbid, this time too something went wrong. The thought
kept nagging me that I must be setting a family record for
unsuccessful engagements.

The weeks passed. I began to notice that the further
negotiations that should have followed the Firpo's interview
had mysteriously fallen behind schedule; there was no sign of
the mounting activity that overtakes a Hindu household
preparing for a wedding. Uncle Kunjar, who had been at the
forefront of the negotiations, went about as though he had
nothing more serious on his mind than the amateur point-
to-point races that the Cavalry School officers held every
winter.

Our house in Sagar housed a very large number of people.
Apart from uncles, aunts and cousins, there were at least fifty
second- or third-generation servants attached to the family
who were forever in and out of our rooms. In such a ménage,
secrets were almost impossible to keep. You only had to keep
your ears open to learn the latest gossip about pregnancies,
illnesses, quarrels, about which aunt had purchased new saris
or jewellery and which uncle had lost money gambling, and

how well or badly their sons were doing at school.

So I listened. I discovered that my grandmother as well as my uncles were having second thoughts. Perhaps they had been a little too precipitate in arranging the match between a young man who was altogether too Westernized, and someone like myself, brought up in strict Hindu orthodoxy?

'But he didn't seem all that Westernized to me,' I was bold enough to point out to Uncle Kunjar. 'I remember he didn't even have a drink when you offered it.'

'That was merely his politeness. He found out that you did not approve of people drinking.'

That revelation made me think even more highly of Durjay. Someone who had gone to the trouble of finding out my likes and dislikes in advance, so that he should do nothing that might earn my disapproval, had shown the sort of consideration that did not come naturally to most Indians. If that was a sign of being 'Westernized', I found nothing wrong with it. After all, I reminded myself, it was not as though there was anything deep-rooted or inflexible about my objection to alcohol, it was merely a new-found prejudice generated by my involvement with the struggle for independence. All my life I had lived among people who drank fairly regularly. Alcohol to the Gurkhas was a necessity of life – indeed, during certain festivals, it was actually a sacramental requirement. Perhaps, it occurred to me, I was even marked by destiny to transform this deep-dyed product of British imperial culture into a properly committed freedom fighter?

Within a few days of this conversation, Uncle Kunjar went off to Tripura, ostensibly to discuss the arrangements for the wedding, but, in fact, to take a closer look at the man he had so fervently hoped I would marry. Now Uncle Kunjar was a real country gentleman, as conservative as they come. He asked nothing more of life than to be able to hunt and shoot regularly, ride with the officers of the Cavalry School and go on living in the more than moderate comforts of the parental home. His horizons were conveniently walled in by the tiger jungles of the Central Provinces; his social circles did not extend much beyond the Sagar Club and the Officers' Mess of the Equitation School. His values were those of suburban officialdom, buttressed upon Rana traditions and taboos.

On the home ground of the Manikyas he must have felt like a fish out of water. In Calcutta they had seemed to form the hard core of its highly Westernized social circle, and this was something he could have reconciled himself to. But here he saw a different facet. Around them congregated artists, writers, dancers and actors. What he must have found even less palatable was their closeness with the Brahmosamajists, a group of articulate intellectuals bent upon purifying the Hindu religion of its accretion of orthodoxies.

To Uncle Kunjar the chasm between his favourite niece and the Manikyas must have looked wider than ever. But there was no question of his breaking off the engagement which he himself had so assiduously brought about – not unless, that is, he found another prospective husband about whom he felt less apprehensive.

If, as they say, marriages are made in heaven, how devious must be the ways of heaven! And how unlikely its instruments! Imagine, for instance, my uncle, a polite and even deferential guest in the house of the groom, determined to call the whole thing off, but giving away nothing as he joined in the interminable talk about that other broken engagement between Princess Kamal Prabha and the Maharaja of Gwalior.

As he listened to the talk about the Maharaja of Gwalior, his way of life, his views, his likes and dislikes, the thought suddenly crossed his mind that here was someone much closer to his own ideas of the sort of man his niece should marry. Practical to the last, he even managed to get hold of a copy of the Maharaja's horoscope, just in case.

The Maharaja of Gwalior, His Highness Jivajirao Scindia: right age, right caste, right everything. You could not aim any higher. He was one of the five premier Maharajas who were what were termed 'twenty-one-gunners', which meant that they were entitled to a salute of twenty-one guns on their 'official' visits.

In the private ranking order of the princes themselves, the gun-salutes conceded by the British stood for less than the fact that he was one of a handful of princes who were also known by their family names. He was 'The Scindia', as the ruler of Hyderabad was 'The Nizam' and that of Baroda, 'The

Gaekwad'. The Scindias were a part of the folklore of the land, a family that had changed the course of history itself.

It is possible that, if my uncle had given himself time to think, he would have been too daunted by the audacity of the idea to have gone on with it. Princes rarely married girls from outside their own order, and the Gwalior rulers, in particular, had traditionally found their brides from among a handful of old Maratha families from their homeland in western India. Around the Maharaja of Gwalior were his conservative and intriguing sardars, vigilant as hawks to guard clan interests and traditions, as they had so recently demonstrated by baring their teeth at the Tripura alliance.

But Uncle Kunjar took the bit between his teeth. As soon as he came home, he wrote a letter to his brother-in-law Chandan Singh, in Gwalior, enclosing the photograph of me which had been taken for the proposed Tripura alliance. How Chandan Singh was to approach the Maharaja, when he was not even in his service, and to speak to him on so delicate a subject as his marriage – a subject made all the more sensitive by the adverse publicity surrounding the breaking off of the Tripura engagement – was not my uncle's problem. He had the fullest confidence in the tact, energy and ingenuity of his brother-in-law.

For a week or so after his return, he went about looking stern and preoccupied. This was so unnatural that I began to wonder if something had gone wrong in Tripura. Apart from my grandmother, who could be trusted to keep the information to herself, the only person to whom Uncle Kunjar had given a hint of what was afoot was his wife, Mamiji. So when, a few days later, he received an answer from Chandan Singh assuring him that the initial reaction from the Gwalior camp had been favourable, he had gleefully read out the letter to his wife. Their son, Devendra, a bright boy in his teens, happened to be within earshot. He came running to my room to tell me what he had heard.

This news gave me the right opportunity for letting off steam. I sought out my uncle and told him that neither he nor anyone else had the right to arrange my marriage without so much as asking me what I thought of my proposed mate. As it was, I had plenty to say about the Maharaja of Gwalior.

'Don't you know how callously he broke off the Tripura engagement?' I charged him. 'It was the talk of our college. How can you even think of marrying me off to someone so fickle-minded – agreeing to marry a girl and, when the preparations are nearly complete, breaking it off after the invitations had been issued?'

My uncle kept reassuring me with sweet reasonableness. No one had given me away; everything was still at the proposal stage.

'And what happened in Tripura?'

'Oh, we discussed things.'

'You haven't gone and broken it off or . . .'

'Whatever could have given you that idea?'

'Then what about this new thing . . . Gwalior.'

'Don't you worry your head about these things,' he told me in his uncle-to-niece tone. 'You just relax, and let us do the worrying. How do you think you girls are to be found good husbands if their relatives don't do everything possible – huh?'

'But a girl has to be able to say yes or no,' I protested.

'Without doubt. She must.'

He was still in the grip of his gut-feeling that he was on to a winner. He made me feel that I was being unreasonable and that I had no cause to grumble. But I could see what my uncle was up to. He was keeping Tripura 'on hold', just for a couple of weeks, while he tried his hand at being an instrument of heaven.

My grandmother was no more forthcoming. 'We'll wait and see,' she told me. 'Let your uncle see what he can do. Meanwhile, try and put on some weight. Just look at how your collar-bones stick out.'

Looking back on these events, it seems to me to have been a kind of Lewis Carroll creation, with logic taking a back seat to Alice. My uncle's emissary, Chandan Singh, had somehow managed to force his entry into the looking-glass world of the Gwalior court. In an arena where angels would have feared to tread he had marched in stamping. He kept Uncle Kunjar posted of his day-to-day progress.

At Sagar Uncle Kunjar went about looking even more distracted, as though bowed down with the weight of secrets, while the rest of the household became visibly twitchy with suppressed curiosity. Then one day he announced that he was taking his wife and me to Hardoi, where my father had been transferred. 'We have to get his agreement to everything we have settled in Tripura,' he told me somewhat pointedly. 'He has to give you away, after all.'

I noticed that my uncle and aunt were taking with them rather more luggage and servants than was normal for such a trip. Mr Dubay, an elderly friend who was an important local official, had been invited to go with us. Mamiji was also taking along her eleven-year-old niece Riddhi, ostensibly for a treat. All this should have made me suspect that our real destination was not Hardoi, but then, as I discovered, not even Uncle Kunjar had a precise idea of where we might end up.

Towards noon we reached Jhansi junction, where it was necessary to change trains. Here Uncle Kunjar had our luggage unloaded and bustled us into the waiting-room. Then he dashed off to catch the waiting train from which we had just alighted. After it had pulled out, Mamiji revealed to me that he might have gone to Gwalior, a three-hour journey from Jhansi.

Hanging about at Jhansi railway station was a familiar feature of our railway travels. The waiting-room was large and high-ceilinged and it was furnished with comfortable cane sofas and lounging chairs; it had a bathroom at the back. The catering was adequate, the waiters and attendants knew us and there was an excellent bookstall on the platform.

It was late in the evening when my uncle returned. We could see from the way he walked that he was bubbling over with excitement. 'We're going to Bombay,' he announced. 'We'll have to hurry up, for the train is due any minute.'

Hardoi, which was to have been our destination, lies 200 miles to the north of Jhansi; Bombay is certainly five hundred miles or so to the south. Instructions were shouted at the bewildered servants to get our things together and porters were ordered to take them to the right platform. Between trying to get reservations, changing tickets and tipping the attendants, my uncle told us that he had gone to Gwalior. The Maharaja of Gwalior had seen my photograph and had suggested that we should all meet in Bombay.

'So that the two of you have a chance to see each other and decide for yourselves,' my uncle told me.

I had been fuming for hours, conscious ever since being bundled out of the train at Jhansi that the whole idea of the visit to Hardoi was an elaborate trick. But the first-class waiting-room at Jhansi was hardly the place to throw a tantrum. What little I managed to say was brushed aside. My aunt, on whom I had hitherto depended to take my side, kept darting warning glances at me to remind me that there were other passengers present.

After we had found our berths on the Bombay train my uncle tried to smooth things out. 'We have met all your conditions, haven't we? You wanted others to be present when you first met His Highness. Well, there is your aunt, and there is Mr Dubay, a family friend. And then, after you two have met and you still find that you don't want to marry him, no one is going to force you.'

'So long as that is clearly understood.'

'But it would be a crazy thing to do,' my aunt put in, now batting openly on her husband's side. 'And I know you're not crazy.'

So everyone else had made up their minds; if the Maharaja of Gwalior said yes, there was no question of a refusal – unless I was crazy, of course.

CHAPTER EIGHT
I Meet the Maharaja

THE ROOM IN the Taj Mahal Hotel in Bombay faced the sea. The afternoon sun came straight through the bay window and cast a watery sheen on everything in it. I sat in a chair, feeling dowdy in a long-sleeved close-necked 'Cossack' blouse of my grandmother's design. Flanking me were my uncle, my aunt and my cousin. Mr Dubay hovered discreetly in the background, making it abundantly clear that he was not participating but was, nevertheless, on call.

Opposite us sat the Maharaja of Gwalior, Jivajirao Scindia, and one of his sardars, Krishnarao Mahadik, a family elder who was married to his aunt.

The Scindia was typical of his Maratha race: compact, stocky and sunburnt. He had muscular shoulders, bright eyes, a soft almost gentle voice, and an easy impish grin. With my uncle and aunt he exchanged only formal pleasantries, but little Riddhi seemed to have made an instant hit. He discovered that she spoke Marathi fluently, which, Mamiji later told me, was why she had been brought along, to 'break the ice'. Beyond greeting me on arrival with folded hands, he addressed not a single remark to me. It was Sardar Mahadik who engaged me in conversation.

The war was in its second year: it was after Dunkirk and the fall of France. British cities were being given a daily pounding by Hitler's bombs. At home, the provincial government run by the National Congress had resigned en bloc, and our political leaders had been clapped into jails. As far as I remember nobody talked of the war or of the freedom struggle; it was not the occasion. Mamiji dispensed sandwiches and poured tea.

Riddhi and the Maharaja chattered away in Marathi and seemed to find a lot to laugh at. I watched the warships at anchor, with their guns pointed directly at us, turning now and then to answer a question from Sardar Mahadik.

'And what about music, Princess; are you fond of music?'

'I like music. But you must not call me "Princess". I am not a princess.'

'How am I to address you, then?'

'Lekha devi, I think. That's how visitors to our house address me.'

He went back to his tea, and I to my ships, and then:

'Classical music or film songs?'

'Both, I suppose, each in its place.'

'And do you play any musical instrument?'

'No, but I did study vocal music. I didn't pursue it.'

'Yes, of course. Did you study history at college, Princess?'

'No, not history – and please don't call me "Princess".'

There was a subdued twitter of laughter. 'You said films. Do you like the cinema?'

That was how it went on, stiff, polite and formal. Presently the Maharaja and his sardar made their farewells and were gone.

It could not have been much more than an hour later when the telephone rang. Mr Dubay, who had taken upon himself the duty of answering all telephone calls, told my uncle that it was Sardar Mahadik on the line, who wanted to speak to him.

My uncle went to the telephone, and I saw Mamiji folding her hands in an involuntary gesture to will the telephone into being the bringer of good news. It was neither yes nor no, however; the Maharaja wanted us to have lunch with him the next day, at Samudra Mahal, his seaside palace in Bombay.

After only a little hesitation, accompanied by wondering aloud whether it would look all right 'at this stage of the negotiations' for us to visit the Scindia's house, Uncle Kunjar had said yes. But, as he told us later, Sardar Mahadik had also made a request:

'His Highness wants to invite someone else to lunch. I take it that will be all right.'

'Well, so long as it is someone from His Highness's family,' my uncle had answered.

'Not family, but as good as. A close friend. His Highness the Nawab of Kurwai.'

On this point my uncle had taken a firm stand. 'Well, I don't know. I'd just as soon it was a private luncheon party, with no outsiders.'

'Of course, of course, Rana-Saheb. No, no, there'll be just ourselves. No outsiders.'

So the next day we all sat down to luncheon at Samudra Mahal. This time the talk was a little less strained, but we still didn't know what the Scindia had decided. He and Riddhi seemed to have taken up their cross-talk exactly where they had left it the previous afternoon. Towards the end of the meal I overheard the Maharaja telling Uncle Kunjar that he would like us to go with him to see a film at the Excelsior Cinema. I saw my uncle turn to his wife before saying yes.

Later that same evening, as we walked into the gilded lobby of the Excelsior, the Scindia was waiting at the foot of the stairs, with a more impish smile than ever. This time he was not accompanied by a member of his staff but by a friend whom he introduced to us.

'The Nawab-saheb of Kurwai. He was supposed to join us at lunch, but couldn't manage it.'

That was when Mamiji became absolutely sure that our marriage knots were already tied. 'Look how anxious he was for his best friend to see you,' she whispered to me. She was convinced that the Maharaja had invited us to go to the cinema to show his bride to the Nawab.

The next morning the telephone rang even before we had breakfast. It was Sardar Mahadik again. The Maharaja would be delighted if we would be his guests at the races that afternoon. Uncle Kunjar, suppressing his initial inclination to refuse, had asked to be rung back in ten minutes to see what the ladies had to say about it. 'I'll tell him "no", shall I?' he said to Mamiji.

'What nonsense? We must go.'

'But at the races! The whole of Bombay will see us in the Gwalior box.'

'But that's just what he wants. To show off your niece — can't you see that?'

'But . . . but it is all so unconventional . . .'

'This is not Sagar,' Mamiji retorted. 'Ask Lekha what she thinks.'

'If Mamiji says it is all right to go, we should go,' I said.

Was that how marriages arranged themselves, I wondered. At some stage they slipped out of the clutches of the arrangers and took off on their own. For even though no one had said anything definite yet, I had already become convinced that the Maharaja of Gwalior had made up his mind. And so had I.

I decided not to put on my Cossack blouse for the races. Mamiji gave me a hard look, but did not say anything. My uncle, I'm sure, did not notice what I was wearing. He was already looking a little lost, having had to relax the ground rules he had believed were inflexible.

So we drove to the races, through the special owners' entrance and were received by the Maharaja, this time with an ADC in attendance, Captain Vithalrao Lagad. We were handed badges, escorted to the Members' stand and settled into a box.

Even I, who knew very little about horse racing, had heard that the Scindia was by far the largest and most successful breeder and owner of racehorses in India. From the race cards that Captain Lagad had pressed into our hands I saw that four of his horses were running that day. Surely it was not too much to ask of the fates that at least one should win, to provide the day with its own good-luck omen? Mamiji had come more formidably equipped to lobby the fates. When we went to see the horses parading, being saddled or just led around in the enclosure between races, she would fall behind, dropping little silver coins. We memorized the Scindia's colours and the number that his horse had drawn. And then we sat in the box, with every nerve knotted and fingers gripping our seats, as though we were ourselves on horseback. Only by an effort of will did we manage to prevent ourselves from yelling out as the terracotta and blue colours streaked ahead of the others. After a chilling few seconds, the number went up on the indicator and the inner knots unravelled.

The fates was benign. Two of the Scindia's horses won. Even after more than forty years, I still remember their names: Pushpamala, meaning 'Garland' and Fire Alarm.

So the wonderful afternoon ended. In the evening shadows

we walked back to the car park. While my uncle lingered to say thank you and goodbye, Mamiji and I got into the car. Captain Lagad, who had held the door open for us, then did a strange thing. He bent low and made as if to touch my feet with his right hand before lifting it to his chest three times. *Mujra* is the mode of salutation with which the courtiers in Maratha princely states greeted their Maharaja and Maharani and their children, but no one else. It is performed with a good deal of flourish and style, and does not come easily to outsiders. Indeed, it is still the proper mode of salutation among the families of the Maratha ex-princes; my own son and other relatives invariably greet me with a *mujra*.

In that instant I knew. Nonetheless, I managed to protest: 'You mustn't do *mujra* to me, Captain!'

'I must, to our Maharani.'

So the members of the Maharaja of Gwalior's staff had been already told what none of us from Sagar knew, that I was to be their Maharani.

Soon after we had reached our hotel room Sardar Mahadik rang again. The Maharaja had charged him to tell us that he had made up his mind to marry me and that he would greatly appreciate it if the date for the wedding was fixed before we left Bombay. 'His Highness would like it to be before the end of February,' he told my uncle.

He and Mamiji looked very solemn and humbled by success. I fled into the bedroom and bent my head in prayer before my bedside gods.

*   *   *

I shall never forget my grandmother's spontaneous gesture when I returned. She took off the diamond ear-rings she had always worn and put them on me. They were big diamond solitaires, the most precious items of her jewellery.

After a brief shopping trip to Delhi, I found the Sagar house gratifyingly astir with activity, with jewellers and dressmakers squatting in the corridors. The priests of both sides had agreed that 21 February was the right day for the wedding. We set off by special train on the nineteenth. I had left Sagar many times before, but this time it was different. I was leaving it to make a new home for myself in Gwalior. As the train chugged through the hills that surrounded Sagar, I burst into tears.

PART II
THE SCINDIAS

CHAPTER NINE
Mahadji Scindia

OF THE SCINDIAS I knew very little, except that they ruled an enormous tract of land. Once, I remember, we had made a night halt at Indore on one of my grandmother's car journeys from Bombay to Agra. We left Indore early the next morning, and within a few miles we had entered Gwalior. Towards sunset and some three hundred miles later, we were still in the Scindia's territory. Now I discovered that what the Scindia still possessed was but a sixth of what his ancestors had once ruled.

They did not, like the majority of Indian princes, lay claim to a celestial, or even a lofty origin. On the contrary, they took pride in the fact that they came from honest peasant stock, the Marathas of western India, and rose to fame and power through grit and hard work, buttressed by an abiding conviction that they had been chosen by destiny to establish Maratha supremacy across the length and breadth of the subcontinent.

Destiny brought them dazzling successes; it also brought them heroic failures. At the beginning of the eighteenth century, their estates had been reduced to a few fields; at the beginning of the nineteenth, they were by far the strongest power in the land and held more territory than any other ruler. In the process more than a dozen sons of the family had left their ashes in distant parts of India.

Their original family name was Shinde. It was the British who took to calling these rulers with whom they came into conflict 'the Scindias', and over the century and a half of British rule this came to distinguish the Gwalior rulers' family from the other Shindes.

The Scindias came from a small village tucked away among the hills south of Poona, in western India, and thus from the very heartland of Maratha country, and their rise coincided with the rise of the Maratha kingdom which, in the mid-eighteenth century, had supplanted the Mughals as the supreme power in the land. My husband was the ninth Scindia from the founder, Dattaji.

Of my husband's ancestors, the one who towers above the others like a colossus is Mahadji. In a portrait of him by James Wales, he looks soft and benign, wearing chains of implausibly large pearls and gazing at the world with calm eyes, a jewel-encrusted sword in his lap. But this portrait was painted in 1792, only two years before his death, and does not show him as his contemporaries saw or imagined him, against the parched brown vastness of Hindustan itself, with little yellow tents and smudges of smoke in one corner, directing military operations from some vantage point, his brass English telescope tucked under his left arm, his face burned black by the sun and grimed with the dust of battle, but his eyes shining with the anticipation of victory; a man as hard as rock and capable of undergoing astonishing hardships, who never lost his cool no matter what the odds, shrewd and calculating to a fault and yet daring as a gambler who risks his all on the single throw of a dice, because he was certain that God was on his side,* almost in return for his own motto: 'Ever alert in the service of the cone of divine power', which is the family's motto still.

Such was Mahadji Scindia in the seventh and eighth decades of the eighteenth century, and the British, with the scent of the Empire strong in their nostrils, recognized him as their principal rival and enemy. It was during these years that they took to calling the Maratha Confederacy 'the Maratha Empire', and the maps accompanying their official dispatches show the entire stretch of continental India, from the desert of

---

* Mahadji did literally carry his own god with him. It was a little Shivling, the phallic symbol of the essence of Hinduism, carved out of an emerald that must have been the size of a hen's egg. As an outsize chunk of flawless emerald, its intrinsic value must be well over a million pounds, but its sentimental value to the Scindia family is literally incalculable. This linga is still worshipped daily in the private shrine in my house in Gwalior.

Rajasthan in the west to the Bay of Bengal in the east, as coming under the authority of that empire.

To be the overlords of the Mughals had been the Maratha dream, and Mahadji Scindia had made it come true. And yet although Delhi was in his charge, it was not where he chose to live. A thousand miles to the south of Delhi was Poona, the nerve centre of the Confederacy, but he had no special fondness for there either. Instead he found himself a place about midway between Delhi and Poona, Ujjain: Ujjain, holy, historic and battered. Here the line of the Sun, the Tropic of Cancer, made a neat cross with the River Sipra; here Lord Krishna himself had done his schooling under a wise sage; here the poet Kalidas, India's Homer, had written his epics on palm-leaf segments. And here Mahadji built himself a grand house with a hundred rooms,* and around it his sardars built their own mansions. He restored the temples and built new ones. Ujjain flourished, and even during Mahadji's lifetime it became known as the Scindia capital.

Towards the end of his days, Mahadji became to his own people and his state what the Duke of Wellington was to become to England, a great military hero, a wise statesman, even a sort of national monument endowed with oracular propensities, and it was a minor jest of history that it was the Iron Duke himself who, as Colonel Arthur Wellesley, defeated Mahadji's successor in battle, and thus made the way clear for the British conquest of India. But the future Duke might not have been victorious if Mahadji Scindia had still been alive. For Mahadji had convincingly demonstrated his prowess in battle. He had crushed the Rajputs into submission, defeated his single rival among the Marathas, the Holkar, and put the Mughal Emperor on a pension. What was more, he had fought two wars with the British. In one he had inflicted a humiliating defeat on them, and in the other had compelled them to break off hostilities and agree to a treaty in which both sides had come out shaken and bruised but with honours roughly even. And since that time Mahadji had improved the strength as well as the fighting capacity of his army.

Mahadji Scindia had read the British as well as they had read him. He knew that they were not merely the group of

* It is now called Maharajwada and is used to house a high school.

inoffensive traders they made themselves out to be, but a band of tough adventurers in the grip of an insatiable lust for plunder and the conquest of India. He, for his part, had sought to shape his military policy to counter the transparent designs of Warren Hastings, the Governor-General of the East India Company, a man of piratical scruples and Machiavellian duplicity. When he saw that Hastings was making a bid to bring the Mughal Emperor Shah Alam under the Company's 'protection', he moved in to forestall these designs.

In 1771 Mahadji captured Delhi, the Mughal capital, and took the demoralized Shah Alam under *his* 'protection'. He installed Shah Alam on the throne of his ancestors and, as the price of his protection, extracted from him two *sanads*, or patents. One conferred on the Peshwa, who was the head of the Maratha Confederacy and Mahadji's master, the title of *Wakil-i-Mutallaq*, or Viceroy, and the other made Mahadji himself the irremovable and hereditary deputy of the Peshwa. The environs of Delhi for nearly a hundred miles all round became Mahadji's personal fief.

*   *   *

For the next twenty-one years, till the time of his death, Mahadji Scindia was the real ruler of the greater part of North India, for all practical purposes a sovereign and independent state. If he had wanted to set himself up as an independent ruler, as the erstwhile Governors of the Great Mughals had done, the Peshwa could have done little to prevent it. Equally, he could have set aside the phantom Emperor and taken his place.

That he did not do either has perplexed Western historians. They see in it sinister motives: oriental cunning, the double duplicity of a man who preferred to operate from behind two masks, who enjoyed the substance of power but was prepared for some cunning reason to eschew its trappings. The less jaundiced ascribe it to a hard-grained pragmatism. His breaking away from the Peshwa would have encouraged the other members of the Confederacy to do the same, and that would have brought the whole edifice toppling down. But this argument, too, while it recognizes a nobler motive, is not really convincing because it smacks of the logic of hindsight.

The fact is that logic had little to do with the arrangement that Mahadji had worked out. It was founded on old-world notions of loyalty, and there are scores of letters written by Mahadji himself in which he explained his stand in precise terms: that it was merely a projection of his rocklike loyalty to the Peshwa.

Possibly his deep faith came into it too. He was a devout and intensely religious man, who believed that prayers made one's dreams come true. In later life, he spent an inordinate amount of time every day – between two and three hours – in prayer and other religious observances, and the trail of his victories is well marked by the shrines and ghats (riverside bathing steps) that he had put up. One of his chief relaxations was to compose *artis*, which are devotional songs, and some of these are still sung in the temples of his homeland.

His preoccupation with religion gave him a finely tuned sense of right and wrong which, at times, affected his military decisions. Once, after surrounding the fort of Chittore with troops, he held back his attack because he did not want to fire the first shot at what he regarded as a shrine – for was not there some legend that Chittore had been founded by none other than Kusha, the younger son of Rama, who is one of the most prominent deities of the Hindu pantheon? The defenders, routinely or chivalrously, obliged him by firing the first salvo.

'I desire no honour save that of being able to serve the Peshwa,' he was to assert again and again to those who questioned his motives, and there is no reason to doubt his sincerity.

Mahadji died in Poona on 12 February 1794, in his sixty-fifth year. He had no son of his own, only daughters, and he had made it known that his grand-nephew, Daulatrao, should be recognized as his heir. As it turned out, he was the first Scindia to be affected by this propensity (or was it some sort of a curse?) of not having a son, or a son who survived childhood, to ensure direct succession. As many as four Scindia rulers from Mahadji onwards were adopted as heirs from collateral branches of the family, and it was not until 1878, with the birth of my father-in-law, Madhavrao, that the curse or whatever it was may be said to have ended, after nearly a hundred and fifty years.

Mahadji was the greatest among the Scindias, but he did not belong only to the Scindias. His name means much not only to my own family and to the families of those who were his subjects, but to vast numbers of other Indians too; to them he was both liberator and saviour, the man who built temples, won battles, and in the process made a national dream come true, for had he not helped to set up Hindupad-Padshahi, 'The Empire of Hindus'? And only those who have lived as slaves in their own land for centuries can fathom the true intensity of that dream. He had become a legend in his own lifetime, and people sang rousing ballads to commemorate his exploits and parents told their children bedtime stories about him. His memorial in Poona is still regarded by many as a shrine and a place of pilgrimage.

CHAPTER TEN
Daulatrao Scindia

IT WAS MAHADJI SCINDIA alone who had stemmed the tide of British conquests. With his death, the British armies fanned out across the length and breadth of the subcontinent, seizing provinces and deposing kings.

Mahadji's successor, Daulatrao Scindia, has gone down in history as one of its less savoury characters, a sort of Nero who fiddled while his kingdom burned. But I cannot help feeling a little sorry for him. The challenges he was called upon to face while still a young man were altogether overwhelming, and he did not, like virtually all the major Rajput rulers, and indeed his own master, the Peshwa, give in meekly to British threats and accept their vassalage as some kind of a boon. Instead, he chose to fight.

It was his misfortune that the general who opposed him was perhaps the most brilliant military commander of the times and had under him certainly the best trained and equipped army of the times. To be beaten by the man who was soon to defeat Napoleon Bonaparte, was no disgrace.

And certainly not when General Wellesley also possessed the advantage of a formidable fifth column in the form of the entire officer corps of the Scindia's best regiments, all of them Europeans, who had no loyalty to either their employer,* or the land, and were out-and-out mercenaries. Many of them had been planted in his army by the Company's agents, to provide

---

* There were honourable exceptions. A year earlier one of his commanders, Michael Filose, on being accused by Daulatrao of disloyalty in the face of the enemy, had in a fit of indignation committed suicide by slashing his own neck with his sword.

for just such an eventuality. Now they were sent open orders to quit the Scindia's service and take away with them as many of his troops as they could. They obeyed without demur, but not before subverting the soldiers under their command and organizing some ingenious sabotage. On the very day of the battle, the men from two brigades declared a sudden *dharna* or strike, ostensibly for arrears of their salaries, and all the artillery bullocks were driven away into the jungles by their drivers.

But what had caused the Company to declare war against the Scindia? Nothing but the burning desire of the Governor-General, Lord Wellesley, to build an Empire. 'I will heap kingdom upon kingdom, victory upon victory, revenue upon revenue,' he had written in a private letter. Combined with this was the equally intoxicating dream of military glory with which the Governor-General's brother, Arthur Wellesley, was obsessed, to say nothing of the scent of 'Prize Money', which was the Company's euphemism for plunder. Arthur Wellesley, who had arrived in India without having seen much warfare, had tasted blood in the campaign against Tipoo Sultan and had come in for a major share of the loot of Tipoo's capital. With it he had not only paid off his debts, but had put aside a tidy fortune. Now, before his brother and patron finished his term as Governor-General and he himself was recalled to home service, here was an all but ready-made victory and the prospect of the lion's share of 'Prize Money'. Was not the Scindia supposed to be even wealthier than Tipoo Sultan?

The two armies met on 24 September 1803, in the field of Assaye, not far from the famous Ajanta Caves. In the event, it was neither a walkover nor a cheap victory for General Wellesley. Even when the artillery could not be brought into action because of the missing bullocks, and with literally all the European mercenaries having decamped and the striking troops not participating, the Scindia's army put up a desperate fight. The casualties on both sides were roughly equal, and, at the end of the day, when Daulatrao disengaged his force and took it beyond the range of the British guns, Wellesley did not go charging after him in pursuit. He too felt the need to make camp and regroup for the next round.

Assaye, for all that the name is emblazoned on the battle

honours of a dozen British regiments, was no victory for the British. Because, even if Daulatrao did not lose the battle, the war itself had been already lost in the other theatre in which it was also being fought. Indeed the surprise is that Daulatrao should have fought it at all and fought so well in spite of his handicaps, knowing that he had no alternative but to accept whatever terms the British offered him.

Daulatrao, young and unworldly as he was, seems to have devised a sensible plan for meeting the British threat. He knew that the Company's Governor-General had despatched two columns against him, one under its Commander-in-Chief General Lake, and the other under General Wellesley. Lake's column was heading towards Agra, where the Scindia's main army was based under its French general, M. Perron. Perron commanded four highly trained brigades of infantry under European officers and had his own pack of artillery. Daulatrao had every reason to believe that Perron would not have much difficulty in defeating Lake's numerically inferior and untried force, and that after that he would lose no time in rushing to his master's aid so that, between them, the two could finish off Wellesley's force. And even if that plan did not for some reason work out, he was quite convinced that Perron would go to ground in one of the several well-fortified and provisioned forts that were placed in his charge, to keep Lake's army occupied while he regrouped to give battle to Arthur Wellesley.

Alas, Perron did nothing of the kind. He, too, behaved as despicably as most of the other European officers who had flocked to the Scindia's army for money. On 20 August 1803, more than a month before Assaye, he sent a secret letter to Lake announcing that he would be prepared to abandon the Scindia's cause and even bring with him his personal body-guard, if he was given permission to travel with his family to Lucknow.

General Lake, it is recorded, 'courteously accorded the request of the fallen general'. But the irony is that the general had not fallen, indeed he had not even been engaged in battle. He had 40,000 crack troops under him, and he was protected behind the walls of the fort of Aligarh. Was it not Napoleon who said: 'In war, the moral to the physical is as two is to one'?

*   *   *

Poor Daulatrao Scindia. He was twenty-four years old. He did not even know what he had done to make the British declare war on him. He had made a creditable showing in the field, but he had lost the war; defeated not by General Wellesley but by the treachery of his European officers. He sued for peace.

General Wellesley may have been sorely disappointed that he was denied the opportunity of plundering the Scindia's capital, Ujjain,* but he may have been relieved and agreeably surprised that there were to be no further hostilities. The letters he wrote to his brother reveal his uncertainties. Nonetheless, when the Scindia emissaries came to him, asking for easy terms, he told them: 'I am not prepared to go into a discussion as to who was responsible for starting this war. What is undeniable is that you have lost it, and we have won. You have to make reparations.'

This was the logic of victory, and Wellesley made Daulatrao Scindia pay a cruel price. His brother, the Marquis, had vowed that he would 'heap kingdom upon kingdom', and Arthur Wellesley's contribution to the heap was truly munificent: the Scindia's province of Agra and Delhi and Jaipur and Jodhpur, Bharoch and Berar and, for good measure, a vast tract around the field of Assaye which had now become hallowed ground. Superimposed on a contemporary map of India, these areas cover the states of Haryana, Rajasthan, Delhi, and a half of Uttar Pradesh, plus generous chunks of Gujarat and Maharashtra.

*   *   *

I, who nearly a century and a half later was witness to the dissolution of whatever was still left of the Scindia domain, can sympathize with the agonies of someone who underwent a similar trauma. Here was Daulatrao, at an age when most men are barely on the threshold of their careers, with his career already ended. On the day of the Dassera festival of 1803, when he fought the battle of Assaye, he had been master of a kingdom that was at least as large as France. The Hat Men to

---

* General Lake fared much better in the way of 'Prize Money'. In the fort of Agra, he found treasure worth a quarter of a million pounds.

whom he had done no harm had come and taken away most of its populous and fertile territory, leaving behind only a mangled portion about one third its original size. In the process, they had demolished the Maratha Confederacy itself, so that even though he was, in theory, still an independent ruler who possessed a fairly formidable army, he was hemmed in by all sorts of controls. He, who had been acknowledged as the 'Protector' of the Mughal Empire, had himself been made a ward of a company of traders. The shock was enough to derange a more sensitive mind, as it did derange the mind of the Holkar, the other 'pillar' of the Maratha Confederacy, whose position was also reduced to a size acceptable to the British and who literally went mad.

Daulatrao did not quite lose his mind, but neither was his future life that of a balanced man. He was consumed with a hatred of all Europeans and paranoiacally suspicious of all contact with them, but at the same time he was acutely aware that his best interests lay in making a pretence of treating the functionaries of the Raj with exemplary decorum. These two traits, intense distrust and outward politeness, became incorporated into the policy of the Scindias towards their British overlords right through the days of the Company and then of the Raj, down to my husband's time. My father-in-law named his two children George and Mary, ostensibly as a token of his esteem for George V and his queen, but no one ever dared to call them by these names in his hearing. My husband, the one who was named George, never set foot in England so long as the English were ruling India.

*   *   *

Daulatrao Scindia became, quite early in his life, a dilettante and a voluptuary, but luckily he had innate good taste too. He made a habit of enticing to his court the most skilful or at least the most seductive dancing girls from all parts of the country, but he also came to be recognized as a discriminating connoisseur of classical dancing and, incidentally – since the dancers usually preferred to be accompanied by their own band of musicians – of classical music too.

Gradually, music took over as his principal addiction, and with his resources he was able to set up what even in his own times acquired an identity as the Gwalior *gharana*, or 'school of music', which, I am happy to say, still flourishes.

Thus did Daulatrao make amends for his shortcomings as a soldier, statesman or administrator. He joined the ranks of the other princely patrons of the arts of India, such as the Maharajas of Jaipur, Baroda, Travankore, Mysore, and the Nawab of Rampur, to name only a few, who between them managed to keep alive the arts and music of India during the hundred and fifty years of alien rule. To the British, the very idea that there could be any music or art outside that of Europe was totally unacceptable, and it is not surprising that in the British parts of India it had quite ceased to exist. There can be no doubt that, whatever the real or supposed benefits of the Raj, under its dismissive estimation of their merits, the art and music of India would not have survived if there had not been a princely India to preserve it.

The head of the Gwalior *gharana* during Daulatrao's times was Mohammad Khan, and it was the practice of these *ustads*, or maestros, to choose from among their more promising pupils just one who would be raised to the level of chief disciple, trained with extra-special care and at a relentless tempo, and subjected to special disciplines of diet and exercise so that, in time, he could take over as the *ustad* of the *gharana*. The fourth *ustad* after Mohammad Khan was Nasiruddin Khan, and it was he who, at the end of the nineteenth century, taught music to my father-in-law, Madhavrao. His star pupil, Pandit Krishnarao, made valiant attempts to get my husband to learn vocal music, but alas without much success. Nonetheless, he was able to instil in him a genuine love of classical music. I have seen him sit through the marathon sessions in which *ustads* try to score points off their rival *ustads* and in which the best performances come only towards the pre-dawn hours. Indeed, Indian music is a mainly nocturnal pastime, and it has never ceased to puzzle western observers why the best musical performances come only after most of the audience has gone home or fallen asleep. For instance E. M. Forster, after 'nautch girls had howled and a military band moaned', went to bed at midnight and woke up at 3 a.m. to find that:

> The music had become beautiful; so I fitted my turban and rejoined the company. H. H. (Maharaja Tukojirao of Dewas) was

asleep on his bed and the townsfolk had gone off to their homes, and only a few experts survived. I am as far as ever from understanding Indian singing, but have no doubt that I was listening to great art, it was so complicated and passionate. Why save your best singers until 3 a.m.?

Why indeed. I, supposedly far more musical than my husband, find these all-night sessions far beyond my powers of endurance. But I must not end this musical digression without paying tribute to my own favourite, *Ustad* Hafiz Ali Khan, who headed the *gharana* when I came to Gwalior as a bride. He used to tear his plentiful hair in sheer vexation at my not keeping to his disciplines or hours of practice in playing the sitar or voice-training and thus wasting what he was convinced were my god-given talents. Alas, I had no intention of qualifying for ustadship, but what he taught me while my enthusiasm lasted remains with me, doubling up as an emotional heritage capable of exercising its own spell, so that when I hear a raga sung in a clear trained voice, or someone like Ravi Shankar playing the sitar or Amjad Ali Khan the sarod, my head sways to the rhythm and I keep time with the big right toe in the approved fashion, at times even brought to tears by their sheer perfection.

*   *   *

Daulatrao Scindia died on 20 March 1827. He too had no son, only daughters, and since among Hindus succession passes only in the male line, his wife Baijabai, a renowned beauty of her time, had to resort to the device of adopting a male child of some close relative as her son and her husband's heir. This boy, whom she named Jankoji, was eleven years old. Until he came of age, Baijabai herself ruled the Scindia domain.

In the Gopal temple in Ujjain, which after its destruction by the Mughals was rebuilt by the Scindias, is a special shrine. Its door-frames are solid silver and the door itself is formed by two panels which, in the manner of a stained-glass window, are a mosaic of segments of precious jade.* Framed in this

* This door is one of a pair which, in medieval times, adorned the inner sanctum of one of the richest Hindu temples on the Gujarat coast and formed part of the loot taken away by Mohammad Gazni in the eleventh century. Both doors were brought back by one of the Scindias from an expedition to the north as part of his loot. The other jade door now belongs to the family shrine in my house in Gwalior, Ranimahal.

Arabian Nights splendour is a chaste white statue of a woman. This is Baijabai in middle age, still a remarkably handsome woman and almost saintly in her widow's white. But she was strong-willed, proud and domineering, and the British did not trust her to toe the line and watched her activities like hawks. Finally they declared her to be a rebel and forced her to leave Gwalior and settle down in Agra in quiet retirement.

Meanwhile, the boy she had adopted, Jankoji, had come of age, and in 1836 he was installed as the Maharaja of Gwalior. But he was not destined to rule for long. Six years later, as he lay dying, the consternation in his court was increased by something that no one could believe was possible: the British had suffered a shattering defeat at the hands of an Asian power. The army they had sent to Afghanistan, in what was patently a bid to take over that country, had been wiped out. The Governor-General who had ordered the operation had been sacked, and the new Governor-General, Lord Ellenborough, had to do something spectacular to salvage the loss of face. Gwalior, still by far the largest kingdom in India, was his obvious target.

And here was the ruler of Gwalior dying without a son to succeed him. What was to prevent Ellenborough from swallowing up Gwalior on the pretext that there was no heir to the kingdom.

The crisis brought to centre-stage the towering figure of a trusted nobleman and family advisor, Sambhajirao Angre, who was the Dewan, or Prime Minister. He it was who mounted his horse and went clattering through the streets of the city on a self-imposed mission: the search for a boy from among the closer Scindia relatives who could be given in a death-bed adoption to Maharaja Jankoji.

Angre came upon a clutch of boys playing a game of marbles. He reined in his horse and watched, shivering in the midwinter cold as one of the contestants took an implausibly long shot and broke his opponent's marble with an accurate hit. Taking this as a sign from the gods, he bent down and picked up the boy, and putting him in front of him in the saddle galloped back to the palace in triumph.

The pandits hurried through the adoption ritual and the eight-year-old Bhagirath Shinde was given a new name,

Jayajirao, and declared to be a Scindia. It is said that throughout the ceremony the boy kept protesting that he had been done out of the marble that he had won from his opponent, and that he even attempted to run away to go and claim it. Anyhow when, a few hours later, Jankoji Scindia breathed his last, he had left behind a ritualistically adopted heir to succeed to his possessions.

CHAPTER ELEVEN

Jayajirao Scindia

ODD AS IT may seem in the context of the East India
Company's appetite for military conquests, forty years after
Assaye Gwalior was still more or less the same size and shape
and still retained the status of an independent kingdom. The
newly arrived Governor-General Lord Ellenborough obviously thought it intolerable that there should exist another
power in the land which could, even theoretically, claim to be
an independent kingdom, and he applied himself energetically
to the task of remedying that situation. The remedy was war.

His difficulty was that the ruler of the kingdom happened to
be a small child, and his guardian and adoptive mother was
not much older. He could not blow up either into the sort of an
ogre who constituted a threat to the British presence. His best
bet would be to go to war against Gwalior in the role of a
protector of these two innocents. But a protector against
whom?

Ellenborough had heard that the Gwalior durbar had
unanimously elected one of the hereditary noblemen, Dada
Khasgiwale, to act as Regent during the minority of Jayajirao
Scindia. Ellenborough peremptorily ordered his Resident at
Gwalior to prevail upon the durbar to remove this Regent who
enjoyed all-round support and to put in his place someone
who would carry out the Resident's behests without protest.
The Resident, Colonel Robert Spiers, rather thoughtlessly
chose a man called Mamasaheb Kadam who, according to Dr
John Hope, the Residency Surgeon at the time, 'was an upstart
with the most repulsive manners'. Much to Lord Ellenborough's discomfiture, the Gwalior durbar gave in to this

outrageous demand of the Resident, and obediently removed
Khasgiwale and appointed Kadam in his place.

Clearly this was not what Ellenborough had anticipated. He
wanted the durbar to resist his demands, thus providing him
with a cause for the war on which he had set his heart. Surely
now that they had succeeded in planting their own man as the
Regent, he could be relied upon to needle the durbar into
providing Ellenborough with the excuse he so desperately
longed for.

From here onwards, the situation developed into sheer
farce. Kadam, no doubt in an effort to feather his own nest
while at the same time promoting the Governor-General's
schemes, proceeded to get his own eight-year-old daughter
married to the nine-year-old Maharaja. This move was bitterly
resented by the ex-Maharani and by the Maharaja's adoptive
mother, Tarabai. A violent quarrel ensued between her and the
Regent in which Tarabai's maidservants became involved.
Some of them chased Kadam out of the palace premises, and
he is said to have 'fled with bag and baggage' to the British
Resident. 'Here,' he triumphantly announced, 'is your chance
to act.' Tarabai's maidservants had risen in revolt against the
Regent, who was a British nominee. Their leader was a slave-
girl called Narangi. To put down this revolt, the Regent
needed the help of British regiments.

Dr Hope dismisses this fatuous story as a patent fabrication.
'We, then residing on the spot, could never believe that
Narangi was anything better than the ordinary slaves,' he
scoffs. Now Ellenborough found himself in the ludicrous
position of declaring war against Gwalior to suppress a revolt
of maidservants, and he blamed his man on the spot, Colonel
Spiers, for bungling things. He recalled Spiers and in his place
sent one of the most promising middle-rank servants of the
Company, who had been waiting for just such an opportunity.
This was none other than Major (as he then was) W. H.
Sleeman, who was soon to acquire fame as the exterminator of
the gangs of thugs, professional bandits and murderers who
used to infest Central India. As soon as Sleeman was in
position, Ellenborough ordered two military columns to
advance to the borders of Gwalior and himself proceeded to
Dholput, which is about forty miles to the north of Gwalior, so

as to be on hand to take overall command of the operations.

Meanwhile, Gwalior's British-appointed regent having run away, the durbar brought back Khasgiwale to run the affairs of the state, and thus at last gave Ellenborough the excuse he had been waiting for.

'He was like a hungry fox with a goose,' wrote Dr Hope. He issued a long-winded proclamation to the people of Gwalior. It is a fascinating mixture of distorted logic and bombast, of verbiage used as camouflage for defending the indefensible. It is crammed with pompous phrases such as 'out of a sense of duty not to ourselves alone but to humanity', and 'moved by sentiments of pity towards the Maharaja'.

Then, for no apparent reason, he unleashed both his columns against the unprepared contingents of Gwalior. His troops fought two battles and won them with relative ease, even if their casualties were disproportionately heavy. After that, the victors proceeded to help themselves to the fruits of victory in a style that had become almost a regular drill, plundering villages and subjecting their prisoners to gruesome tortures. All of this was faithfully put down in his memoirs by that detached ringside observer, Dr John Hope.

Despite Ellenborough's declarations, neither pity nor sentiment prevented him from abrogating the earlier treaties between the Scindias and the Company and imposing a new one. By this treaty, Gwalior was divested of its independent status and declared to be a feudal state under the East India Company. A new contingent of troops was raised in Gwalior, ostensibly for the Scindia's protection and paid for by him, but it was trained and commanded by the British. Edward Thornton, in his *History of the British Empire*, believes that Ellenborough declared this war 'merely to gratify a desire for treating the Gwalior State as a conquered country'.

* * *

So while still a small boy Jayajirao Scindia had his wings drastically clipped; from being a king, he was demoted to being a vassal, a dependent prince. During his interview with Ellenborough, 'he had wept most of the time', and as he grew up the British grip visibly tightened. He awoke to the sound of British bugles and saw battalions drilling to English words of command. A British resident directed the affairs of the state through a council of Regency which he could override at will. All this lasted for ten years. But if Jayajirao came to look upon the British as a prisoner looks upon his custodians, he also developed an exaggerated respect for British might, British cunning, British capacity for intrigue. No one could oppose them.

When, in 1845, he attained the age of nineteen, the British installed him as Maharaja of Gwalior with what were called full ruling powers. But these powers had to be exercised through a Dewan, or Prime Minister, whom the British foisted on him.

With all these restraints, it is not surprising that Jayajirao Scindia grew up into an enigmatic character, given to weighing the odds too much before acting, preferring silence to speech, devious and secretive, yet managing to give the impression of a happy-go-lucky prince who enjoyed the good things of life, music, hunting and pageantry. He reminds me of the Roman Emperor Claudius as portrayed by Robert Graves, for he was the same size and shape and even had Claudius's tendency to stammer. Both had developed an uncanny capacity for survival.

*   *   *

Twelve years later came the Indian Mutiny or, as the Indians themselves call it, their first war of independence. It began with the Company's sepoys in the cantonment town of Meerut killing their British officers and their families. Within a month, the uprising had reached Gwalior, where was stationed a brand new contingent that had been raised, trained and commanded by the British. This contingent too joined the revolt and promptly slaughtered the British officers, although at Jayajirao Scindia's urging their women and children were spared. Jayajirao gave them shelter and sent them off under escort to the fort of Agra, which had remained in British hands.

Both sides in the conflict, conscious that the prestige of the Scindia name and his still considerable military force would prove a formidable asset, were desperate for Jayajirao to join them. But for a whole year he remained immune to their appeals or threats. It was only when he saw for himself that the revolt had all but died out and the British were on the brink of victory that he finally went over to their side.

Normally the Company's satraps would never have condoned such vacillation; that the Scindia had held back to see which side was winning instead of joining them at the very outset would have been regarded as sufficient to merit the severest penalties.

But the days of the Wellesleys and Ellenboroughs had gone. Indeed by the time the revolt had been put down, the process of winding up the East India Company itself had reached its final stages. The British Parliament, horrified at the bitterness that the Company's rule had aroused throughout India by its policy of ruthless annexations, had decided to end its charter. A few months later, on 1 November 1858, Queen Victoria, in a statement she herself had helped to draft, solemnly announced that 'for divers weighty reasons' the Company had been taken over by the British Government. The Queen further declared that the treaties and engagements made by the Company with the Indian rulers would be 'scrupulously maintained', and that she would 'sanction no encroachment' of their rights. She desired 'no further extension of our present territorial possessions,' and guaranteed that her government would 'respect the rights, dignity and honour of the native princes as our own'.

Every ruler in India, large or small – and there were nearly six hundred of them – heaved a sigh of relief. This was a reprieve. As for Gwalior, the Queen's proclamation had saved it from being transformed into a province of British India.

To be sure, the Indian Princes had not regained their independence, but as least what they still possessed was to be theirs for ever and ever. The fence that the Company's officials had devised had been made a permanent fixture, and if they had to live within its confines, at least they were now assured that there would be no further contractions of the fence.

Over the years this segregation was carefully nurtured and reinforced by the princes themselves. The less contact they maintained with the overlords, the less cause they would have for interference. Thus the two Indias, British and Princely, shown on maps in splotches of pink or yellow, established themselves as separate worlds. Princely India became more ingrown and insular and developed an identity of its own as a repository of the culture and traditions of a land from which the Industrial Revolution had been kept strictly at bay. To visitors from Europe and America, it represented a quaint, well-preserved tableau of the past – a panoramic Williamsburg encrusted with medieval trappings.

*   *   *

Jayajirao Scindia ruled for more than forty years. His was a happy if circumscribed life, that of a man possessed of rude good health and seemingly unlimited wealth. He became a renowned shot and a superb horseman who, as seen by a French visitor, 'mounted on a magnificient stallion, went through all the evolutions of the high school of India. The animal reared, plunged, started off precipitately, stopped short, pranced and jumped at his master's will.'

He made himself a reputation as someone who loved the good life, a man who patronized music and the arts and who could match the flamboyance of the imperial satraps. At banquets he drank implausible quantities of a mixture of old brandy and champagne in enormous golden goblets and, according to the same French visitor, delighted in creating spectacular effects as, for instance, at a party he gave for the Viceroy in the courtyard of the Taj Mahal at Agra:

> The garden was like a gigantic fairy-scene, the fountains throwing up showers of glittering spray, the trees covered with fruit and flowers and the air filled with enchanting music from the orchestras . . . the Maharajas sparkling with diamonds presenting a spectacle of which no European ceremony can give an idea.

Then came a special effect which was obviously intended to impress the guests. Hitherto, the Taj itself had been kept in darkness, but

> Suddenly, about ten o'clock, there appeared at the farther end of the avenue a snow white mass of colossal proportions, suspended in the air. The Taj . . . lit up with electric lights. The effect was magical.

Nonetheless, for all his gaiety and high spirits, Jayajirao himself considered that his life had been blighted by two inflictions, one ordained by the gods, and the other by the British. Both were to relent, but not until towards the end of his days when he had all but given up hope.

Three of Jayajirao Scindia's sons had died in their infancy, one after the other, and the ferocity with which the fates had acted to maintain their peculiar affliction on the head of the Scindia family, that he should leave no son to succeed him, had filled his mind with an overpowering sense of futility. Then, at the age of forty, he had taken yet another wife, his fourth. She was the daughter of a Gwalior feudatory, Sardar Jadhav, and it was this wife who a year later blessed him with yet another son, to whom they gave the name of the greatest of the Scindias: Madhavrao.

The British, for their part, took much longer to relent. It was not until 1884 that they offered to exchange the fort of Gwalior for the Scindia's fort and the town of Jhansi and its environs, where they intended to set up a new cantonment.

It was an extortionate price, but Jayajirao jumped at it. On the appointed day, the Union Jack was lowered from the fort's flagstaff and the British battalion stationed in it marched out of the Elephant Gate and filed past the naked stone giants carved into the hillside, their band playing 'Tommy make room for your uncle'.*

For Gwalior's army it was a truly memorable occasion. It was going back to its home fort after an absence of forty-two years. The 'uncle' who took charge of it after Tommy had made room for him was, appropriately, the most formidable figure in the Scindia's court, decked out in the most splendid of uniforms, that of the Commander-in-Chief of the army. His name was Sardar Baburao Appasaheb Angre, and he was said to have been as broad as he was tall. He was the son of Sambhajirao Angre, who had all but kidnapped Jayajirao Scindia to be adopted as heir to the Scindia inheritance, and upon Sambhajirao's death he had become head of the family.

From all accounts, this Baburao Angre was a truly

* Their well-appointed barracks were later used to set up India's first public school, the Scindia School. Its spacious grounds are studded with ancient monuments of archaeological interest, and the platform round the historic Teli temple is used as a stand to watch schoolboys playing cricket where once Tommy Atkins drilled.

Falstaffian figure, who filled out more and more into the role
he had created for himself. He was a physical culture fanatic
and wrestler and stories of his feats of strength, his size and
weight, and above all of his gargantuan appetite, are treasured
by the Angre family. The pair of wooden clubs with which he
exercised every day at dawn are preserved and periodically
polished almost as a dare to any professional strongman
visiting the house. It is difficult for an average man to lift even
one of them off the ground with both hands; he, it seems, used
to take one in each hand and twirl them about for a hundred
times as part of his routine for keeping himself in training. The
size of the meals he ate may well have grown with the telling.
That his breakfast consisted of a spiced scramble of twenty-
one eggs and a dozen or so thick parathas, washed down with
a gallon of buttermilk, and that he ate a medium-sized goat
every day, may well be apocryphal. But the fact that for his
morning round of various parade grounds, which took him
two hours, it was customary for him to use eight strong horses,
one after the other, is a matter of official record.

Lady Dufferin, in her book *Viceregal Life in India*, describes
the scene of the handing back of the fort to the Scindia by her
husband, who was the Viceroy:

> The fort looks like a Gibralter guarding his palace. He has been
> waiting for it for years; and when we see how completely it
> commands his town and his home, one can quite understand what
> a thorn in his side it must have been.

The actual ceremony took place in the enormous durbar hall
at Jaivilas Palace, which Jayajirao had built and which, nearly
a century later, was to be the scene of some of the most painful
and horrifying experiences of my life. Here is how Lady
Dufferin describes it:

> The Viceroy read out the Foreign Office despatch handing over the
> fort to the Maharaja. Scindia made a short reply in a very low
> voice . . . and though he showed little emotion of any kind, we all
> knew that the great wish of his life had been fulfilled. He said to the
> Resident as he left: 'Now I must go and tell my boy.'

The 'boy', Jayajirao's eight-year-old son, was not present at
the durbar. He lay ill in bed.

He was regarded as a boon child, a gift of the gods – a

'natural-born' son as defined by Dalhousie in a line that had not seen a father-to-son succession for a century and a half! A son who would one day, by the mere act of lighting his father's funeral pyre, send his father's soul soaring up to heaven and at the same time ensure that whatever he had left behind was not swallowed up by the British on the grounds that they were somehow the legal heirs of all sonless Indian rulers – for few in those early days of the Raj were prepared to believe that Queen Victoria's promises were proof against the land-hunger of the Hat Men.

So the festivities, for Jayajirao, were shadowed by anxiety. Madhavrao was now eight years old. Was some capricious fate going to take him away too – merely to give point to a family curse?

Surely this was the reason behind Jayajirao's 'very low voice' and his strange lack of emotion at so exciting an event as the restitution of the ancestral fort: he did not want to antagonize the fates by showing too much joy. The niggard-liness of the gods in providing male heirs has always been a source of nagging worry to the Scindias; I remember how after my two daughters were born I myself was conscious of whispering among the courtiers that my husband might have to resort to the expedient of adoption, or even of finding himself another wife, and how after the birth of my third child, who was a son, there was wild rejoicing all over what had once been the Gwalior state as at some national victory.

So I find it easy to sympathize with Jayajirao's sentiments on the day he got back his fort while his 'boy' lay ill with a fever. It couldn't have been a serious illness, however, and Madhavrao soon recovered. Though he was to be my father-in-law, I never saw him, for he died when his only son, my husband, was himself a boy aged nine.

CHAPTER TWELVE
The Building of the Palaces

THE JAIVILAS PALACE having, as it were, strayed into this narrative without a proper introduction, I should like to explain how and why it came to be built.

The Scindias had established themselves in the north of India by conquest, and at first their capital was Ujjain, an ancient and holy city in the very heartland of India. It was not until after the turn of the century and the indecisive war with the British that Daulatrao Scindia took his army well to the north of Ujjain. He wanted to be close to his kampoos stationed in Agra in case the British forced yet another war on him, so he pitched his camp near the ancient fort of Gwalior and Gwalior became his principal place of residence. Daulatrao's tented camp blossomed into a bustling town, and this part of the city is still called Lashkar, which means 'cantonment'.

By 1870, the Scindias had built themselves three palaces in Gwalior, which must have been perfectly adequate for the family's needs. By this time too the Raj, after the period of turmoil consequent upon taking over from the East India Company, had settled into its proper stride. Its style of functioning had changed and order prevailed across the length and breadth of the subcontinent. India was no longer the land of the pagoda tree, made to order for British adventurers to make quick fortunes in, but it had come into its own as a hunter's paradise for those who had a lot of money or, better still, the right connections with the Raj's élite. No Viceroy, as the Governor-General was now designated, would think of completing his tenure of duty unless he had shot his fill of tigers as the guest of some Indian prince. Aside from the Raj's own satraps, there were a fair number of Grand Dukes and the royals of several European duchies and monarchies who had taken to visiting India in increasing numbers under the auspices of the Raj, and they too were passed on to some Maharaja or the other to shoot their tigers.

In those days, and indeed until the advent of independence, Gwalior was regarded as India's tiger-land. This was because its rulers took great care to preserve the numbers of tigers at a level that would have gladdened the heart of the most rabid conservationist. Admittedly the reason for this protectionist zeal was so that there should be plenty of tigers to provide sport for the Maharajas themselves as well as their guests, but the overall result was nonetheless laudable. And because they had all these tigers in their preserves, they were regularly called upon to host shoots either for the Viceroy or for the Raj's most privileged guests who came from the highest levels of Europe's aristocracy. These people invariably travelled with large retinues, and the Viceroy himself went from place to place in a special train with its carriages painted ivory and gold, and with an entourage of officials, hangers-on and servants that seldom numbered less than a thousand.

Normally, these guests were put up in tented camps.* And though the tents were like bungalows, with stout double roofs and hung with silk and velvet draperies, richly carpeted and provided with brick fireplaces, they still gave the impression of makeshift hospitality. It was to be able to accommodate these frequent influxes of European guests that Jayajirao Scindia decided to build himself yet another palace, one so spacious that it would never cause him an accommodation problem.

So he commissioned one of his favourite sardars, Sir Michael Filose, the grandson of the Michael Filose who had committed suicide to demonstrate his loyalty to Daulatrao Scindia† and known in Gwalior as Mukhel Sahib, to build him

---

* Even as late as 1911, the famous Delhi Durbar attended by George V and his Queen was no more than a city of tents, but with its own gardens, artificial pools, lawns and well laid out drives, and with electric lights indoors and outdoors.

† And the grandfather of Colonel Agustine Filose who, when he decided to emigrate to Italy, left his entire estate to my daughters.

a palace. He told Filose to visit the capitals of Europe, study the architecture of famous royal residences, buy whatever he thought necessary in the way of materials, fittings, furniture, carpets, pictures, statuary and curtain material, hire craftsmen, engineers, plumbers and other skilled workers, and get his palace ready as soon as possible.

So Mukhel Sahib went all over Europe and decided to build a palace which borrows heavily from both Versailles and the Place Vendome in Paris, but still manages to retain an oriental look. There were, too, necessary variations to suit the climate and the lifestyle of its putative inhabitants. For instance, there is an entire wing with walls of pierced stone where the ladies of the house who observed purdah could roam at will, unseen by outsiders. He scoured Europe for furniture, mirrors, pictures, chandeliers, velvets, silks and tapestry with little thought of expense, and brought back enough of everything to fit out at least two Jaivilases.*

Michael Filose was a sardar, or hereditary nobleman, of the Scindia's court. He was the descendant of Jean Baptiste, an Italian gentleman who had taken service under Mahadji Scindia as an officer of the kampoos, and who in Daulatrao's time had become one of the principal supporters of the regime. As such, it was perhaps natural that Mukhel Sahib should have derived his inspiration mainly from Europe. Nonetheless, the structure he put up shows evidence of an earnest desire to synthesize the style of the Mughals with that of the Medicis. For the exterior and much of the interior he relied upon a versatile local stone which could be quarried in enormous chunks† and cut into the required shapes and sizes to form

* Seventy years later, the huge, barn-like storage sheds which housed the surplus and were called the Aarayash Karkhana were still crammed with furnishing fabric which crumbled at the touch, carpets which had been eaten up by moths or white ants and reduced to powder, pictures that had buckled and cracked, mottled mirrors with their gilt frames peeling, and chairs and tables in tottering piles. Filose must have bought Hepplewhite and Chippendale chairs by the gross and curtain material from Prato by the mile. From whatever furniture that could be salvaged or cannibalized and lengths of material that were still whole, I was able to furnish much of the portion of the house I now live in, plus two fair-sized villas in the palace premises.

† Two of these immense stone beams still lie in Phulbagh, the park at the back of the palace, looking like relics from some pre-historic ruin of truly Brobdingnagian proportions.

pillars, beams and wall-sections, and which, when polished, acquired the translucence and sheen of marble. For the interiors of some of the grander rooms and for more decorative pillars and bannisters, he imported Carrara marble and brought in Italian craftsmen to execute the work.

Jaivilas was an Indian answer to the magnificence of the Imperial style which the Raj had adopted from the Mughals, and every major Indian prince was soon to have his own Jaivilas but bearing his special imprint. Sheer bulk combined with ornate elaboration were its mandatory requirements. The main reception rooms were built with grand levies in mind, such as coronations or investitures. The durbar hall of Jaivilas in which Lady Dufferin saw her husband formally handing back his fort to the Scindia, is one of the largest of its kind in India, measuring fifty feet by ninety, with a roof forty feet high. The ceiling is vaulted, painted pale green and picked out with heavy gold scrollwork, and the floor is covered with a single wall-to-wall carpet which is believed to be the largest one-piece carpet in the world. It was woven *in situ* by the carpet makers of Gwalior.

Mukhel Sahib saw to it that most of the other things in his palace matched the durbar hall in scale and splendour, and nowhere else is his propensity for the grandiloquent more in evidence than in the crystal chandeliers he ordered for the durbar hall from Vienna. The two main ones, which are very nearly a pair, are said to be the largest ever made, with the possible exception of the one which hangs in the Czar's Winter Palace outside Moscow.

The story is told that, when the time came for him to hang these chandeliers with their combined weight of nearly six tons from the ceiling of the hall, engineering experts feared that the roof might collapse. Mukhel Sahib rose to the occasion and carried out a practical demonstration to test the strength of his roof. He constructed a broad wooden ramp from the ground level to the top of the roof, and coaxed a dozen elephants up the ramp and on to the roof. These elephants who, between them, weighed at least twice as much as the chandeliers, were made to go round and round the top of the roof for several days. If it could sustain that sort of pounding, Mukhel Sahib argued, it would surely hold the weight of his Viennese chandeliers. It did, and still does.

The larger of the chandeliers holds 248 lamps, and when they and the pedestal and wall lamps are lit, according to one writer their effect is 'like stepping into a petrified waterfall' with the icy-blue and gold of the room and the lights reproduced infinitely on the wall mirrors strategically placed on the opposite walls. The one trouble with this room has always been to find enough people to fill it, and I have often agonized over whether the number of guests we had asked for some party would really fill the corner we had decided to use. Lady Dufferin too, when she and her husband were entertained in it in 1884, and when the Viceregal party and the Gwalior courtiers must have been there in strength, speaks about the durbar hall as 'the magnificent room in which we lost ourselves last night'.

*   *   *

Not that there was much of a problem filling up the durbar hall on the first occasion it was put to use; the real problem must have been that it and the palace itself might not be ready for occupation in time. The Prince of Wales – the future King Edward VII – was coming to Gwalior, ostensibly to pay a state visit, but in truth so that he and the dozen or so members of his party could shoot tigers.

It was while the elephants were still going round the roof and everyone was on tenterhooks about whether they and the roof would come crashing down, that a message was received from the Viceroy that the Prince would have to be put up for four days. This was like being asked to play host and provide sport and entertainment for a travelling circus of truly Mughal dimensions.

Filose was confronted with a new challenge to his organizing capacity: to get the palace ready for occupation in less than ten months. He rose to the task as one steeped in the ways of princely caprice. While the palace itself was being plastered, painted, furnished and curtained, and the weavers were busy on the carpet, he engaged hundreds of masons and gardeners and put them to work in day and night shifts to get the surroundings ready. He finished the job ahead of his deadline, so that when the Prince of Wales came to stay there was not only no smell in his apartment to offend the royal nostrils but the acres of lawns overlooked by his private verandah were green and lush, the fountains spouted merrily, and water cascaded in ripples over the pink channels that sloped down to the sunken garden; the rose bushes were in full flower and the bougainvillaea 'a surf of crimson'.

Michael Filose was to be rewarded with a knighthood, and it was well deserved.

*   *   *

The Prince of Wales came in December 1875, shot his tigers, and went. Not long afterwards, Jayajirao Scindia decided that he did not really like the palace that Mukhel Sahib had built for him. It was too large and open, and it was designed more for a European style of living than for an eastern prince. He was passionately fond of listening to Indian classical music and watching dance performances that went on for most of the night, and he loved to gamble. And yet in the two hundred odd rooms of Jaivilas there was not a single one in which he could hold his song and dance parties with his cronies, squatting on soft mattresses spread on the floor and leaning against bolsters instead of sitting up stiffly on chairs and sofas, smoking their hookas and drinking what were called Raja Pegs, which were made of brandy topped up with champagne instead of the usual soda-water. So he set about building himself yet another palace.

This new palace, Motimahal, owes little or nothing to European models. It is an elaboration of the medieval buildings in the Gwalior fort and completely at home in its setting. Its main feature is a curving, colonnaded terrace flanked by high, square towers. Directly behind it rears the great fort; in front is an artificial lake. Inside, it could be an old princely abode in northern India, with narrow passages linking a multitude of dark, low-ceilinged rooms . . . there are more than nine hundred.

Years later, while the Scindias still ruled Gwalior, Moti-mahal was given over to the state's administrative offices, and still soldiers on manfully in that plebeian role. Ranks of underworked clerks bend over piles of files in its rosewood panelled rooms; its intricately carved lotus-patterned pillars are festooned with notice boards and dusty cyclostyled pronouncements, and its music room, which was like a private theatre and in which Jayajirao Scindia held his gambling parties and nautch-sessions, is a conference room fitted out with metal-topped tables. Its exquisite murals of the major *ragas* or melodies, which were painted by some of the most renowned artists, are criss-crossed with clumsily laid electric wiring.

*   *   *

'The Maharaja gave the order and Yakub Sahib made the garden,' wrote Rudyard Kipling, and perhaps that was what it meant to be a Maharaja: the capacity to order gardens or palaces without bothering too much about how much they were going to cost. It was to be demonstrated yet again when my father-in-law became the Maharaja and refused to step into the Kothi Palace that had been built for him in Ujjain, not because he did not like the palace, but because he disliked the man who had had it built for him while he was still a minor and thus not allowed him to oppose its construction.* Instead, as soon as he was given ruling powers, he proceeded to put up his own Xanadu on Kalia Deh, an island in the river not quite ten miles from Ujjain. This now belongs to me and I still use it occasionally when I visit Ujjain.

My husband too ordered the building of houses as another well-to-do person might order cars. Luckily, by his time, the lifestyle of the princes had changed. Ordinary dinner parties had shrunk in size from around a hundred guests to a score or so, and houseguests did not travel with battalions of servants. Then again there was my husband's well-known aversion to the grandiose. As such, the houses he wanted built were not palaces even though they would, I'm sure, qualify as elegant mansions. Almost as soon as he became the Maharaja, he commissioned the Bombay architect John Ritchie to build him a house in Poona, where he maintained a racing establishment. This house, built in a park which the Scindias had owned in Wanawri, near the memorial of Mahadji Scindia, did in the

---

* The vast park which surrounded this palace was given away by my husband for the campus of Vikram University; the Kothi Palace itself houses the local collectorate.

end acquire the lineaments of a palace. While it was being built, John Ritchie and his wife Irene, who had a flair for interior decoration, became our friends, so it was natural that we should entrust the decoration and furnishing of the house to Irene. Thanks to her impeccable good taste, the Poona house, Padma Vilas, became one of the most attractive of our residences and my husband's favourite. When we went to live in the house for the first time, I was expecting a baby: Irene had even stocked its nursery with baby furniture and a freshly laundered stock of nappies, baby clothes, booties and blankets.

Even before the Poona house was finished, my husband commissioned John Ritchie to build him another house in a place called Tekanpur, barely twenty miles from Gwalior. Its compound enclosed two fair-sized lakes which were the Scindias' wild-duck preserves, and where during the winter months we took our guests on duck shoots. Here Irene chose a more contemporary style for the decorations and furniture, which John ordered to be made in Bombay. Today our Tekanpur lake house serves as the Officers' Mess for the Training School of the Central Reserve Police Force.

Now, because it was later to be the scene of one of the most unpleasant experiences of my life, I must prolong this digression from the story of Jayajirao Scindia to bring in the third house my husband built, at 37 Rajpur Road, Delhi.

The British were keen that the Scindia, from whom they had taken away the city and environs of Delhi, should build himself a palace in their new imperial Delhi, but my father-in-law's sense of family pride made him resist their blandishments. With the coming of independence, the old objections were no longer valid, though my husband had no reason to feel especially friendly towards the new rulers of India either. But, to demonstrate that he was fully reconciled to both independence and democratic rule, he had accepted a sinecure as the Rajpramukh, which was a sort of super-governor, of a new state they had created by amalgamating a dozen or so princely domains. This made it necessary for him to visit the capital more often than he would have wished to.

The Scindias had always owned a bungalow in Delhi, situated in a quiet locality and surrounded by a large compound full of old trees. My husband decided to pull down this bungalow and in its place build a modern house more suited to his needs. This house, 37 Rajpur Road, was designed by Narendra Kothari and was much more modest than most of our other houses. It had a dozen bedrooms, three reception rooms, and a separate guest-house with its own suites of rooms, garages, servants' quarters and stabling. After my husband's death my growing involvement with politics necessitated prolonged stays in the capital, and I began to use it more and more so that it became almost my second home.

I was in this house on 25 June 1975, when I had to run away and go into hiding to avoid being arrested. The subsequent indignities that this lovely house was subjected to were as much a part of the nightmare that followed as of a relentless political vendetta. It was broken into and made into the headquarters of a particularly unattractive organisation: the Twenty Point Programme. I was so sickened by what they had done to my lovely house, that when the emergency ended and people like myself could move about freely again, I never wanted to enter it again. Since then, I have avoided even driving along the street on which it stands.

*   *   *

If a man can die happy, Jayajirao Scindia did so. What Lady Dufferin had described as his 'great wish' had been fulfilled when he got back his fort. As though after that there was little to live for, he died on 20 June 1886 at the age of fifty-two. One of the British writers, M. Griffith, in a very brief sketch of his life, mentions the immense treasure he had amassed. It seems that he had hidden it so well in ingeniously devised hiding places, 'that no one could find it, until some time afterwards, Colonel Bannerman, the Resident' managed to discover it. The estimated value of the horde was Rs 62,000,000, or about £5,000,000:

> In addition to coin, there was an inestimable quantity of jewels which rivalled Aladdin's store. This collection . . . was the largest in the world. He had in his vaults, silver coin that could be counted in millions, magnificent pearls and diamonds by the ten thousands, rubies, emeralds and other gems by the thousands, and wrought and melted gold by the maund.

A maund was a measure of weight normally used for the wholesale purchase of grain, and equalled fifty-six pounds. A maund of gold, at today's price, would be well over half a million pounds sterling.

CHAPTER THIRTEEN

My Father-in-Law Madhavrao Scindia

THE MONTH OF July is unbearably hot in north India. But an accession ceremony, in which a ruler is installed on the *gadi* or seat of his ancestors, cannot be held up for the weather to turn mild. It has to be performed on the first auspicious day as soon as the mandatory period of mourning – thirteen days – has passed. On 12 July 1886 the precise moment at which the stars were at their most propitious fell at forty-two minutes past 5 p.m.

At five, the guns began to boom from the battery point of the old fort at thirty-second intervals. When the twenty-one gun salute had been fired, the heralds began to announce the approach of the Maharaja, making a recital of his titles interspersed with calls of warning to those assembled in the durbar hall to remain alert, to mind their manners, and to observe silence. The hall was packed to capacity with a full contingent of Gwalior's courtiers and officials and with a fair sprinkling of Englishmen in uniform. The din in the hall became hushed as the nine-year-old Scindia, dressed 'in rich, brocaded yellow silk sewn with diamonds' and holding the hand of a bearded giant of an Englishman with the face of a visionary and dressed despite the torrid heat in a sombre grey woollen suit, entered the hall and walked up to the *gadi*. The Englishman was Sir Lepel Griffin, and he was the man who had been appointed as official guardian of the Maharaja during his minority. Guardian and ward had no language in common, and they communicated through interpreters. But the details of the day's events had been carefully rehearsed. There was a short wait before the precise moment arrived, during which Sir Lepel sat down in an ornate chair kept for him, but there was no such chair for the Maharaja. Instead, in a gesture that must have instantly won the hearts of the Gwalior contingent in the hall, Sir Lepel picked up the boy and placed him on his knee. There was a murmur of approval.

But soon they rose. The moment had come. Sir Lepel, Wagnerian in presence and ponderous in his movements, placed a beautiful necklace of pearls around the young king's neck and seated him on the *gadi.*

Thus in the same ceremony that made Madhavrao Scindia Maharaja of Gwalior, the Raj made it clear to the people of Gwalior that it had taken the upbringing of the Maharaja into its own hands. It had been his father's expressed wish that Madhavrao should be brought up in the traditions of ortho-dox *kshatriya* Hinduism. But the British had, as they put it, 'rightly determined that it was their duty, as the guardian of a young prince who was to rule over several millions and whose wealth was enormous, to give him the best education procur-able in both eastern and western learning.'

A photograph of Madhavrao Scindia taken at this time shows him smothered in fold upon fold of silk and velvet with heavy gold-thread embroidery, and hung with jewels, but between the ropes of pearls and diamonds that would look flashy on the vainest of women, and the boat-shaped Scindia pagree worn at a rakish angle, are the bright Scindia eyes in a rounded, full face, wide and slightly staring, 'eager and interested' as one writer has described them. To me they have always been the most conspicuously recognizable feature of the family in four generations. My husband inherited them and so have my children and their children.

*   *   *

The education of the prince went on as planned, its principal aim being to mould him in the image of that imperial ideal, the product of a British public school. Luckily he had already been weaned on its basics, having as a boy been taught to ride and shoot and to love the outdoors. And when they tried to interest him in 'mechanical hobbies', they found that he couldn't have enough of mechanics; he was never happier than when tinkering with some machine or the other. When his guardian, Mr J. W. Johnstone, whom he called *Masterji*, went on leave to England, all he asked him to bring back was a toy train in which he could take himself for a ride.

The 'toy' railway that *Masterji* brought back for his pupil came in several wagonloads, for it consisted of a steam-engine, six carriages, and half a mile of railway track, all in a two-foot gauge. For the next few weeks Madhavrao bustled about laying the track around his palace and, in the process, breaking down any compound walls that got in its way. When, however, the train made its trial run, the track was found to be too short because 'by the time the engine had gathered speed, it was necessary to close the throttle to avoid running into the dead end.' So two more miles of track were ordered, and because there was not enough room for it within the palace precincts, it was extended as far as the suburb of Morar.

This created an awkward political situation between the Resident and the Government. For while a railway train that could carry passengers and freight might be thought to be a toy if it operated within a private compound, when it ran from one part of the city to another it became a 'railway system'. And the British had always been most particular about not letting Indian princes build their own railways, communications being a jealously guarded imperial preserve.

In normal circumstances, the Government might well have demanded that the track should be dismantled, but since the violation was an offshoot of their own method of bringing up the Maharaja, they were prepared to 'regularize' the lapse. Indeed, a year or so later, they even sanctioned extending the 'railway system' as far as Sussera, about eight miles from the capital, which was a hunting preserve where Madhavrao's father had built a shooting box.

Thus the Gwalior Light Railway (GLR) came into being as a princely toy. When completed years later, its track was more than 250 miles long, and it served the remoter parts of the Scindia's domain as a passenger and freight carrier in the days when motor vehicles were rare, and between the two World Wars became a part of the Indian railway network. Of late, with the burgeoning of road transport and the development of bus services, the railway became uneconomical, and much of its track was dismantled. Luckily, however, a section of about a hundred miles has been spared, and you can hear the little trains tooting impatiently and racing with the auto rikshas and tongas as they run through crowded localities, their carriages crammed to capacity, stopping at little stations which themselves look no bigger than ordinary railway carriages.

*   *   *

Between them *Masterji* Johnstone and his colleagues seemed to have managed to hold Madhavrao Scindia's enthusiasm for railway engines, cavalry drill and hunting sufficiently in check to have been able to impart to him the sort of education that a normal schoolboy received. But they had to contend with other priorities. As soon as their pupil passed his fourteenth birthday, he was married. The bride was the daughter of Sardar Bhausaheb Mohite of Satara, in Maharashtra, and her name was Chinkuraje. After this interruption, however, his education seems to have proceeded smoothly enough, and when Madhavrao was sixteen they began to put him through a course of administrative training. Thoughtful as ever, *Masterji* set up a new school for this purpose in the shooting preserve of Sussera, so that from the windows of his classroom Madhavrao could also select the black buck which he would shoot for the evening's dinner.

*   *   *

On 15 December 1894, when he was in his nineteenth year, Madhavrao Scindia was invested with ruling powers. The stewardship of the guardians was over, and so was the authority of the Regency Council. One of his first acts as ruler of Gwalior was to appoint his guardian, J. W. Johnstone, as his Secretary for Education.

The officials of the Foreign and Political Department of the Government of India, who had evolved their own intricate code of grading Indian princes, watched his every move like hawks, sniffing the air for proverbial eastern weaknesses of character. But as time passed they found that Madhavrao was not only proving to be a capable and diligent ruler, but he was filling out into the precise image of the ideal prince that the department had drawn up, combining flamboyance with common sense, exemplary loyalty with self-respect, sub-servience with leadership. He was someone they could hold up as a bridge between the twain, who, rooted in the arcane orthodoxy of inherited beliefs, was yet fully at ease among the miracles of steam and electricity. Even if they themselves had little to do with shaping his career after he became Maharaja, the Scindia had turned out to be the sort of Indian potentate of whom the Raj could justly be proud.

H. F. Prevost Battersby, a journalist who accompanied the Prince of Wales and his wife (the future King George V and his queen) on their visit to India in 1903, was greatly impressed by Madhavrao. He had found the endless military parades 'monotonous and depressing', but when the Royal train arrived in Gwalior, for the first time he saw the East as he had imagined it:

> Scindia's thirty-six elephants are drawn up at the station to mount the Royal party, gorgeous with their painted faces, their howdahs of beaten gold and silver, their golden earrings and necklaces, each a strongman's burden, the great silver-gilt bells and heavy anklets, the gold embroidery and trappings, these great beasts, filling the whole station yard, cheered, as nothing before, our disappointed vision.

And on the platform stood the master of ceremonies, the Scindia himself, wearing rich ceremonial robes and the terracotta tricorne Maratha *pagri* at a jaunty angle, a crimson caste-mark daubed on his forehead and a cascade of pearls and diamonds 'which would seem exuberantly magnificent on a woman'.

But behind this regally eastern façade ablaze with caste-mark and jewellery, Prevost Battersby discovered a man of boundless energy and an alert mind. He noted with approval that the Scindia's main concerns were schools, markets, hospitals and drainage, finance and municipal affairs. He found it almost paradoxical in such a setting that the Scindia should own his own railway system and a garage full of motor cars, and was amazed at his ability 'to drive car and locomotive or strip the works of either, as skilfully as a chauffeur or an engineer'.

Inevitably there was a military parade. But it included a sally by 'old-time warriors in full cry and ancient batteries for horse, ox and elephant', and its climax was a cavalry charge at full gallop, led by the Scindia himself.

And at the tiger hunt, which one suspects may have been the main purpose of the Prince of Wales's visit, Prevost Battersby saw the Scindia 'tramping with his beaters up and down the thorny hills in search of a tiger' that a hunter from the Royal party had wounded, and they all saw the Scindia 'rolling the tiger over as it charged him not thirty yards away'.

In those days, Europe had its own array of potentates, in the form of a score or more of kings and grand dukes. Prevost Battersby thought Madhavrao Scindia more progressive and capable than most of them, and concluded:

> It would not be easy, even in England, to match the capacity, breadth and variety of his mind: to find a man who has proved himself so sound a financier, so practical a philanthropist, so astute a soldier, so good a sportsman . . . He does not seek his pleasures in Simla or Paris, he finds them in work among his own people.

*   *   *

It was a vanity of the times that the man who shot the biggest tiger attained an eminence that could not be matched by the recipient of a Nobel prize. It was therefore only right and proper that the man who claimed the record for having bagged the largest (or certainly the longest) tiger should be the Bada Laat, or 'Biggest among the Lords', the Viceroy himself.

The Viceroy was Lord Hardinge, who held office from 1910 to 1916. And the man who provided him with the tiger that made him the envy of big-game hunters, was none other than Madhavrao Scindia. To this day, driving along the main Bombay-Delhi highway, you can see between the 101st and 102nd kilometre stones from Gwalior, the pink sandstone slab held up by two uprights:

NEAR THIS SPOT ON 11TH APRIL 1914
A TIGER MEASURING 11 FEET 6¾ INCHES
WAS SHOT BY
HIS EXCELLENCY THE RIGHT HONOURABLE
CHARLES BARON HARDINGE OF PENSHURST

P.C., G.C.B., G.M.S.I., G.C.M.G., V.O.I.S.C., VICEROY AND GOVERNOR GENERAL OF INDIA

What sort of social order had the Raj devised in which its proconsuls could invite themselves to shoot tigers, accept all the hospitality that the host was capable of offering, and yet treat him as some kind of social inferior? The requirement that a native must never appear bareheaded in the presence of the sahib must have been particularly irksome, because in April the weather in this part of India can be unbearably hot, with the temperature hovering well above the 100° mark. How the Indians, rulers as well as their staff officers, who attended upon these exalted British guests must have longed to take off, even for a minute, their pagris or turbans, if only to be able to wipe off the rim of sweat round their heads.

It is easy to imagine the scene around the dining table in the stone villa that the Scindia had had built in the jungle in imitation of some Scottish castle. The hunting party were partaking of the gourmet dishes concocted by cooks brought over from the palace and thirstily gulping down Dom Pérignon. Lord Hardinge, as he waited for his glass to be refilled, noticed that the Scindia had surreptitiously shifted his pagri to ease the pressure against his temples and probably said: 'Oh, do remove your pagri, Your Highness; we're in camp after all.'

Of course this may not be precisely how it happened, but the point is that the liberty was permitted, even though some of the Viceregal aides may have disapproved. Surely, H.E. had gone too far. Imagine Curzon letting the side down like that, no matter how many tigers he was given. At least the Scindia should not have taken the Viceroy at his word and removed his pagri.

Two years later, he did so again; this time at a Viceregal dinner in Simla in the summer of 1916. The Viceroy, Lord Chelmsford, had already left the room and his guests were in all probability exchanging risqué stories over brandy and cigars when Mr H. Wood, the Foreign Secretary, noticed that Madhavrao Scindia had removed his pagri. As it happened, the British guests were bareheaded themselves, but the Indian guests, though they too wore white ties and tails and medals, had to keep their hats on.

The file on the 'incident' makes interesting reading. Mr Wood wrote to the Resident at Gwalior, a Mr W. E. Jardine, to demand an explanation from the Scindia. Jardine, it seems, did not feel all that strongly about the lapse, and pointed out that the Scindia had already been permitted to remove his pagri by a previous Viceroy, even in his presence. Whether Jardine's view prevailed over that of Wood, who was his official superior, never became clear. Even as the two protagonists were getting set for one of those long wrangles that are so dear to the hearts of bureaucrats, the Scindia managed to put the case virtually out of court by bringing off a coup. He secured the agreement of the King and Queen to becoming the godparents of his two children, Jivajirao and Kamalaraje, on whom he proposed to bestow the additional names of the royal couple, George and Mary.

So despite an annual pinprick or two to remind him that they had not quite forgiven him (he was once prevented from visiting a fellow Maharaja, the Gaekwad of Baroda), the Scindia continued to rise in official estimation as the most loyal of Indian princes, properly intolerant of the agitation of the Nationalists and a man to rely on in a crisis.

In 1921 yet another Prince of Wales (the future Duke of Windsor) came to Gwalior, and like his father and grandfather before him went off happily, having shot his bagful of tigers, full of praise for his host. Then the very next year came yet another Viceroy, Lord Reading, the first Jew to become Viceroy and also to rise to such eminence from the humblest beginnings – having begun life as a ship's boy in a merchant vessel. He failed to break Lord Hardinge's tiger record by the proverbial whisker. His tiger, shot in the same jungle as that of Hardinge's, measured 11 feet 5½ inches. Hardinge's, it will be remembered, was 11 feet 6¾ inches.

Madhavrao Scindia's attitude to the British may be said to exemplify that of the average Indian of the pre-Gandhian era. The Indians had settled down to the British over-lordship and, by and large, they strove hard to cooperate, to win the good opinion and, if possible, the friendship of their rulers. It was the British who, by their arrogance and prejudices, managed to alienate them. Even the most broadminded of them tended to be excessively sensitive, and the line between subservience and an acceptable level of familiarity was very thin.

In the summer of 1921, while Madhavrao Scindia was staying at Ujjain, the Maharaja of Dewas, Tukojirao, who knew him well and was distantly related to him, went there to invite him to visit Dewas, and took his English secretary, the writer E. M. Forster, with him. It seems that the Scindia did not want to go to Dewas, but for Tukojirao it was a matter of prestige that he should come. Forster describes the mood of the meeting:

> At Ujjain we passed a most ignoble evening. The great man wouldn't say yes, and wouldn't say no, he teased and swanked. (At the end of a 'slipshod' dinner.) I remember that when it came to smoking and I wanted a match, Scindia bounced the match-box at me on the tablecloth although he was near enough to hand it.

It is quite possible that Madhavrao Scindia wanted to register his annoyance at a minor prince's secretary asking him to pass the matches – he could not envisage even the Viceroy's secretary taking such a liberty. (Indeed, an Indian private secretary would have eaten his dinner in the staff dining room, in the company of the Scindia's own staff.) The throwing of a matchbox was in the mood of the evening, half-petulant, half-jocular, an uncle being made to do something against his will by his nephew's unwillingness to take no for an answer – and the repercussions that would follow in the closed-circuit world of Princely India when it became known that the Scindia had refused to visit Dewas! I am almost certain that even if the Maharaja of Dewas had asked his host for the matchbox, he would have bounced it across, just as I am certain that if at a similar dinner in some cantonment bungalow or officers' mess an Englishman had chucked a matchbox at him, Forster would have put it down to playfulness or high spirits. But not here, for as Forster noted elsewhere, complete with a triple mark of exclamation: 'This doesn't do in India, you know; it doesn't do!.!.!' He was not prepared to make allowances. 'The Maharaja of Gwalior was a bounder' was the verdict.

*   *   *

It is a shame that Mr Forster was so put off by the towering presence of Madhavrao Scindia, or by the awe and esteem in which his employer Tukojirao held him, that he failed to mention the amazing house in which he spent the best part of a day, for I have always believed that it is the nearest anywhere in the world to Kubla Khan's Xanadu, complete with a sacred river, though it was not called the Alph but the Sipra. Surely, Mr Forster could not have been entertained in a house quite like that in all his wanderings.

The house was called Kalia Deh and it was built, as I mentioned earlier, out of a fit of pique.

Madhavrao's choice of the site may have been influenced by the strong religious streak in him. It was, nonetheless, inspired: an island in the River Sipra, about ten miles north of Ujjain, an island which, since ancient times, was believed to be situated exactly on the line of the Tropic of Cancer and had thus come to be regarded as a *Tirtha*, a place of pilgrimage for the Hindus. Several temples had been built on it, the chief of them being, appropriately enough, that of Surya Narayana, the Sun-God, and the arm of the river overlooked by the temple was known as Suraj Kund, or the 'Sun Pool'.

Over the centuries of Muslim rule, the island had become a private pleasure-garden of the ruling Sultan, and later, in Mughal days, of the local Viceroy. The Muslims were lovers of the good life, and one of the Sultans, Nasiruddin, built a house for himself on the island and joined it to the mainland with a stout stone bridge, strong enough to take the weight of elephants. Later, Nasiruddin and his successors transformed the island into an oriental dreamland, with rose bushes, trees and pavilions, and a system of bathing pools with water cascading through stone channels at varying speeds and levels, forming shallow or deep pools, little waterfalls or rapids, and – shades of Xanadu – even disappearing into arched recesses built like caves along the river bank for more private bathing or aquatic dalliance.

But when Madhavrao Scindia decided to build himself a house on the island, most of these buildings had fallen down, the garden had become a wilderness, and the bathing pools a bed of slime choked with water-hyacinth. The only structure that still remained virtually intact was the mansion in which the later Mughal Viceroys had lived and which may well have begun life as a tomb or a mosque, built as an act of revenge upon a hated religion on the very site of the original Sun Temple. It was a domed structure built of pink sandstone with four minarets at its corners, and it resembled a medium-sized, rose-coloured Taj Mahal without the fussy ornamentation of the original.

Madhavrao Scindia entrusted the task of converting this structure into a princely residence to one of his principal sardars, Chandrojirao Angre, who was also the keeper of his privy purse and who, through his recent marriage to the junior Maharani's sister, had become almost a member of the family; and it was Bade-Angre-saab, as I used to call him, who, like Mukhel Sahib in an earlier generation, proceeded to create for his Maharaja a twentieth-century Xanadu.

He called on the help of a well-known Bombay architect, and between them they decided that the building might look better – or at least less like a mausoleum – if it was divested of its four minarets and promptly dismantled them.* Then, pleased with the effect, they divided the building into living rooms and bedrooms and put in waterpipes, sanitary fittings and electric fittings.

Adjoining the house they put up a large colonial bungalow with a wide verandah and six spacious bedrooms, and behind the bungalow they built rooms for about fifty servants. After that they set about restoring the surroundings to what they might have been like during their heyday under the later Mughals. Rose gardens sprang up, lawns at different levels, and poolside pavilions. The bathing pools were reconstructed, right down to the channels running through the arched recesses, and indeed they improved on the original facilities by erecting a dam a little higher up the river so that the pools and fountains would not run dry even during the summer months. They constructed a broader bridge to take cars and lorries, and across the river from the main house they built more bungalows and staff quarters and stables and garages. Luckily the trees that the Mughals had planted served them well as

---

* In this they anticipated Aldous Huxley's disappointment with the Taj Mahal, for he too believed that the artistic effect of the main building was diminished by the minarets at the four corners of the platform. Mr Huxley's visit to the Taj took place in 1926.

screens, and few of these outbuildings can be glimpsed from the island itself.

This was Kalia Deh, which Mr Forster visited in the spring of 1921. It is possible that it did not conform to his ideas of comfort or elegance, but I doubt if he had ever been a guest at a more exotic house, and I do wish he had somewhere made a note of what he thought of it. There was so much to see and comment on, such as the outlandish baobob trees which the Pathans had brought over, the medieval bridge, the Mughal gardens neat as a chessboard, and the sacred river which, in those days, was full of crocodiles which often came to bask on the banks and offered sport and diversion to guests.

I bought Kalia Deh from my son in 1980. Nowadays I seldom go to Ujjain, perhaps not more than half-a-dozen times a year, and I rarely stay for more than a couple of days at a time. I use the bungalow built by Madhavrao Scindia, not the pink Taj Mahal built by Nasiruddin. That house I have restored to what it had been since ancient times, a temple, and it now has a new idol of Surya Narayan, the Sun God. And every time I pass the bridge, I am struck by the grace and space of Kalia Deh, the bungalow concealed among the trees and waiting to be occupied; the river, holy and luminous on one side and, nowadays alas, altogether free of crocodiles, and, on the other, rushing in little torrents through cracked and broken stonework; all of it takes you back in time, making it a place for contemplation and study; it is a strange, haunting place, linked through many historical changes with antiquity, and perversely named after a mythical serpent of biblical malignity, Kalia; for Kalia Deh means the Pool of Kalia.

Some day I propose to turn it into an institute for advanced Sanskrit studies. Already I have restored the Sun God to his rightful place. What would be more fitting than to transform his surroundings into a refuge for Sanskrit scholars? Ujjain, after all, was the city where Kalidas lived. He was India's – and Sanskrit's – greatest poet and what better use for a property such as this than to dedicate it to the language he served and enriched.

*   *   *

Parades, durbars, tiger hunts, railway engines, cavalry

charges, music: these were Madhavrao Scindia's *shauks*, a word that means something more than a hobby but less than an addiction. The main concern of his life was the running of his state, which he took as seriously as the managing director of a company takes the running of his company. But the centre of his life was his family which, for a man of his inclinations, was pathetically small, consisting of only two members besides himself, his mother and his wife. He was absolutely devoted to both.

He had been married at a very young age, and right up to his thirtieth year he went on hoping that his wife, Chinkuraje, would bear him children. But all the prayers and penances which the astrologers they consulted had advised had been in vain, and specialist doctors in Bombay had confirmed that Chinkuraje would remain childless. His mother urged him to take another wife, but he was too fond of Chinkuraje to think of taking such a step lightly. In the end, however, his wife too joined his mother's entreaties and reminded him of his twin obligations to his inheritance: the first was not to damage or diminish it in any way, and the second was to make sure that there was a son to carry on the line.

In 1911 Madhavrao Scindia went to London to attend the coronation of King George V, and there he was approached by a fellow Maharaja, Sayajirao Gaekwad of Baroda, who proposed that he should marry his daughter Indira. Indira was one of the acknowledged beauties of her time. 'Wherever she went, she broke hearts like eggshells,' wrote John Lord in *The Maharajahs*, and predictably enough Madhavrao Scindia was captivated by her charms. Dynastically it would have been a perfect match, for both families were rooted in the country's past and both were immensely rich.

No doubt the horoscopes too were found to match. But if the stars were compatible, many other things were not. There was the difference in ages. Indira was only seventeen, Madhavrao thirty-four. And the cultural gap between the two was far wider. He was rooted in tradition, in the cult of masculine superiority, and he was a believer in purdah, the seclusion of women behind veils or at least in a part of the house exclusively set aside for them. She was outspokenly 'modern', having attended a co-educational school in Baroda and spent a year at a finishing school in Eastbourne. She sometimes wore European clothes and even went to dances, behaviour which would have outraged Gwalior's sardars. She was rather like most well brought-up Indian girls of today; indeed like my own daughters, whom, I'm sure, the Gwalior of my father-in-law would have found outrageously westernized.

But all this was overlooked in the euphoria of a union between the two highest princely families of India. The engagement was announced, and Indira's father gave a party at Ranelagh, on the Thames, at which the cream of English society came to congratulate the couple. Then Madhavrao went back to India, no doubt to make preparations for providing yet another record tiger for George V, who was due to visit India in the coming winter for his *Indian* coronation. And the bride-to-be went on a shopping spree around the capitals of Europe, to put together a trousseau befitting the daughter of the Gaekwad and the wife-to-be of the Scindia.*

In December 1911 the two families met again, this time in Delhi, where the coronation durbar was held.† The date for the marriage had been set towards the end of January, and the plan was for the Gaekwad to proceed immediately after the

---

* She bought on a scale that would have shown up even Sir Michael Filose, for we are still – after seventy years – using some of the table and bed linen she ordered to be sent to Gwalior from some of the most famous Irish and French looms, complete with the intertwined letters of her married name, IS, Indira Scindia, embroidered in matching silk on each piece under a crown of her own design.

† It was at this durbar that Indira's father, Sayajirao Gaekwad, caused a furore of indignation by failing to conform to the precise drill laid down for the princes on this occasion; either he did not make a low enough obeisance to his monarch, or he turned his back too soon on him when he should have 'walked backwards'. To these lapses were added other minor 'offences': someone noticed that the Gaekwad was dressed too simply, instead of wearing a florid oriental costume such as the princes were supposed to flaunt (and for which they were made fun of), and someone else saw that in place of the sword he should have carried he had brought a gold-topped cane; that he had presented himself at the durbar not only without any of his fabled jewellery but – the ultimate sin – even without the latest decoration that the Raj had conferred on him, the insignia of the G.C.S.I. In all this the officials of the Raj detected 'sedition', and Miss E. W. Tottenham, the English companion of Indira's mother, wrote: 'Loud were the howls of the wolves . . . no epithet was bad enough for the Gaekwad. "He should be stripped of his rank and deported", "his salute of twenty-one guns reduced", etc. etc.'

durbar to his own capital, Baroda, which had been preparing for the event for months. Elaborate arches were erected at strategic street corners and special stands were constructed along the route of the marriage procession. Troops of musicians and drama companies had been invited from all parts of India for the entertainment of the thousand or so guests who were expected. The Gwalior party was to reach Baroda only two days before the day of the wedding.

But when the bride's father returned to his palace in Baroda, a telegram was waiting for him. It was from Madhavrao Scindia and it read:

WHAT DOES THE PRINCESS MEAN BY HER LETTER?

The princess was summoned, and it all came out. Just before the Gaekwad's special train had left Delhi, Indira had posted a letter to Madhavrao Scindia breaking off their engagement. Over the ensuing weeks she revealed that, during her stay in England, she had fallen desperately in love with another man, Jitendra, the brother of the Maharaja of Cooch Behar, and that while they were all in Delhi, she had been secretly meeting Jitendra there, since the Cooch Behar party too had been there for the coronation.

*   *   *

A terse notification in the papers announced the cancellation of the wedding. The street arches were quietly dismantled and the special trains cancelled. One or two newspapers hinted darkly that the 'intending bridegroom, having disapproved of the conduct of his prospective father-in-law at the durbar,' had broken off the engagement.

In Baroda, Indira's parents did their utmost to end her romance.* In Gwalior, the custodians of its orthodoxy, the

* Without success, however. Forbidden to see Jitendra and kept under constant watch, she managed to send letters to him nevertheless, made it clear to her parents that she was determined to marry him, and even threatened to elope. They took her to Europe in an effort to make her get over her infatuation, and did not realize that Jitendra was following their party wherever it went. He often managed to see Indira, sometimes 'disguised as an old man with a beard'. In the end they gave in, and she married Jitendra in London in the spring of 1913. Neither of her parents attended the wedding. One of her daughters, Gayatri Devi, became the Maharani of Jaipur. During the 'Emergency' of 1975, she and I were fellow prisoners in the criminal ward of the Tihar Jail in Delhi.

hereditary sardars of the Scindias, such as the Shitoles, the Angres and the Phalkes, must have heaved a tremendous sigh of relief at being providentially saved from an infusion of westernized femininity into the Scindia household and from a threat to the system of purdah. The two ladies of Madhavrao Scindia's family took matters into their own hands and sent emissaries to their homeland in Maharashtra to find a suitable second wife for him. The girl they finally chose came from Goa, from the Rane family of Sanquelim, and her name was Gajraraje. She was taken to Gwalior and married to Madhavrao at a quiet ceremony on 8 May 1913.

The Maratha princely houses such as the Scindias, the Holkars, the Gaekwads and the Pawards had established their rule in the northern parts of the Indian subcontinent, well away from their homeland, Maharashtra, which lies in the peninsular portion of India. Caste and clan considerations made it obligatory for them to find their brides from among their own people, and from within a hundred or so families which possessed the proper origins and ancestries. Indeed the main objection of Indira's parents to her marrying Jitendra Naraian was that he was not a Maratha. In Gwalior, the northernmost of these domains, attitudes were especially narrow, and the taboos all but inflexible. Indeed, apart from Mahadji Scindia's mother who was from a Rajput princely family (and whom many of his fellow Marathas regarded as an outsider), I was the first non-Maratha bride to marry a Scindia in almost two hundred years. My coming to Gwalior as its Maharani was strongly disapproved of by virtually all the Maratha sardars, who would greatly have preferred a girl from their own part of India and belonging to one of the families on the approved list.

Those who had taken a leading part in bringing a bride for Madhavrao all the way from Sanquelim in Goa had reason for self-congratulation. Gajraraje, who was now designated the junior Maharani, was soon with child. As the time of her delivery drew near, the entire population of the state was on tenterhooks. Guns would boom from the fort, riders would go galloping through village streets announcing a public holiday, sweets would be distributed by officials as well as by the richer citizens, and a hundred and one prisoners would be released from the city jails to announce the birth of a son. But none of this happened. The child was a girl, whom they named Kamalaraje.

The Scindia's subjects had to wait another two years for all this to happen. Gajraraje's second child was a boy. He was born on 26 June 1916, and given the name of Jivajirao.

*   *   *

If I myself grew up without a mother's care, my husband had to contend with the coddling of two mothers, both of whom competed for his affection. They spoilt him outrageously, and each in subtle ways tried to prejudice him against the other. There was, too, at the back of his real mother's mind the ever-present fear of some harm being done to him by the senior Maharani, who was herself childless, with the result that she was never at peace unless he was within her sight. She had his crib placed next to her own bed and later, even after he grew up, made him sleep in her room.

His father, pleased as Punch with his now well-rounded family, was keen to bring up his son in his own image, as a man's man who was yet deeply religious. He could hardly wait to teach him riding and shooting, and made him participate in his own elaborate ritual of prayers and penances. When he was four years old, he was 'recruited' as a trooper in the senior Maharani's Household Guard on a 'salary' of one rupee a month. A photograph of him, dressed in top boots, riding breeches and a uniform jacket, hair cropped in a severe roundhead tonsure, signing the register to receive his salary, was displayed in the great durbar hall. His sister, Kamalaraje, who was two years older, was also put into military uniform, and both were taught arms drill with toy rifles and words of command by instructors especially chosen from the state's army for their smartness and swagger. E. M. Forster saw my husband in 1921, 'dressed as a Tommy in khaki', and a year later his father made him give the words of command for the general salute at a full-dress parade of the entire Morar garrison comprising a mixed brigade of cavalry and infantry. He was also put under a regime of physical instruction and, from the age of seven, given lessons in music.

I would now like to pay tribute to my father-in-law's

remarkable business acumen, if only because it is due to one of his industrial ventures that I owe my house in New Delhi and the privilege of affording the luxury of peacocks sporting in the yard. For he was a firm believer in industrial progress and had an instinct for picking the right industries – or at least the right entrepreneurs – to support.

Madhavrao Scindia broke his own rule against setting up industries himself to start the Gwalior Potteries, and he did this because he wanted to give India's traditional village craftsmen a new outlet for their wares. He set up factories simultaneously in two places, in Gwalior and in Delhi.

The Delhi factory, which occupied a thirty-acre plot, was situated about ten miles south of the Delhi of those days, which was a walled Mughal town with marginal British extensions outside the walls. The factory plot was typical of the thornbush wilderness of the north Indian plains, and formed part of the hunting country of the Mughals as of the British.

Then in the twenties and thirties a whole new town, designed jointly (but not, alas, without incessant mutual friction) by Sir Edwin Lutyens and Sir Herbert Baker as an epic memorial to the Raj, sprang up in the open plains that separated the factory land from Mughal Delhi (which, ever since, has come to be referred to as Old Delhi). With the coming of independence, New Delhi began to grow and grow like a river that had burst its banks, and by the 1970s it occupied more than ten times the amount of space that its planners had provided for forseeable extensions. In the process, it not only engulfed the factory but went on for a couple of miles beyond – and it is still spreading. The factory has thus become merged into the metropolitan area of New Delhi, and forms part of one of the capital's most fashionable residential areas. The New Hyatt Hotel is just across the road from it, and high-rise office and residential blocks gleaming with glass and metal are rearing up all around it.

Since the pottery thus came within the residential area of the city, it was ordered to close down, though not all the other factories that lie within the city's extended limits have been similarly affected. The stoppage may well be part of the harassment which has become a normal occupational hazard for people like myself who were prominent opponents of Mrs Gandhi's increasingly imperious style of running the country. In the chequered course of my political life I have been subjected to a full range of penalties for not toeing the line, and the stoppage of our factory may well have been one of them. Whatever the reason, the work of the potteries in Delhi came to a sudden halt, its workers were given compensation and dismissed, and the premises were shut down. These included a score or so of single-storied yellow-brick structures of assorted sizes, from large hangars which housed the kilns and the machinery to staff quarters, a manager's bungalow with an annexe, a couple of guard-houses, and about half a dozen nondescript sheds for the storage of the raw materials or finished products.

One of these storage sheds, set well away from the main factory complex and converted without in any way altering its shape or size for residential use, now serves as my New Delhi residence; almost a home away from my real home, which is Gwalior. As houses go, it must surely be one of the smallest I have owned, with only four bedrooms and an annexe which has another two. But the extent of the land belonging to the defunct factory that surrounds it, makes it a delightfully non-urban residence; like the keeper's shed in one of London's parks, but with the whole park as your property.

Ironically enough, it is a sort of gift conferred on me by the prohibitions imposed by two sets of laws. One forbids the construction of any new buildings or the slightest alteration to the plinth areas or the sizes of the original factory buildings, and the other forbids the use of these buildings for the purpose for which they were originally constructed. How long this anomalous situation will last is anybody's guess. Meanwhile I am profoundly grateful for the space that cushions my little house from the roar and fumes of the metropolis, and that still possesses enough trees to resemble a small forest in which the squirrels obviously find enough nourishment to support a flourishing colony. It must be the only house in New Delhi in which you wake up to the up-country sounds of partridges and quails calling, and from whose veranda you can see a family of peacocks scrabbling for worms among the flower-beds and, for no reason at all, breaking into a dance on the lawn. One of them, a very large male with the plumage of a Maharaja dressed for his own coronation, has the habit of straying into the rooms if he finds a window or door open, only to make tracks for the nearest mirror and sit gazing at himself, testifying to the proverbial vanity of peacocks – but then everything else in the house must seem so drab to him in comparison with his own image.

*   *   *

New Delhi, the Raj's monument of self-glorification, was planned to resemble a durbar in stone. Viewed as its architects meant it to be viewed, from the eastern end of the ceremonial avenue which they had named Kingsway and which has subsequently been renamed Rajpath,* the pink expanse of the Viceroy's palace stood on top of the only hill suitable for such a concept and formed a throne, the Imperial seat. On either side but at a suitably lower level of the hill, were the twin powerhouses of the Empire, the secretarial blocks. Between them, as though pouring out of the Viceregal gates, ran Kingsway, straight as a die for two miles. At the other end of Kingsway, balancing the concept of a Mughal durbar, were the palaces of the feudatories, of the Nizam of Hyderabad, of the Gaekwad of Baroda, of the Maharajas of Jaipur and Patiala. Along other avenues providing the elaborate flourishes at strategic intervals were other princely residences: Kashmir House, Travankore House, the houses of Dholpur, Nabha, Bikaner, Kotah, Mandi and dozens of others.

But not of Gwalior.

This was because both my father-in-law and my husband, who were the ruling Scindias during the quarter century or so it took to build New Delhi, held back from participating in this particular exercise for extolling the imperial presence. To be sure they too, like all their fellow Maharajas, had resigned themselves to their feudatory status; they too, like the others, chafed under the collar about the periodic demonstrations of fealty that they were called upon to make, but nonetheless went through the motions docilely and with good grace. But to make humble courtesies to the Raj by building a grand house in an allotted slot in the imperial city was particularly

* Which means Kingsway.

abhorrent to them. After all, Delhi had been *their* city; it was the Scindias who had replaced the Mughals as its custodians; it was they who had realized the Maratha dream of being masters of Delhi. They were not going to stand up and cheer those who had ousted them from it.

No doubt their intransigence did not escape the notice of the Political Department of the Government of India. The Scindia was being difficult about coming under starter's orders. But there was never any question of his being allowed to get away with it. 'It doesn't do in India, you know; it doesn't do!!!' as Mr Forster had observed. But the sahibs were in no particular hurry. This was a game in which they held all the high cards; above all, it was a game they enjoyed playing. They played it as a sort of slow-motion chess, each move trying to foresee all the likely counter-moves and taking months to execute. Meanwhile, it was a pity that the place reserved for Scindia's New Delhi house, between the Gaekwad's palace and Patiala House, on the outer side of the great semicircle around the monarch's statue, remained vacant, like a missing tooth.

But forces even more powerful than the political service of the Raj took a hand in the proceedings. First, the First World War brought the building of the new capital to an abrupt halt. After the war, victorious but shaken, it took them some time to resume the pre-war tempo as though, as James Morris put it, 'the fire had left the imperial idea'. Five years later, they had just finished laying out the roads and putting down the foundations of their major buildings, and had also obtained the consent of most of the major princes to start work on the building of their palaces. The exception was Madhavrao Scindia, who tried to make out that he didn't really need a large house in Delhi, and that the bungalow he already possessed in Old Delhi was quite sufficient for his needs.

Before they could get down to persuading him that he did need to have a house in the new capital, the Scindia died. After that, they had to wait for another ten years till his son came of age. By that time, the building of New Delhi had been completed. The roadside trees had grown and begun to flower and the Viceroy had moved into his house, and the Scindia, not having built a house even though a plot* had been set aside for

* During the war, a temporary mess for army officers was built on this plot, and given the name Prince's Park Mess.

him, had become a subject of dinner-table gossip. And then they discovered that Jivajirao Scindia seemed to be just as reluctant to build a house in New Delhi as his father had been.

They were still trying to work out the best way to bring him into line with the other princes when they found themselves caught up in another war, and when that war was over, they themselves were on the way out.

And so, as it turned out, were the Maharajas. As to the magnificent houses many of them had built in New Delhi, they were taken away from them and adapted to the needs of a muddled democracy. Baroda became a railway office, and the Nizam's house the headquarters of the five-year plans.

*　　*　　*

For Madhavrao Scindia, the coming of the year 1925 had been marked by a series of evil omens. During the Mohurum festival, his personal *tazia*, the elaborate replica of a mausoleum that is taken out in processions, had caught fire and burnt to ashes. Then one of the most cherished of Scindia emblems, almost the equivalent of the sceptre, the Mahi-Maratib, had been broken by accident. Most horrifying of all, an elephant pulling a heavy gun up the slope of the fort had slipped and come crashing down a precipice 400 feet high.

He was not yet fifty years old but, as though convinced that these events foretold his own death, he not only made a will disposing of his possessions but left detailed instructions as to how the administration of his state was to be carried on and the manner in which he wished his son to be brought up. He wanted a Council of Regency to be formed, with the Senior Maharani, Chinkuraje, as its president, and he was particularly anxious that his son should not be sent to England for schooling but trained, as far as possible, to be familiar with the traditions and living conditions of his own people.

In the spring of that year, he embarked on a journey to England in answer to a summons from King George V, with whom he had developed the most cordial relations. He was taken ill on the way, so that when the ship reached Marseilles, they had to remove him to hospital. From there he was rushed to Paris and operated upon for the diabetic carbuncles that he had developed. He died in Paris on 5 June 1925, far away from his beloved Gwalior, his tigers and his railway trains.

*   *   *

His nine-year-old son woke up with a start, and then realized that what had woken him was the silence: the clock on the tower which had chimed every quarter-hour ever since he could remember, had not struck for some time. He sat up in bed and listened. All the clocks in the vicinity also failed to chime. And suddenly he knew that his father had died, for it was the custom in Gwalior to stop the clocks for a day when the Scindia died.

PART III

THE MAHARANI OF GWALIOR

CHAPTER FOURTEEN
My Husband

ON 21 FEBRUARY 1941 at precisely thirty-one minutes past ten in the evening – the auspicious moment or *muhurta* decided upon by the priests and astrologers of both sides – I was married to Jivajirao Scindia.

A photograph taken during the ceremony shows what looks like a couple of untidy bundles of washing. The one topped by the tricornered *pagri* can be identified as my husband; the other bundle could be anyone – or, indeed, anything – but is, of course, me. The upper half of my face is covered by the overhang of the *dupatta* or bridal veil, decorously pulled down well below the eyes, the lower half is covered by chains of flowers. The photograph brings back the sounds, the smells and the thoughts they provoked.

The air is heavy with the scent of flowers, and the smoke from the incense makes my eyes smart. The chanting of the wedding service, which has been going on for several minutes, rises to a crescendo. *Shuba mangala savadhan* is its refrain: 'Beware, the moment approaches, beware!'

Through the tiniest slit I have contrived to make in the folds of the sari over my eyes, all I can see of my husband-to-be are his feet, folded under him as he squats on the hard wooden board. I gaze at them as though hypnotized, and suddenly I am struck by the thought that they are the feet of the god I have adopted as mine since childhood, the Bal Krishna who became the Gopal Krishna, and to whom I sang the devotional songs of Meera. Meera had found her god.

The moment had come and gone. We were man and wife.

*   *   *

To me he was a private god; to his subjects he was the *ann-data*, the food-giver, the protector, father-and-mother and king; to the officials of the Raj he was the Scindia; to the crowds of racegoers in Bombay and Poona, who cheered as one of his horses romped past the winning post, he was merely Gwalior. His official title was truly forbidding: Lieutenant-General, Mukhtar-ul-Mulk, Azim-ul-Iqtidar, Rafi-us-Shan, Wala Shikoh, Mohra-Sham-i-Dauran, Umdat-ul-Umra, Maharaja dhiraj, Alijah, Hisam-us-Sultanat, His Highness Sir George Jivajirao Scindia Bahadur, Srinath Mansur-i-Zaman-fidwi-Hazrat-i-Mali-Muazzam-i-Rafiud-Darjat-i-Inglisia G.C.I.E., G.C.I.S.

It was difficult to associate so resplendent an array of titles with someone who made a cult of simplicity, someone so natural and warm and with a marked preference for the outdoors, someone who loved horses and guns and believed in hard exercise and in keeping himself fit. But then it is not easy for me to see my husband as others saw him. I was totally infatuated with him. In marrying him, I had embraced the world which was his by inheritance, its disciplines and orthodoxies. It was a world rooted in tradition and even its language, Marathi – which the sardars and their master invariably spoke among themselves – was a sort of transplant which the Scindias had brought from their homeland.

And it was a firm believer in purdah, the segregation of women. But it was a sensible sort of purdah. Even though my less restrictive upbringing made it difficult for me to be mentally reconciled to it as a system, as a bride I did not find it irksome. I was not required to wear a veil. In the premises of the palace I could go about freely, speak to, and joke with, the menfolk. It took me some time, however, to get used to some elderly manservant turning his face to avoid my face.

The rules required that I should not allow myself to be seen in Gwalior itself. If I went to the cinema, I went in a car with tinted windows and slipped into our box through a corridor of screens held in position by attendants. But whenever we were outside the borders of our state, I did not have to observe purdah at all, except in gatherings in which other princes or their families might be present.

Upon marriage (as is customary among the Marathas) I was

given a new name, Vijayaraje. At all times, I seemed to be surrounded by a platoon of maidservants for whom I could not conceivably have found enough work. I had brought four of my own maids with me,* and the palace, which seemed to have at least a hundred in its employ, had allotted a score to me. I had about a dozen cars fitted with smoked-glass windows and as many chauffeurs. A little saffron-coloured flag fluttered on the bonnet whenever I went for a drive; after dark the flag was replaced by a red light.

My jewel-box was a *jamdarkhana*, or treasure-vault, stacked with jewellery that had been made for the Scindias since the days of Mahadji. I would indicate what colours or stones I wanted to wear, and presently a venerable official from the *jamdarkhana* would turn up, followed by one or two servants carrying a selection of jewellery on silver trays covered with velvet cloths, so that I might choose whatever I fancied. Although the items I took out were allowed to lie around on my dressing-table, outside my rooms there was strict security. Everything I took out was ticked off in a register and checked again when it was returned to the *jamdarkhana*.

Apart from my husband and myself, only the custodian of the *jamdarkhana*, appointed from among the senior sardars, could enter the vaults, which entailed a ritual like the daily opening of an old-fashioned small-town bank, with multiple one-of-a-kind keys in different hands. The only time an outsider entered them was when Jayajirao Maharaja died. The then Resident, Colonel Bannerman, saw what has been described as the 'Aladdin's store', a collection of diamonds, pearls, rubies and emeralds that 'was the largest in the world'.

A sari is more suited to the wearing of jewellery than a dress. A heavy silk sari encrusted with traditional designs in gold-thread, such as wealthy Indian ladies wear at wedding receptions, is ideal for the display of jewellery. Even so, it is difficult to imagine an Indian woman of means decking herself today in the sort of jewellery that the Maharanis customarily wore. But even they could not match the barbaric flamboyance of their consorts. In any photograph of my father-in-law Madhavrao in his court dress, the ornaments themselves must have weighed several pounds. The gems don't really show up

* One of whom, Jamnabai, is still a much valued member of my household.

in these old-fashioned settings, for the turban-clasps and arm-bands are all but embedded in gold. The pearls predominate, emphasizing the fact that the Scindias were known as Motiwalas or 'Pearl Kings'. There is a collar around his neck containing perhaps a dozen strands, and some of the pearls are as large as marbles. Around his waist there is a pearl cummerbund, over which hangs another necklace of pearls and rubies that reaches well below his waist and resembles a garland of flowers. But His Highness was by no means wearing everything that he had in his vaults, for other portraits show him with other items of jewellery.

In our *jamdarkhana* there were boxes and boxes of pearls, and some of the necklaces were so alike that only an expert could have told them apart. Ordinarily, when I was not going anywhere special, I wore one of these pearl necklaces with diamond or ruby earrings. I was most attached to an emerald necklace that had been my husband's very first gift to me, and I remember when returning to Sagar from Bombay my grandmother asking me: 'And what did he give you?' When I showed her the emeralds, she was struck speechless. My favourite among the more valuable items was a pair of ruby ear-clips made to go with a ruby and diamond necklace set in such a way that you could not see the mounting at all, so that the stones seemed to be suspended in mid-air. The necklace was at least an inch wide, with an inner arc formed of pigeon-blood rubies, each of which was the size of half a postage stamp, while the outer arcs were made up of rows of blue diamonds.

The walls of my dressing-room, as well as of a couple of other rooms that adjoined it, were lined with *almirahs* stacked with saris with matching petticoats and blouses. The saris, I discovered, had been bought by teams of ladies from the household of the senior sardars, and the blouses and petticoats had been made-to-measure from samples procured from Sagar.

I still remember my husband showing me round my apartment and throwing open the doors of the *almirahs* to display their glittering contents: the sheerest of French chiffons and georgettes made on sari-width looms and with the palest of butterfly tints, gorgeous silks, Indian and imported, heavily embroidered with gold and silver thread, all bought by the dozen from the most expensive shops in Bombay, Madras and Calcutta. After showing a properly demure enthusiasm for them, I was reduced to a speechless silence. Sensing that something was wrong, my husband turned to me and asked: 'But don't you like them?'

'I do, oh, very much! But . . . I don't wear them. I gave up wearing such saris when I went to college . . . when I made a resolve to wear only Indian-made cottons.'

For our honeymoon we went to Bombay. The train was drawn up in the porch and all we had to do was to go down to one of the side entrances of the palace and step into the cream and gold saloon with the Scindia crest emblazoned on its door. It was a carriage of Edwardian elegance, with looped velvet curtains and sofas upholstered in heavy apricot silk. It had its own dining room containing one long table and two smaller tables, its own well-stocked bar, its own kitchen and three bedrooms with wide beds. We were waited upon by our own servants, giving one the feeling that one had merely stepped into another part of the palace. On both sides, joined by corridors, were the carriages of the servants, the ADCs and the secretaries. At some point this chain of four coaches was mysteriously joined to a train going to Bombay. I was woken up in the morning just as though I was at home, to find myself among the sights and smells of the outer reaches of Bombay.

In Bombay, we lived in Samudra-Mahal, built by my husband's father at Worli Point; of the dozen or so houses of the major princes in town, it must have been the most desirable. It certainly had much more land around it than the others, with a low hill and a spur of the coastline all to itself. The main house faced the Arabian Sea, and it had a long drive that ran through palms, shade-trees, sloping lawns and a formal garden; the compound was so large that you could just glimpse the top of the main house from the main road leading out of Bombay.

On the second afternoon, as my husband and I walked back into our apartment after a drive into town, I saw perhaps a hundred saris put out on display wherever place could be found for them; on beds and draped over bedheads, on the backs and arms of chairs and sofas, and even in disciplined rows on the carpet. Suddenly I realized that they were all made of pure *khaddar* – the hand-spun and handwoven cotton material which had been adopted by millions of Gandhi's followers as a hallmark of their nationalist zeal.

With rare exceptions such as the muslin of Dacca, for which the fashionable women of Europe pined during the eighteenth century, *khaddar* is a knobbly and coarse-grained material. While it is good enough for making the simpler garments such as the *sadra* (shirt) and pyjamas that many Indian men wear, it is hardly right for saris. It doesn't wear well, wash well or iron well; it looks dowdy and is far from cheap. Even the poorest woman field-hand, if she went about wearing *khaddar* saris, would be considered either an eccentric or a flag-bearer in the Mahatma's crusade for independence.

I was neither. Here I was, presented with a life-time's stock of pure *khaddar* saris, and beside me stood my husband, who had obviously gone to a lot of trouble on the previous day to hunt out these treasures in the less fashionable markets of Bombay, beaming in triumph.

I could have cried. What I had given up wearing was imported fabrics. While I believed that the finer quality of a mill-made cotton sari was suitable for everyday wear, I had no objection to decking myself on occasion in the shimmering and embroidered silks for which many Indian towns were renowned.

Then and there my earlier resolution crumbled. Such a touching demonstration was something that I could have expected only from Muan. I made up my mind that I would wear all the silk saris I had been given for my marriage and even those in chiffon and georgette that the more fashionable women had begun to wear. How fragile are one's resolutions when one is young, lighthearted and in love!

Above all, I certainly did not want to earn myself the title of the most dowdily dressed Maharani in India, even though my husband had so obviously resigned himself to the idea of his wife accompanying him into the saddling enclosure of the Royal Western India Turf Club on Derby Day looking like an imitation of Kasturba Gandhi.

I was too new to the business of being a Maharaja's wife under the Raj to have realized what a serious risk my husband had exposed himself to. The Raj's guardians would never have allowed such a lapse to pass without a snarl of disapproval. This would have been even more outrageous than his father having removed his *pagri* at a Viceregal dinner. How could the Scindia, with the empire grappling for life against Hitler's armies, permit his wife to adopt the uniform of those who were inciting sedition?

But the spontaneity and generosity of his instincts, together with a childish joy in the simpler pleasures of life, were among Jivajirao Scindia's most endearing traits. If he had led a too sheltered life, which had cushioned him from its harsher realities, it had also preserved intact his natural instincts, which were deeply rooted in his proud ancestry.

*   *   *

Very soon after this I broke another of my teenage resolutions – vegetarianism. In Gwalior, there were twelve head cooks, each with his team of assistant cooks, all practising a subtle game of oneupmanship. It seemed churlish to go on refusing the delicacies they had gone to so much trouble to prepare. During the shooting season, for example, wild duck, part-ridge, green-pigeon, quail or some variety of deer was always on the menu. So, while I continued to keep to a predominantly vegetarian diet, I also began to help myself to the meat and fish dishes so temptingly arrayed. Sometimes we ate in the Indian-style dining room, squatting down on individual silver boards with our *thalis*, usually of silver but, occasionally, of gold with matching *katoris* or bowls, and sometimes we ate our meals in the European-style room, brought up by relays of waiters.

*   *   *

In his will my father-in-law had appointed his first wife, Chinkuraje, to act as Regent during his son's minority. She was a warm and engaging woman, popular alike with officials and sardars. My mother-in-law resented her influence in Gwalior's affairs. She herself was a strong-willed woman, prickly over questions of protocol and given to fits of temper and prolonged bouts of sulks whenever she felt that her wishes were thwarted. It was she who had forced her son to break off his engagement with Kamal Prabha, the Maharaja of

Tripura's sister, by threatening to go on a fast to death. Her resentment manifested itself in keeping her son isolated from the senior Maharani and her entourage.

In 1930, when Jivajirao was fourteen years old, Chinkuraje died. Madhavrao had been genuinely fond of her and had made provision for her that, if he died before her, she should continue to live in the style to which she had been accustomed as the Maharani. In her will she had left her considerable fortune to her step-son, Jivajirao. Brought up to regard her as someone who was opposed to his interests, he was deeply touched that she should have chosen him as the recipient of her wealth. After the death of the senior Maharani, my husband's mother was appointed as Regent.

The Raj took its obligations towards the Indian princes with self-conscious seriousness; when a ruler died leaving his son a minor, that son became their ward. The Government took a hand in his upbringing and provided him with a guardian who enjoyed its trust. In the case of my husband, as a counterweight to his mother's influence, they appointed one of their most experienced civil servants, Sir Terence Keys. But he was hardly a match for my mother-in-law, whose natural wiles and wilfulness were now given rein. She had no interest in the running of the state, which she was quite willing to leave to the other members of the Council, but she was not averse to using her authority as head of the state to see that only such officials who enjoyed her trust and were personally loyal were appointed to be in attendance upon her son.

In this environment Sir Terence seems to have found himself hopelessly at sea, particularly because, whenever he wanted to make a protest to her, purdah etiquette required that she remain invisible. He found himself arguing with a bamboo curtain lined with dark-blue muslin. He must have quickly resigned himself to letting her have her own way in the upbringing of his ward. There is a story that he was once pulled up by Lady Willingdon, the masterful wife of the Viceroy, for taking the young Scindia to a Viceregal levée dressed in a purple velvet robe and hung with chains of pearls.

It must, therefore, have come as something of a relief both to Sir Terence and his ward when the Political Department decided that Jivajirao Scindia should be sent to Bangalore to learn the ropes of running a princely state. Bangalore was the administrative capital of Mysore, which was also a major princely state, and its Dewan, Sir Mirza Ismail, enjoyed the special confidence of the British.

*   *   *

Under the Raj, an heir to a princedom was deemed to have come of age on his eighteenth birthday and was invested with his ruling powers soon after. But since such investitures were important events in the lives of the princes concerned, occasions for public rejoicing and stiff with rituals, the Government usually announced its intentions well in advance to allow the princes enough time to prepare for them.

When Jivajirao Scindia returned to Gwalior, he was in his eighteenth year. Soon after, Sir Terence Keys was recalled to his parent service. This Jivajirao saw as a sure sign that he was soon to be given his ruling powers. Instead, he found that he was to be saddled with yet another guardian, Sir Humphrey Trevelyan, who, fortunately, was a man of extraordinary charm, understanding, and tact; and very soon Jivajirao began to look upon him as a real guide and mentor.

Something must have gone wrong, but this time the Raj was not to blame. The Regency Council of Gwalior, headed by Jivajirao's mother, had requested the Government to hold back his grant of powers. Jivajirao was aware that his mother was merely the nominal head of the Gwalior Council, and that the real power was wielded by Sir Kailas Narayan Haksar, an astute and ambitious Brahmin from Kashmir, with powerful contacts in the Political Department. It was clear that Jivajirao was not going to be allowed to occupy the seat of power.

Humphrey Trevelyan, in his book *The India We Left*, recalled how, over a stiff whisky and soda in the burning midsummer heat of Gwalior, Sir Kailas told his ward in an avuncular tone: 'Young man, I've looked after this state during your father's time, and I have dandled you on my knees. You had better let me run it for you.'

On 16 June 1934 Jivajirao Scindia celebrated his eighteenth birthday. There was still no nod from the Viceroy. The Council went on initiating major projects as though settling down for a protracted tenure, and his guardian took him on a tour of northern India, ostensibly to show him how the Raj ran its administration, but, in fact, to remove him from an environment of mounting intrigue which he considered detrimental to the mental peace of his ward.

*   *   *

Another year passed before my husband did what he should have done much earlier. He solicited the help of a senior sardar, who was also his uncle, Bade-Angre-saab, in resolving the situation.

Sardar Angre had a larger than life-size presence. He had a full face adorned by a fierce Kaiser Wilhelm moustache and a prominent vermilion caste-mark daubed on the forehead. His extra-large eyes seemed to have an accusing stare, possibly because one of them was slightly askew having been damaged in a hunting accident. He stood out in a crowd as much by his imperious bearing as by his immaculate attire – his suits were made by a Savile Row tailor. He lived in great style and entertained lavishly. Feudal to the bone, he was perfectly at ease in the Westernized society of the big cities, especially in Bombay, where he maintained a sumptuous establishment. He was popular in British official circles and counted the Viceroy, Lord Willingdon, among his friends.

Angre-saab seized the challenge with relish. His old-world notions of family loyalty to the Scindia in his hour of need were reinforced by a personal animus towards Sir Kailas, whom he regarded as an outsider.

An old hand at the game of court intrigue, he put his secret weapons to work in the very heart of the Raj, its secretariat. He camped in the capital, and bustled about making friends and influencing people in the highest echelons of the Political Department, even managing to make an appeal to the Viceroy. That same summer, a terse announcement issued from the Viceroy's secretariat. The Maharaja of Gwalior, Jivajirao Scindia, would be invested with ruling powers on 22 November 1936.

*   *   *

The first thing Jivajirao did on becoming the ruler of his state was to shift his residence to Usha-Kiran, a mini-palace his grandfather had built about a hundred yards from Jaivilas as a guest house. He was anxious to free himself from the influence of his mother, who continued to live in Jaivilas. It was to Usha-Kiran that I went as the Maharani of Gwalior. The big palace was used only for ceremonial and official entertaining.

My husband retained the system of administration which his father had initiated of having a team of councillors who headed their own department. But he made Angre-saab his Huzur or Chief Secretary which, in practice, was a position above that of the councillors. However, in time my husband wanted to be left to make his own decisions. So Angre-saab, who had his own considerable estates to manage, withdrew more and more from the day-to-day administration of the state, contenting himself with the role of a family elder whose advice was invariably sought on matters connected with the immediate family.

Unfortunately, my husband by marrying me had flouted Angre-saab's advice and gone against the grain of Maratha sentiment. This had driven the two even farther apart, and Angre-saab had virtually given up coming to the palace. It was only during our honeymoon in Bombay, when my husband took me to pay a call on his aunt, Angre-saab's wife, that I realized how much opposition from his family and courtiers he had had to contend with.

Sardar Angre lived in a fourth-floor flat on Marine Drive. There was no one to meet us at the street entrance, as custom demanded, with garlands and butter-lamps in a tray. Nor were we received by our host and hostess at the door to the lift. Over tea my husband and his aunt carried on a polite conversation in Marathi, but she scarcely addressed a remark to me, which I put down to her knowing neither Hindi nor English. When we got up to go, we were seen as far as the lift, as though we were everyday callers not a Maharaja bringing his wife to be presented to his aunt.

As we drove back along the sea my husband was fuming. 'I shall never forgive myself for exposing you to such incivility,' he said. Beyond thinking that his aunt and uncle were rather cold and had been far too formal, I had not noticed that anything was amiss, but he knew that the rules of feudal courtesies had been flouted. As I looked at him, it dawned on me that I had contributed a new feud to the prize collection of feuds that had gone on for centuries. Sadly, this particular one was not resolved until well after the traumatic changes which followed in the wake of the British withdrawal.

CHAPTER FIFTEEN
Life as a Maharani

I WAS TO discover that the glimpse of my husband's life I had been given as a child was amazingly representative of his concerns. They centered round his sister and his horses. He adored and loved Kamalaraje; she was his boyhood friend, the sharer of his doubts and uncertainties, the custodian of his secrets. Horses were his passion, and I was to be aware time and again that he had some sort of a sixth sense about them, for he really 'understood' them, as only someone who has lived among horses since childhood can.

Kamalaraje was two years older and, as children, she took the leading part in all their activities. But as he grew up their relationship began to change, so that she became more and more dependent on him. Perhaps the first really grown-up thing he did as the head of the family was to arrange Kamalaraje's marriage.

It was not easy, in the days when the Indian princes were real rulers of territories and people, to find suitable husbands for the daughters of the major princely houses. The choice was restricted not only by insuperable considerations of lineage and caste, but also of wealth. A Scindia or a Gaekwad could not give his daughter to someone who had to work for a living, no matter how impeccable his antecedents. Often enough, an otherwise eligible prospective son-in-law had to be elevated in the social order by the grant of a few villages in fief and thus made a *jahgirdar* to enable him to support his wife in something like the style she had been brought up in.

In the case of Kamalaraje, the bridegroom was a ruling prince, a Maratha, the scion of a family going back to the seventeenth century. His name was Vijaisinghrao Bhosle, and he was the Maharaja of a state called Akkalkot. A young man of pleasant appearance and charming manners, he had had a college education and been trained at Bangalore at the same time as my husband. Even the Scindia sardars were delighted with the alliance, and played their full part in the festivities. The wedding took place in Gwalior and Kamalaraje Scindia became Her Highness the Maharani of Akkalkot.

Eight days later she was dead. She, her husband and her maternal uncle had gone for a drive near Akkalkot. The car was caught up in a whirlwind of such ferocity that it was swept off the road and fell into a ditch. It was Kamalaraje who helped to take her husband and her uncle out of the overturned car. They were all driven to Akkalkot in another car, and a team of doctors was rushed in from Bombay to see to their wounds. It turned out that the other passengers were barely shaken, but Kamalaraje's lung had been punctured. Two days later she died.

Her death was the first real shock of Jivajirao's life. The person whom he had thought of as being nearest to him and whom he could trust had gone. He was desolate with grief, and could not help feeling a vague sense of guilt that it was he who had taken the lead in arranging the marriage that had led her to her death.*

*   *   *

My husband's reign as the Maharaja of Gwalior coincided almost precisely with the period that has been described as the 'Twilight of the Princes'. But, paradoxically, that same span of time was also their heyday. Never since their rude take-over by the East India Company had the princes been so completely the masters of their domains. British control had relaxed to the vanishing point and the princes had become real kings.

If the British were becoming increasingly aware that their days in India were numbered, the princes knew equally well that they would not last long in a free India. The Raj had

* It speaks for the old-world decencies of the times that the Maharaja of Akkalkot returned every single item of jewellery and money that Kamalaraje had taken with her as her dowry. My husband made a trust of it, devoted to women's education in Gwalior.

received some nasty shocks. Self-admiring sahibs were becoming increasingly aware of their unpopularity. The world of Kipling had vanished. Indians had not only rejected Pax Britannica, but they were also booing it from street corners.

Adding insult to the injury was the fact that, while the British administration of India was in turmoil, the princely domains, which it had always tended to dismiss as pockets of misgovernments, were barely touched by it. This was not, as the Indian leaders of the time tried to make out, because the princes' subjects were ignorant of their plight, but because they were genuinely contented with their lot. In states like Gwalior, Baroda, Mysore, Gondal and a dozen others I could name, the people regarded their rulers not merely as their providers and protectors, but as benefactors conferred on them by history. They had learned to live under the princes, and were too remote from the British presence to have developed an active dislike of it. I am convinced, at least as far as Gwalior was concerned, that, if, at the time of independence, its subjects had been given the choice of remaining under their Maharaja, rather than accept the rule of the Indian National Congress, they would have overwhelmingly opted for it.

My father-in-law, Madhavrao Scindia, had been the Gwalior people's ideal of a ruler. While he was their Maharaja they were convinced that they were living in *ramrajya* or Utopia. And they could see for themselves that his son patterned himself on his father. Here was someone who had the authority to take quick decisions and who, since he himself had no axe to grind, could be depended upon to take these decisions with fairness. Rough and ready justice, dispensed without the unconscionable delays unavoidable in bureaucratic systems, was one of the most endearing features of autocratic rule.

But those who were waiting to take over the Raj looked upon a popular prince with suspicion and hostility. Having trained themselves to rant at the princes for being oppressors of their subjects, a fifth column of the Raj, they were outraged by the reality that some princes were genuinely liked by their subjects. While my husband's popularity among his subjects was a matter of pride and joy to me, I took little interest in the way our state was run. My husband preferred that I should keep myself aloof from the state's politics, which I believed was right. Indeed, to the subjects of the Scindia I was not even visible, being *pardanashin*, a presence behind the trellised wing of the palace. Besides I was enjoying the experience of my married life far too much to want to take an interest in things that were of no immediate concern to me. To parody Wordsworth, bliss it was to be alive in that world, but to be the Maharani of Gwalior was very heaven.

*   *   *

It was a fantasy world, Byzantine in its splendour with more in common with the French kings of the *grand siècle* than with the world of today. Who, after all, can count his servants in thousands, or the tigers in his hunting preserves in their hundreds, maintain half-a-dozen enormous palaces and a dozen or so hunting lodges or country houses, give sit-down dinners for a hundred and fifty guests on special family plate that had been used for the banquets in honour of at least three British monarchs and one Czar?

The Indian feasts were far more frequent and far more festive. They were heroic repasts, such as might have been served by the ancient Hindu kings, Ashoka or Porus, for little could have changed over the centuries in the type of food served or the manner of its serving. The places for the diners were arranged in a neat rectangle in a large hall the size of an indoor tennis court, and everyone sat according to rank. The Brahmins only ate vegetarian food, which had to be cooked and served by Brahmins; the Muslims had their own prohibitions. The rest of us partook of everything and, as we ate, the servants kept replenishing our plates with more piping hot delicacies.

We sat on silver boards, with our legs folded under us in a standard yoga position, and before each of us was a low silver table. On this table was kept one large plate surrounded by as many bowls as there were dishes to eat. My husband and I ate and drank from gold plates, bowls and glasses; the others, not in our row, from silver. We drank water as no alcohol could be served at Indian meals.

There was always far too much food and our plates seemed

to be just as full when we finished the meal as when we began. There were far too many dishes too, and some of the double-parked bowls were invariably out of my reach. Since it would have been inelegant for a Maharani to be seen bending forward to pick up some morsel from a dish at the corner of her table, two maids were always in attendance to shift the bowls around. Often some sauce or sweet I particularly liked was whisked out of my reach to make room for something that they thought I had neglected. But then there was little I could do to remonstrate.

Like most other princes in India, my husband never carried cash on his person; it was the duty of the ADC to pay for whatever purchases he made. I doubt if any of the other princes believed, as he did, that to ask for the price of anything was somehow an unprincely gesture. He was by no means a spendthrift, but whatever he wanted to buy he bought without ever demanding to know how much he would have to pay for it.

This quirk I remember most forcibly on my twenty-second birthday. I never think of it without a surge of affection; it set the pattern for my subsequent birthdays throughout his life. We were living in Bombay. After breakfast, my husband invited me to go with him to one of the downstairs reception rooms. The room had been transformed into a jeweller's shop. Nanubhai, Bombay's leading jeweller, had brought the most precious items in his collection to our house for a private showing, and from these I was to pick my birthday present. As I went round looking at the shining ornaments displayed on blue or black velvet trays, none of them bore a price tag. My husband did not want me to be put off from having something I liked because I thought its price was too high.

*   *   *

Through the summer and the rains, which roughly coincided with the English spring and summer, we stayed in Poona. Here my husband had his main stud farm, which had as many as two hundred thoroughbred horses. He was one of the two biggest race-horse owners in India, the other being his friend, rival and fellow Maharaja, Sir Hari Singh of Kashmir. He was in his element on the race course, a popular and respected figure in turf circles, with an enviable record as a 'clean' owner. When the Royal Western India Turf Club was in danger of being taken over by gambling bosses, he and Hari Singh were invited by an overwhelming majority of the club's members to become stewards, so that their presence in the control room would restore the confidence of the racing fraternity. It did.

He loved horses. Once, having told some of the sardars that he wanted to get rid of a dozen or so of his horses, he rode over to see them inspecting the horses. After they had made their choice, he told them that he had changed his mind about selling the horses; instead, he invited them to take the horses out whenever they wished, 'as though they were your own'. It was just that he could not bring himself to part with them.

However keen he was for his horses to win, it gave him particular satisfaction if he was on the spot to cheer them on and to lead them in. His trainers had instructions not to enter any of their charges in the major races if there was a possibility of his not being able to attend. Over the years the shrewd Bombay punters had cottoned on, so that the odds on the Gwalior horses tended to fluctuate according to whether the Scindia was present on the course or not. I like to think of him leading in a winner, glowing with pleasure and pride and looking as if he was walking on air. Happily, his horses won with heartening frequency and I am sure they were a great help in enabling him to accept with impeccable good grace the traumatic upheavals that his order was subjected to in the wake of freedom.

*   *   *

Our first child, a girl, was born almost exactly a year after our marriage, on 23 February 1942. We named her Padma, which means Lotus. With Padma's arrival our family life took on an extra dimension; it became fuller, richer and somehow more integrated. By this time I had settled down into the routine of being a wife as well as a Maharani, and had begun to take an increasing interest in women's education and welfare and in the activities of the Gwalior Ladies Club.

I had always been interested in Indian classical music, and had studied it somewhat perfunctorily at Benares. In Gwalior for a while I resumed my study of the sitar under the famous teacher, Hafiz Ali Khan, who was then head of the Gwalior *gharana* or school of music. This was rather like being taught the piano by Sir Thomas Beecham. But I soon found that the rigorous disciplines demanded of me took up too much of my time and, much to Hafiz Ali's disappointment – for he was a dedicated teacher who believed that I had talent – I soon gave up taking lessons from him.

My husband and I shared a passion for listening to music. As a boy, he had been taught music by another pillar of the Gwalior *gharana*, Pandit Krishnarao. Although he had not been able to make a musician of my husband, he had inculcated in him a liking for music strong enough to enable him to sit through and to enjoy the periodical *biathaks* at which the *ustads* of the Gwalior school or other invited guests gave virtuoso performances. Anyone familiar with Indian music will tell you that these *baithaks*, or *mahfils* as they are also known, begin sometime before midnight and end sometime before dawn (and, occasionally, not even then). To enquire in advance as to when the singing will begin or end is not merely to show ignorance, but is a major solecism. *Baithaks* are strictly for those who have been caught by the bug, and my husband called for one at least once every two weeks when we were living in Gwalior.

My most cherished memory connected with music, or rather with a maestro, is of Alla-ud-din Khan of Maihar, a small princely state lost in the jungles of central India. Its school of music was believed to be the best in India, a reputation, of course, which was the reason for the bitter rivalry that existed between the *gharanas* of Gwalior and Maihar.

Chandan Singh, who, you will recall, was instrumental in arranging my marriage, had a son called Jitendra Pratap. From childhood Jitendra had been devoted to classical music and was learning it under *Ustad* Alla-ud-din Khan. One day Jitendra fell off his motor cycle and broke his wrist. When I heard of his accident, I sent a doctor in a car to Maihar to bring him to Gwalior for treatment. Jitendra took advantage of the doctor's visit to get him to examine his music teacher as well, who was suffering from a painful stomach complaint. The doctor told him that, unless he was operated on in a properly staffed and equipped hospital, he would not survive. Jitendra tried to persuade his teacher to accompany him to Gwalior.

Alla-ud-din was shocked. 'Gwalior! But how can I ever go to that place?', he told Jitendra. He then revealed that he had previously paid a visit to the memorial of the great eighteenth-century musician, Tansen, surreptitiously so that no one should know that the head of the Maihar school of music had made a trip to Gwalior.

Jitendra, who had grown up among musicians and knew how to find his way through the feuds of music, was able to persuade his teacher that going to hospital for treatment was almost like going to Tansen's memorial. No one could think he had lost face by it, so long as they knew that he had not given a performance in Gwalior. He gave him his word that he would not be called upon to give a recital in Gwalior and, on that promise, both *ustad* and pupil were bundled into the car and brought to Gwalior. Jitendra's wrist was set and put into a cast, and Alla-ud-din was successfully operated on for stones in his bladder.

When he had recovered, he was gracious enough to want to see me and thank me. So Jitendra brought him to the palace and they both sat in one of the waiting rooms. Alla-ud-din apparently expected an ADC to escort him to wherever I might be holding court. I went to the room where they were sitting, bowed to him and sat down. After a somewhat one-sided conversation on my part and the offer of refreshment, I heard him ask Jitendra in a whisper how long he was going to be kept waiting before the Maharani sent for him. When Jitendra explained that I was the Maharani, he was so overwhelmed that he rose and made as though to touch my feet, which I prevented him from doing.

After Alla-ud-din Khan returned to Maihar, I received a long letter from him and with it the full notation of a *raga* he had composed for me and named after me. This letter, with its notation of the tune, disappeared in the raid on Jaivilas Palace carried out during Mrs Indira Gandhi's Emergency. Perhaps the officials who conducted the raid thought that they had come upon some mysterious code which enabled me to send secret messages to the enemies of the nation. Of all the valuable things I lost then I miss this heartfelt and spontaneous tribute from India's foremost musician of the times the most.

Luckily, however, a couple of years later I was able to persuade him to return to Gwalior to sing at a musical evening I was arranging. He came, breaking God knows what mental vows, and gave a performance that held us spellbound and drew praise even from the stalwarts of the host *gharana*. Alla-ud-din Khan remained a friend until he died in 1953. His school at Maihar has been lately transformed into an officially-supported institution of no special distinction, but I am happy to say that its tradition survives. His son Ali Akbar Khan is perhaps India's most renowned tabla and sarod player, and his son-in-law, Ravi Shankar, has been almost uniquely responsible for popularizing Indian music in distant lands and has himself become a cult figure.

*   *   *

We were, like most of the princes, essentially a country family. Animals seemed to be part of our lives. In Gwalior, besides the horses which my husband used to get up at five every morning to ride, there were *his* dogs and *my* dogs which lived in our apartments, in addition to a score or so of *our* dogs which lived in large kennels at the back of Usha-Kiran. Our evening stroll through the garden usually ended at the kennels during the dogs' feeding time.

On the lawns there were peacocks; in the fields, left open by the landscapist, partridges rocketed in ones or twos as the dogs nosed through. Quails in their well-regulated families of eight or less seemed to hang in the air just long enough for their number to be counted; there were ducks in ponds and cranes parading at the edges, parrots, mynahs, crow pheasants and pigeons by the hundred, jackals, wild dogs, monkeys and squirrels, an annual cobra or two and more frequently encountered benign snakes. In Ujjain we even had a profusion of crocodiles basking among the lilies.

The age of elephants had gone; but we still kept more than a dozen. We had dairy cattle and draught animals. In the patch of carefully preserved jungle at the back of the Jaivilas Palace was an enclosed depression which we had named Hiranvan, or 'deer-forest'. It had its own water-hole and an artificial salt-lick. Here sambhar, cheetal, neelgai, barking deer, as well as one or two varieties that defied classification, lived and multiplied, so that it was always something of a problem to keep their number within manageable proportions. The deer sometimes attracted the attentions of an itinerant leopard, which was like the proverbial cat straying among the pigeons and had to be despatched with promptness.

Over the years we grew increasingly attached to Hiranvan. We began to recognize some of its more prominent denizens and to have favourites among them; afternoon tea on the platform overlooking the deer park became a routine of our life in Gwalior.

Hiranvan was violated and destroyed in the Emergency. The bars of the fencing were sawn off and the deer were shot as they tried to escape. Local poachers muscled in and made more gaps in the fencing; the deer wandered all over the palace grounds and even strayed into the city streets, where they fell prey to anyone who possessed a gun, an axe or stout staffs.

And yet, miraculously, a few escaped the slaughter. Even today, as your car winds over the labyrinth of lanes that surround the palace complex, you can sometimes see a sambhar or cheetal streaking in the direction of its one-time sanctuary. Here, behind the sagging fencing, the thorn hedges have grown thick, tall and unsightly, but they offer the inmates wonderful protection, and mercifully their waterhole never seems to run dry even in midsummer.

*　　*　　*

And there were tigers, if not a staple of our daily life, at least its spice. Tigers were what Gwalior was known for in distant lands; tigers were what emperors and kings came to Gwalior to hunt.

In India tiger-hunting was the sport of kings long before the British or the Mughals came to India. The kings preserved them and protected them in jungles to provide sport for themselves and their friends. Not even the most fanatical conservationists could have done more to protect wild animals and forests than the Maharajas. Their methods were indisputably efficient, and the results exemplary. Twenty years after the Maharajas were shorn of their powers, both the tigers and the jungles had vanished, plundered and vandalized by those who replaced princely rule.

In my husband's time as Gwalior's ruler there were at least a dozen hunting preserves strategically scattered across the state. The best and biggest was near Shivpuri, our summer capital, about a hundred kilometres south of Gwalior. Part of this preserve has now been set aside as a wild-life sanctuary and named after my father-in-law, who created it at the turn of the century: the Madhav National Park. It has a number of deer, hogs, hyenas and a bear or two, but not a single tiger; in my husband's day it must have held at least a couple of dozen tigers.

I can think of few more enchanting places than this park: it had that freshly minted, expectant look of a landscape waiting for an explorer to pitch his tent. Here the jungle belonged to its inhabitants and no one else. The only houses within its perimeter were the cottages of the gamekeepers and the stone villa which was our hunting lodge, George Castle.

The road up to the lodge snaked through low hills covered with jungle and waving grass. The jungle was sparse on the upper slopes and denser and greener in the valleys. Numerous watercourses fed a large lake with tiny shrub-covered islands. The lake had been artificially created by damming a small river. On the dam was a green-painted wooden cabin with peep-holes through which you could look into the valley below. And there, barely thirty yards away, were the tigers.

To say that the tigers were enticed to haunt this precise spot by providing them with an unending supply of bait buffaloes, just so that the Scindia would always have a tiger on hand to offer to some important visitor, is to distort the whole concept of conservation for sport. It is also to take away all the romance. Of course, the tigers were shot for sport, but it must be remembered that they were shot selectively and in strict conformity with the rules of sportsmanship. But then that was also a way of keeping their number at a manageable level. Luckily, the oldest tigers were also usually the biggest and made the best trophies.

In my time it was rare for one of these animals to be shot. In Shivpuri they served the same purpose as the deer in Hiranvan. Our cabin on the dam was our private Tree-tops; only, instead of elephants, we had tigers, great orange beasts with black stripes and trim white beards, gambolling like kittens. We occasionally had afternoon tea served in the cabin and took our guests to it as a special treat. So long as we spoke in low voices, the tigers were not disturbed.

Approaching the cabin by road, the cars had to be stopped at some distance from the foot of the dam. We had to creep up a narrow path so close to the tigers that we could sometimes hear their purring. But if the tigers heard the sound of an approaching car, they took fright and disappeared into the surrounding forest. So we usually went by boat, from a jetty at least half a mile away. Long before the throb of the boat's engine could be heard from the cabin, we were within sight of the battery-powered signal lamp operated by the gamekeeper in the cabin. If the light was green, it meant that there was no tiger within sight, in which case we could approach the landing on engine power. But if the light was red, it meant that a tiger, or tigers, had already arrived. It was rare for us to see the green light.

On one occasion I remember, the light was red. The boatman shut off his engine and we were rowed a couple of hundred yards to the cabin steps. It was late afternoon. In the dark glade thirty yards below us was a tigress; behind her we could see the two yellow puff-balls which were her cubs. For a minute or so she lay flat on her belly, only the tip of her tail swaying in slow movements. Not more than twenty feet from her nose was the bait buffalo, tethered to its post, rigid with fear and snorting as though in an effort to frighten its killer away.

Abruptly, the tigress got up and began to circle her prey. The buffalo kept turning as she turned, ready to take on the charge with its horns. This went on in spellbinding slow motion for several minutes, and then the tigress suddenly turned and bounded off into the jungle. Her cubs pressed their heads down and became invisible. For a minute or two, nothing happened, and then she burst out of the forest like a flame, from behind the buffalo, and hurled herself at it. In one fluid and exquisitely co-ordinated movement, she enveloped its body and broke its neck. It was quick, clean and awesome, like the climax of a dance and, I have always believed, as painless as a process of killing can ever be. Within no time the buffalo had ceased to struggle and the tigress had relaxed her death

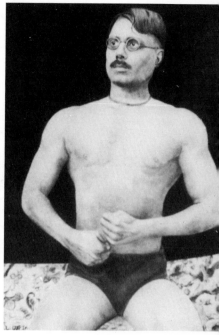

(Above left) My mother in her traditional costume.

(Above) My father's favourite picture of himself.

(Left) My Rana grandparents.

(Above) The house I grew up in: Nepal Palace.

(Middle and below) The palaces at Gwalior, photographed in 1882.

(Above) My father-in-law and Lord Curzon with their tigers. Both are posing in court dress.
(Below) My father-in-law with King George V and Queen Mary. The *howdas* on the elephants are made of gold.

(Above) My wedding ceremony.
(Below left) Myself aged 21.
(Below right) My husband and a fellow prince at a banquet.

(Above) My husband with Marshal Tito.
(Below left) In Hollywood with Bob Hope. He inscribed the picture
'To Her Highness from Her Lowness'.
(Below right) My husband with a winner.

(Above left) My husband with Pushpa, our eldest daughter.
(Above right) Lisha as a bride.

(Above left) Vasu with her son.
(Above right) Yesho, our youngest daughter © *Erica Lennard.*

(Above) My son Bhaiya at the time of his marriage, with Vasu and Yesho.

(Below) Male guests at my son's wedding watch *nautch* girls dancing.

Myself canvassing.

squeeze. As she tore at the soft meat of its thigh, she emitted low grunts. As though answering to a signal, the cubs emerged from the undergrowth and tottered uncertainly towards her kill. Soon they too had buried their fangs into the buffalo's flesh. We watched them until the sun dipped and darkness filled the glade.

The next morning we went to see how the tigress and her family were faring. They were at some distance from the kill and were watching nervously while an enormous male tiger, which had obviously shooed them away, was enjoying their meal with gusto. We could hear the noise of bones cracking. I had never seen my husband so excited by the sight of a tiger. He whispered to me that he was going to kill it and signalled to his gun-bearer to hand him his big rifle.

The sudden urge to kill must have been instinctive, a response to some challenge that was intelligible only to the initiated, the answer to an imagined blast of the hunter's horn, all translated into an irrepressible desire to shoot an animal of unmatchable magnificence. He put the rifle to his shoulder, aimed and killed the tiger as neatly as the tigress had killed her prey, breaking his neck with one shot. Transfixed, I watched the victim. Death seemed to pass in a single tremor along the spine and down to the tip of the tail, which twitched just once and fell still.

The report of the shot had driven the tigress and her cubs into the jungle. But the keepers later told us that they had returned to their kill in the evening.

*   *   *

Such was our life, cushioned, insulated, ornate, taboo-ridden, not much different, I suspect, from the lives of my husband's forefathers. Our family grew. A second daughter, Usharaje, was born on 31 October 1943, and she was followed on 10 March 1945 by a son.

It was an event awaited with trembling anticipation not merely by myself and my husband but also by Gwalior itself. The people went wild at the news; salutes were fired, prisoners were released, sweets were distributed in the streets and blankets and garments were given to the poor. When my husband heard of one old woman who had sold the spinning wheel with which she eked out a living to be able to light oil lamps before her hut, he was deeply moved and hastened to make amends with his usual generosity.

What hopes he and I shared for our son, and how we prayed for them to come true. We gave him the most honoured name in the family, Madhavrao, in memory of his great ancestor, who had virtually made himself the master of north India, and his grandfather.

Much to our delight, and surprise, some of the leaders of the national movement sent us messages of congratulation. The wisest by far, Chakravarti Rajagopalachari, known by his initials CR, came to Gwalior and was impressed by the spontaneity of public jubilation. In a speech to the people he said: 'Such demonstrations of joy as I see in Gwalior today can only have been witnessed in an age long gone, in Ayodhya, when Kausalya gave birth to Rama.'

CR was an expert on *Ramayana*, and his English translation of the epic is still the most authoritative, scholarly and readable. But for us his words were wonderfully comforting. If a top Congress leader such as CR was prepared to express kind thoughts at the birth of a future Maharaja, surely, we naïvely thought, the princes had little to fear from the Congress.

Even if I had not given birth to another Rama, I at least had the satisfaction of knowing that I had provided an heir to the Scindia *gadi* or seat of power. We soon found out that the inheritors of the Raj were not like CR or Gandhi; to them the *gadis* of princes were like the proverbial red rags to the bulls.

*   *   *

The war ended. It had scarcely touched India, which had been steeped in its own age-old troubles: famines, floods, communal killings and police firings. But not, mercifully, in Shindeshahi or the Realm of the Scindia. Here as always the people basked under a special sun, whose image, flanked by two cobras with spread-out hoods, was emblazoned on the Scindia flag. The Maharaja was the surrogate of that sun, whom his subjects looked upon as their food-giver and protector.

And then a terrible event occurred. On the orders of one of my husband's ministers, the police opened fire to disperse a mob of striking workers at a local mill and one man was killed.

It is difficult nearly forty years after the event, when hardly a week passes without some horror in which ordinary citizens are killed by agents of the Government, to appreciate the stunning effect this had on me. While my husband used to share his thoughts with me, he had done his best to keep me away from the problems of his state; and I had happily accepted that position.

Now a tradition has been violated. We could no longer sit back and point a finger at the British who, being outsiders, thought nothing of opening fire on Indian mobs. My husband's officials had proved themselves to be just as callous. He ordered an inquiry. It came out that Vinayakrao Pawar, the minister who had ordered the firing, had over-reacted. There was even a suspicion that he may have been swayed by pressures brought to bear on him by the mill's powerful management, the Birla family. My husband was debating about what action he should take against this minister.

'Sack him,' I advised. 'Show the people that you still care for them, not side with your officials whether they are right or wrong, as the British do.'

I surprised myself by the intensity of my involvement, but I was conscious that I was not speaking as the Maharani of Gwalior so much as a self-appointed spokeswoman of its citizens, who had been let down.

My husband too had been deeply upset. A kindhearted man, he had been trained from boyhood to weigh pros and cons, to balance issues and resist impulsive responses. Above all, he had special ties of loyalty to his officials, ties that were rooted in history. He looked at me in surprise, but said nothing.

We were sitting at table, just about to begin lunch. I don't know what could have come over me, but the words I uttered next had escaped my mouth before I became aware of their import. 'Unless you remove Mr Pawar from office, I shall not take food,' I told my husband and flounced out of the room.

My hunger strike lasted barely the rest of the day. In the evening he passed orders for Pawar to quit office. It was only later that I found out that he had managed to persuade the ruler of another princely state, Narsinghgarh, to employ Pawar in his service. My husband, as the Scindia, looked at things from an exalted level. I, on the other hand, was beginning to think of myself as someone capable of seeing the ordinary citizen's point of view, a quality that I believe has stood me in good stead in my subsequent political career.

CHAPTER SIXTEEN
Integration

INDEPENDENCE CAME TO India in 1947 accompanied by unimaginable horrors. Millions of people were uprooted from their homes, half a million were slaughtered in an orgy of religious killings and thousands of women were raped, abducted or mutilated.

For the princes, independence brought different kinds of shocks: the inheritors of the Raj had decided to abolish their order. Their domains were to be 'integrated'; to them this meant 'liquidated'. The new masters made no secret of their dislike for the princes, whom they regarded as anachronisms. The princes, for their part, returned the sentiment.

There was nothing the princes could have done to oppose 'integration'. They meekly fell into line, some with better grace than others. V. P. Menon, who had been one of the Raj's most devoted servants and who took a prominent part in finishing off the princely states, mentioned my husband as one of these 'good' princes:

> A young man with a progressive outlook and extremely pleasant manners, cautious by nature and deferential to his elders. He has always moved with the times (and) was the first among the rulers of the five 21-gun salute states to agree to integration, a step which was motivated by no other reason than the good of the country.

But then good manners was all that my husband and his fellow princes had to fall back upon in the face of the armoury that Mr Menon and his political superiors commanded. For the princes to have so much as questioned the rationale, legality or usefulness of 'integration' – or to have even hinted that what they were being asked to do was hardly in conformity with the norms of democracy – would have instantly exposed them to the charge of being unpatriotic and anti-national reactionaries. The Indian leaders knew perfectly well that, given the choice, the people of many of the princely domains would have opted to go on as they were. They were determined not to give them that choice; they wanted the princes to surrender their subjects without affording them a chance to say yes or no.

Every princely ruler was hurt and saddened by the deprivation of his ruling powers. But having to surrender their subjects to the care of self-styled democrats was, to some at least, the most painful part of integration. Many sought to cushion its effects by trying to hold out for some sort of safeguards, only to discover that the new masters of the land could be just as tough and imperious as the Dalhousies and Ellenboroughs. My husband tried to persuade Mr Menon that Gwalior should at least be allowed to remain as a separate state, since its territory was large, its finances sound and its people had had a separate entity as the Scindia's subjects for close on two centuries.

'Why not at least ask the people if they want Gwalior to be joined to some other territory?' he pleaded. 'Surely, in a democracy, they should have the right to decide that?'

D. R. Mankekar, recalling these events, mentions how, after my husband had proved obdurate, they had sent a special plane to call me to Delhi. Mr Menon had done his best to wear down our resistance, but found that I was 'indeed a tougher nut to crack. She insisted that the wishes of the people of her state should be consulted in the matter. This the State Ministry did not want to do, as they had no doubt of the verdict of the people on the issue.'

That was the rub. They wanted to bring in democracy in the place of feudal rule, but that democracy did not extend to the people of princely states, who were to be transferred to the new regime without being given an opportunity to decide their fate. They did not want arguments from the princes; they wanted capitulation.

During these days, when Gwalior was about to be steam-rollered into the vast totality of India, my husband came to depend on me more and more. I shared his thoughts and anxieties and became his right-hand man.

So we lapsed into good manners and smiled bravely as my husband signed away whatever territory the Iron Duke and Lord Ellenborough between them had left to his ancestors, trying to make out that the abandoning of four million subjects to the mercies of the Congress nominees was not breaking our hearts. All of which even earned me a favourable mention in Mr Menon's memoirs: 'The Maharani's progressive outlook enabled her to appreciate my arguments.'

So the princes were finished off, a class wiped out, so many different kinds and sizes of eggs broken to make a common hash called democracy. I speak for the whole order, not for Gwalior alone, when I say that only those who have lost their possessions in some natural calamity or in a political revolution can realize the shattering effect this had on the princes and their families. It was not merely a matter of losing their possessions or their hereditary right to rule; they were gnawed by an acute sense of guilt that they had let slip a trust passed on to them by their forbears and even more, as in the case of my husband, that they had failed their people.

*   *   *

So Gwalior was merged with Indore and a few other smaller princedoms and given the name of Madhya Bharat. My husband was appointed to be its *Rajpramukh* or Governor, and the Maharaja of Indore, the *Upajapramukh* or Deputy.

Madhya Bharat was a hybrid freak that never became integrated: its people never thought of themselves as belonging to it, but to their erstwhile states. Luckily it did not long survive and later when the Government was planning to redistribute India into linguistic states, Madhya Bharat became absorbed into one of the four Hindi-speaking states and was given the name of Madhya Pradesh.

The Government agreed to pay the princes annual pensions, which were called 'Privy Purses'. They were also allowed to retain their private possessions. My husband's privy purse was just over half a million dollars which, since these privy purses were also exempt from income tax, was not ungenerous. But then, as Mr Menon points out, the funds he had bequeathed upon his successor administration would from their interest alone have sufficed to cover the privy purse paid to all the rulers of Madhya Bharat. The princes were also permitted to go on using their titles and other symbols of their order, such as flying personal flags on their palaces and their cars. These arrangements were to be permanent and hereditary, and enshrined in the constitution.

* * *

My own feelings about 'integration' were confused. I rejoiced at the advent of freedom. As an Indian, I felt liberated and light. But as a wife I shared my husband's anguish at the sacrifices he was called upon to make. Accustomed to look upon our freedom fighters with starry-eyed admiration, I did not now consider them as the adversaries of the princes. I still did not think of them as professional politicians who were not averse to bending their own principles to achieve their own, or their party's ends, but rather as selfless individuals motivated only by the greater good of the greater numbers.

Integration brought these national leaders suddenly under close inspection, and it was not long before my husband and I were called upon to play hosts to some of them. As soon as Mr Menon reported that he had got his very first twenty-one gunner in the bag, Vallabhai Patel came to Gwalior for the ceremonies connected with the transfer of power.

'The Sardar', as he was called, was known for his toughness, his blunt manners and his contempt for artificiality. But under this rough exterior, he was not only sincere and pragmatic, but also warm and avuncular. Having got his pound of flesh, he was anxious to let bygones be bygones. Almost in spite of ourselves, my husband and I took a liking to him. When I rather hesitatingly asked him if he would address a women's gathering, he at once agreed, but he made it a condition that it should be an open meeting, not restricted to women, and that I must appear with him on the platform.

'If you call yourself the mother and sister of these people,' he argued, 'how can you bear to have a veil between them and you?'

That afternoon he and I appeared in Gwalior's Town Hall. I made a short speech introducing him and he spoke for a few

minutes about the changes that had come over India and
Gwalior. The meeting turned out to have been one of the most
crowded that Gwalior had ever seen. It was quite plain that the
majority of people had come not to hear the Sardar explaining
the transfer of power, but to see what their Maharani, whom
they had never seen, looked like.

The Sardar was perfectly aware of this and made jokes
about it. When he died, a few months later, the princes lost
their staunchest ally, for he was the only man in the party
hierarchy who had the clout to stop its rank and file from
baying for more and more princely blood. He had made a pact
with the princes and he was determined to honour it. If he had
lived for another ten years, Indian politics might have been
saved from many of its follies.

Anyhow, that was how I came to give up purdah, and I have
never worn a veil since.

*   *   *

Jawaharlal Nehru, on the other hand, was not such an easy
guest as the Sardar. Urbane, polished and aristocratic, he took
his role of being a true socialist far too seriously. He was
displeased that the public of Gwalior had not lived up to his
expectations of them. When my husband rose to introduce
him at a public meeting in the heart of town, he was greeted
with wild cheering. But when Nehru began his speech, the
applause was noticeably muted. My husband later told me
how upset Nehru had looked and that he had made no secret
of his displeasure, rebuking his audience with these words:

> Times have changed, and everyone, everywhere else, has come to
> realize how they have changed. Everyone, everywhere else, knows
> that I hold in my hand the key to all cities – all but this perverse
> city, Gwalior. Here people are still mired in the values of the past.

Their applause, when the speech ended, was even less
enthusiastic. My husband, embarrassed as if it was somehow
his fault, saw to it that it never happened again. Whenever
Nehru or any of the major political leaders came to visit
Gwalior to give speeches, he always sent along a hundred or so
of his own men among the audience to act as cheerleaders.

That meeting set the mood for the Prime Minister's first visit to our house and, indeed, of my husband's subsequent relationship with him. Neither readily took to the other, and each bristled with suspicions about the other's efforts to be amiable.

*   *   *

With the disappearance of so many of our cherished land-marks in the wake of 'integration', there was one which particularly affected my husband – the loss of his army. True, it was not as though it was going to be disbanded: the bulk of it was being absorbed into the Indian army. What pained him was that it should be shorn of its unique identity. The Scindia's army was not only the older army, it was the real Indian army; it had fought battles against the enemies of the country. What free India had inherited from the British was, on the other hand, an army that the British had raised for the specific purpose of conquering India. Surely, the Cavalry and Infantry units of the Scindia should have been retained as they were, and their battle honours and flags enshrined in India's military archives? But it was the honours and colours of the regiments which had helped the British to capture India that were retained; the flags and colours of the Scindia's forces were laid to rest. Curzon himself would have applauded.

As his troops marched past him in the farewell parade and the band played the Gwalior anthem for the last time, my husband was close to tears.

*   *   *

My husband was still a very rich man, and his job as *Rajpramukh* gave him plenty to do. He was, however, like the owner of a house who had been dispossessed but allowed to go on living in a small room in it as a matter of favour. A great believer in close personal rule, he was not cut out for the role of pensioner while in his mid-thirties.

Attitudes were changing. His administrators had been absorbed into a pool of bureaucrats. They had to develop new loyalties and take care not to offend their new masters. Even their wives gave up coming to the Ladies' Club, which had been their favourite gathering place, in case they were exposed to the charge of being associated with an institution that bore the taint of British influence.

We began to spend rather more time away from Gwalior. We tried to get used to the attitude of mind which seemed expected of us, that our historic heritage in which we took pride was something to be ashamed of; that we had to make amends by good behaviour, which meant unquestioning subservience to our rulers; that Jawaharlal Nehru and his colleagues who had wound up the princedoms were really our benefactors.

It was difficult not to brood. Whether we were in Bombay or Poona, we could not remain unaffected by the rapid changes that were taking place all around us. So we decided to shake ourselves free from our environment and go to Europe.

In the twilight of the Raj many of the Indian princes had tended to play hooky from their responsibilities and spend unconscionable amounts of time and money in the fleshpots of Europe. My husband had never gone out of India, even for the standard European trip to which most Maharajas were treated by their British guardians as a part of their education.

In 1951 I went with the children by ship to London, where my husband joined me. From there we went to the Hotel George V in Paris. For a few days we enjoyed exploring the town as tourists in anonymity, before an enterprising news-paperman found out who we were and wrote a column about us. As a result of this unsought publicity, people we had never heard of began to send us invitations for parties. Since neither my husband nor I had even a smattering of French, we thought it prudent to ignore most of them.

One invitation we did not ignore was a glossy white card from the fashion house of Jacques Fath for a showing of his latest creations. I had never seen a fashion show and very much wanted to go. So I dragged my husband and my companion, Mrs Sharda Seshadri, to it. We were given seats in the front row. Thin, willowy mannequins, with what seemed to be pained expressions on their faces, paraded before us, postur-ing and turning as though on hidden springs. My husband whispered to me in Hindi that it would not look proper if we went off without ordering anything. So, on impulse, I bought one or two dresses for myself and another for Mrs Seshadri. I chose a blouse and skirt outfit and a party dress.

After the show was over, I was taken to one of the cubicles at the back for a fitting, where the saleswoman told me in her accented English that the clothes I had chosen were just right for my complexion and figure. She then proceeded to sell me various accessories, including a saucy little hat made of black net which covered part of my face and was trimmed with decoration – not unlike the headdress that my grandmother used to make me wear when she had had my head shaved.

When the elegant boxes were delivered to the hotel I could hardly wait to open them. Cushioned in folds of the softest tissue paper and looking like flowers were the clothes that I had ordered. I took them out one by one and gingerly tried them on in the privacy of my room. Wearing the skirt and blouse, I went over to where my husband was sitting; he loyally pronounced that they looked even better on me than they had on the model. That same afternoon Mrs Seshadri wore her new dress and we ventured out into the street.

Paris took not the slightest notice of us, which was a change from the stir we seemed to cause whenever we appeared in our saris. So we decided to wear the clothes we had bought occasionally while we were still in countries where dresses were more common than saris.

A couple of days later we went to Versailles in our smart Western outfits. We had done our sightseeing and were sitting at a table in a nearby café, when among the strolling visitors I noticed a group of Indians, the man of the family in the lead and the women swathed in saris and holding children by the hand. At the same instant I recognized the man. He was one of the senior members of the Birla clan and never failed to call on us whenever he came to Gwalior; moreover, he had known my husband and his father since childhood.

I nudged my husband, and Mrs Seshadri and I buried our noses in our fizzy drinks. To my horror, I saw that Mr Birla had already seen my husband and was shepherding his family towards our table with a broad and mischievous grin, as though he had caught the Scindia doing precisely what Indian princes were accused of doing while they were in Europe: squiring a couple of local girls. When he came close enough to recognize me, the smile on his face froze and gave way to a look of disbelief. For here was someone who had been rarely seen out of purdah turned out like a Parisian girl trying to trap a visiting Maharaja.

The shock was mutual. Mrs Seshadri and I squirmed with shame as Mr Birla, without checking his stride, came up to introduce his family. For a Maharani to be seen dressed like a memsahib was an outrage against the norms of convention. I brooded for days afterwards about what he and his women-folk might be thinking of me.

It was not until we were even farther distanced from the land of saris that I could bring myself to try out my Fath evening gown in public. In New York we made friends with the famous jeweller Harry Winston and his wife, Edna. At Edna's urging, I wore the dress to go and see a play with them and to the party they were giving for us later at their apartment. I was complimented on my choice of the dress, which, coming from those particular ladies of fashion, I took as high praise indeed.

The trip did wonders for us. My husband was like his old self, a bundle of energy and yet mentally more adjusted to living out his days as a gentleman of means instead of as a king. Yet he remained a king, particularly in the way in which he gave to the cause of education. It is of great pride to me that he set up the first ever women's college in Central India and made it possible for that college to give free education. He was happiest with his racing stud near Poona, and he now took to aeroplanes with the same enthusiasm as his father had displayed for railway engines.

He bought a war-surplus Dakota and three smaller planes, including a tiger-moth for training, and engaged an RAF veteran, Captain Roberts, to pilot them. The planes set us free from train schedules and the fledgeling Indian Airlines, and we would often go for joyrides too. My husband took flying lessons from 'Robby' and soon became a proficient pilot. I had developed a superstitious dread of my husband taking a pilot's licence since our close friend, Maharaja Hanwant Singh of Jodhpur, had died in a crash while he was piloting the plane. Although my husband tended to make fun of my sentiments, he respected them, nonetheless, and he never went on a solo flight.

*   *   *

Our family grew. Our fourth child, a girl, Vasundhara, was born on 6 March 1953. A year later, on 19 June 1954, came another daughter, Yeshodhara. The nurseries in our various houses had to be enlarged to accommodate the new arrivals and also because the older children had begun schooling in the charge of an American governess, Mrs Norma Shastri, who was trained in the Montessori method of teaching children. Betty Castelion, who was a trained nurse and had come to look after my first baby in 1942, had stayed on to take care of the later arrivals and by now had become almost a permanent fixture. She was a rare find, a person who had a way with children that was beyond systems, and a balance of indulgence and discipline which seemed to endear her to her charges. Happily, she still visits every winter.

My husband's efforts to bring up his children as those of middle-class parents often presented us with anomalies. Our children, for instance, learned to ride on horses that their parents owned, had the run of a well-equipped riding school and the services of skilled riding instructors. To make it suitably plebeian for our children he made them start riding bareback, graduating to the saddle only after they had learned to ride the hard way.

Similarly – and this may have been a reaction set up by his own overprotected upbringing – he thought it best that the children should grow up without too much parental coddling. Instructions were given in the nurseries not to pamper them. Even though I used to visit the nursery at least once every day, the children were brought to us only to say goodnight. If we happened to have visitors, they had to go round making their bows to each one in turn. At times this presented quite an ordeal for them. Their bows would become mechanical and their voices trembled. Their pleasure at being brought to see us would vanish and they would be on the verge of tears. And so would I.

*　　*　　*

Camelot might have gone, but at least we were happy. Some other princes were not so lucky. They had taken their deprivations so much to heart that they had taken to living outside their states or even in foreign lands. Although we spent more and more time in Bombay and Poona, Gwalior was still our home.

My husband had to spend a good deal of time in Gwalior in his official capacity, and I usually accompanied him. His duties were mainly ceremonial and among those in which I could help him was playing host to visiting heads of foreign governments. For these occasions our special plate would come out in all its unbelievable elegance, the little silver train would go on its round, the great chandeliers would sparkle like myriad diamonds, and our durbar hall and dining room would once again seem like a setting from the Arabian Nights.

Ironically, the guest who seemed most at home in this setting was Marshal Josip Broz Tito. A freedom fighter turned dictator, Tito's uniform had a feminine elegance, as though it was made of silk, and he loved the good things of life. But he also had the hunter's passion for the outdoors. He confided to us that he had come to Gwalior with the intention of bagging a tiger. Since he had learned that most of Gwalior's tigers had been shot by the senior army and police officers, who now had the run of the Scindia preserves, he resigned himself to a camera-safari. My husband went to a lot of trouble to get him close to tigers to photograph, and during their search they seemed to hit it off as though they had a lot in common. The big vase of Czechoslovakian crystal that he had brought along as a present stands in a special place in my sitting-room in Gwalior to remind me of the visit of Jugoslavia's Man of Destiny.

*   *   *

And so we became adjusted to our new life. Our titles, at this time, were still left to us, so that we were still His Highness the Maharaja and Her Highness the Maharani. But these titles were merely shadows; the substance that they had represented had gone.

As time passed, we began to notice that the erstwhile subjects of our state were finding the adjustment to their new status just as difficult to make. Whenever our plane landed in Gwalior, the news that the Scindias had come home spread by word of mouth and we would find the people lining the roads leading from the palace for my husband's *darshan*, which was really an opportunity to offer their greetings.

It was heartening for us to see that the political convulsions had not succeeded in wiping out the past completely. Gwalior remained recognizably what it had been under its Maharajas. In particular, the Scindia sardars were so disoriented and bewildered in the new milieu that they seemed to gravitate back to familiar landmarks. While the people waited outside the gate, they came in by established right, almost as though a court still existed, and enthusiastically participated in the Scindia's traditional rituals.

But it was in our beautiful new house in Poona, where we had taken to spending the monsoon months, that my husband was to be given an even more pointed demonstration of his family's ties with its courtiers. Sardar Angre's eldest son, Sambhajirao, came to see my husband and told him he had come to offer his services in the spirit of the historical relationship that had existed between their two families. My husband readily responded. After all, the two were first cousins who had known each other since they were children. My husband had always called him by his nickname 'Bal', which means 'Kid'. He was from the fold, brought up on the same orthodoxies.

From that day on Sambhajirao Angre became my husband's closest friend and most trusted confidant. Early risers both, they went riding together at dawn and seemed to have enough to say to each other throughout the rest of the day as well. Bal, as I too soon began to call him, became a member of our household and went wherever we went. The children by instinct took to calling him 'Uncle' and our son became especially fond of him.

My husband even took the lead in finding a bride for Bal. The girl came from the princely house of Jodhpur. Like myself, she was a Rajput, and therefore had to overcome the initial opposition of Bal's Maratha parents. My husband bustled about fulfilling the role of family elder and even gave away jewellery to the bride with his customary generosity. I rather think it was his evident high spirits that melted the reserve of Bal's father and mother, who soon accepted their daughter-in-law into the Angre fold with evident good grace.

CHAPTER SEVENTEEN
The Clocks are Silenced

WHEN MADHYA BHARAT was gathered into the larger state of Madhya Pradesh in 1956, the office of *Rajpramukh* was abolished and my husband, much to his relief, ceased to hold a Government position.

Nine years had passed since independence. In these years, the Congress Party, which had inherited India from the British, had so strengthened its hold in what had been British-ruled India that it was accepted as the automatic successor of the Raj. Only in the erstwhile princely domains, such as Gwalior, did it encounter difficulty in putting down roots. Much to the distress of its leadership, the population of these areas had not taken to Congress rule. It was only in such soil, and in those early days of freedom before the Congress had acquired the power and financial resources which made it virtually un-assailable, that there existed a climate in which rival political parties could originate and survive.

That was precisely what had happend. By and large, the people were beginning to wake up to the realization that democracy and Congress rule were not necessarily analogous. Of the several new parties that had sprouted like mushrooms, the Hindu Mahasabha seemed to have a special appeal to the educated middle class and the farming community, and had made considerable headway in the Hindi belt.

*   *   *

My husband, like other princes, looked upon politics and politicians with equal lack of relish; in private conversation, he spoke of both with undisguised contempt. He had no reason to look upon the Congress Party as his benefactor, nor did he consider it the benefactor of the common man. Understandably, his sympathies tended towards those who were opposed to the Congress. But that certainly did not mean that he was going to lend his support to the main opposition party in Gwalior, the Hindu Mahasabha, in the forthcoming elections.

Unfortunately, his unguarded criticism of the ruling party had set up a wave of fear among the rank and file of local Congressmen. In Gwalior, the Mahasasbha was powerful enough; with the Scindia lending it support, it would be unbeatable. The former Gwalior territory covered as many as eight parliamentary constituencies and sixty in the state's assembly. The local leaders ran to New Delhi to get their leaders to stop my husband from throwing his weight on the side of the opposition.

From Delhi came ominous rumblings, which caused me considerable anxiety. I knew that the mildest expression of disapproval from an ex-ruling prince was looked upon as blasphemy; for one of them to join the opposition would be something in the nature of high treason. Had not Maharaja Pratap Singh of Baroda been summarily deprived of his privy purse and privileges for the sin of merely attempting to form a union of ex-rulers?

Jivajirao was in Bombay, immersed in the racing season which was then at its height. From Gwalior I tried to get him on the telephone to find out if there was any truth in what the papers were saying. But the telephone gremlins were particularly devilish that day. After sitting up half the night for the call to go through, I cancelled it.

Improbable as they must seem, these were the circumstances that combined to push me into politics – a tissue of rumours, a wife's anxiety to save her husband from the consequences of such rumours and an abortive telephone call. Spurred on by friends who shared my apprehensions of the punitive action that the Government might resort to against my husband, I decided to go to New Delhi before it was too late and to explain to the Prime Minister, Pandit Nehru, whose patience was proverbially thin, that the rumours of my husband's involvement with the Mahasabha were entirely baseless.

Not that I ever found Mr Nehru anything but urbane,

charming, and even helpful. I was led past the queues that had formed in the corridors and through rooms where Party officials were deposited like left-luggage. Conscious of the pressure on his time, I came to the point. His response shook me. 'Well, if he's not against us, then let him show that he is with us. Let him stand for parliament as the Congress candidate.' And then, for such was the mood of the encounter, he added something banal about the proof of the pudding being in the eating.

'But, Panditji!' I protested, 'he simply hates politics! He will never be a candiate for any party! That is precisely what I have come to explain to you!'

'Well, in that case you stand as our candidate,' he told me glibly. 'Go and see Pantji and Shastriji. They're in charge of giving party tickets . . .'

'But I don't want a ticket,' I protested.

He brushed aside my protests. 'Go and see them. Indu will take you.'

At first I took his remarks to be purely conversational. I had said my piece and now this was my opportunity to explain the same thing all over again to the powerful Home Minister, Govind Vallabh Pant, and to Lal Bahadur Shastri, who became Prime Minister after Mr Nehru's death. Indu, as Mr Nehru called his daughter, was Indira Gandhi. Even though she held no official position in the Party at that time, she sat in on its highest conclaves.

Both Mr Pant and Mr Shastri seemed to treat Mr Nehru's suggestion as some kind of command. Their pressure was concerted. The more I tried to convince them that I had not come to Delhi to seek a ticket for my husband or for myself, the more determined they became to draft me in. Even though neither of them made a direct threat as to what would happen if I refused to cooperate, it was never quite absent from my mind. Here were two seasoned politicians agonizing about who they were going to field against the Hindu Mahasbha in Gwalior when the answer had walked in. The Party's victory in that constituency was assured provided that I or my husband became their candidate. The best I could do was to fend them off by pleading that I could not make such a decision without my husband's approval.

That evening, from Delhi, I was able to get my husband on the telephone. He was horrified at what I had let myself in for, and advised me to return to Gwalior immediately. He flew home the same day, and over the next few days we discussed our possible options. In the end we decided that it would not be prudent for me to refuse the Congress ticket, for it would look like open defiance of the very people I had sought to placate. I agreed to contest the elections but determined that after the elections I should take no part in parliamentary activities except to put in an appearance for the minimum number of days required in order to retain my membership. My husband went further. So distrustful was he of my new-found political associates that he persuaded Bal Angre to join the Congress too, so that he could guard my interests and act as a political advisor.

I don't know what agonies of mind Bal went through in order to perform what was for him an astounding somersault. His affiliation with the Mahasabha was long-standing and sincere. But he took it as a test of his devotion to my husband. Assuming that my own commitment to politics was to be no more than a formality, he knew that there was little danger of his being called upon to show excessive fervour to the Congress cause.

Only minutes before the time for the filing of the nomination of candidates ran out, my name was sprung as the Congress candidate for the Guna parliamentary constituency. The Scindia's subjects, with heartening loyalty, overnight abandoned their allegiance to the Mahasabha. I won with 118,000 votes over the 58,000 votes cast for V. G. Deshpande, the President of the Mahasabha, who had been thought to be unbeatable. Both the adjoining seats, even though they too had been part of the Gwalior state, went to the Mahasabha, a clear indication of the clean sweep the opposition would have made if I had not been the Congress candidate.

I was thus responsible for throttling a party with which I and my husband had much in common and which had a fair chance of defeating the Congress in what had been our state. How hard in later years have I tried to undo the consequences of my impulsive mission to Delhi.

So began my long pilgrimage in politics, against my will. No one could have made a less diligent parliamentarian than I, and my husband simply loathed my association with career politicians. My solution was withdrawal, a retreat into my own world of warmth and plenty and family togetherness, and of the things we liked to do together as a family.

*   *   *

Our son, Madhavrao, whom we called Bhaiya, had been sent as a boarder to the Scindia public school in Gwalior, but the girls were at home with us, two toddlers and two teenagers; and somehow spanning the difference of ages between them was my husband, devising things to amuse and entertain them, teaching them to ride and taking them on drives or on day-long picnics in the mountains behind Bombay. In those days my responsibilities as a legislator did not take precedence over my private life; now, alas, I have no private life, or so it seems.

And then a shadow fell over us. The diabetes, which had afflicted my husband even as a young man, took a turn for the worse. He tried to make light of it and all but refused to comply with the dietary restrictions. 'No one has a right to stop a man from enjoying his mango,' he would protest. The Alphonso mango, which is special to Bombay, was his dream fruit. The fruit merchants of Bombay, who had done business with the Scindias for generations, would send him the pick of this fruit wherever he happened to be staying. It broke my heart to make him give up eating mangoes.

Over the next couple of years few people would have thought of him as an ill man. A lifelong regimen of hard physical exercise and, even more, an attitude of mind that rebelled against the very idea of ill health, seemed to hold his malady at bay. He began to tire more easily, but that was all. And, aside from his health, things were going well for him. His horses were doing better than ever, and in the 1959/60 season he was not only the biggest winner on the course but his horse Ali-Jah had won most of the classics as well.

On 6 March 1960 our eldest daughter, whom we called Akka, was married to the young Maharaja of Tripura, Kirit Vikram Bahadur Singh. Every ex-Maharaja and his family were present at the wedding, which was pronounced to be of a magnificence that Bombay had not seen since the war. My husband threw himself into the hectic round of rituals with gusto, revelling in his role as the father of the bride. After the extravaganza, for which the tempo had been building up for weeks on end, there was a sense of letdown, made worse by Akka's departure to the other end of India. For the first time my husband began to look ill.

Thereafter, I rarely left my husband's side. He began to lose weight, his skin sagged and his walk lost its athletic spring. But the sparkle in his eyes remained as a marker of his ebullient spirit. There were days and even weeks when he seemed to bounce back into his old vitality, as though some miracle, for which the doctors in Bombay and London we consulted held no hope, had actually happened.

The new year brought good tidings. On 16 January 1961 Akka gave birth to a daughter, making Jivajirao the first Scindia in goodness knows how many generations a grand-father in his own lifetime. The next month his Gwalior-bred horse, Flying Carpet, won the season's main event at Bombay. Queen Elizabeth II, who was on a visit to India, was present on the course and gave away the cup. The photograph taken of him receiving the cup from Her Majesty is one of my favourites.

He had set his heart on installing a statue of his mother in the memorial temple erected in a new park which he laid out in Gwalior. The month was April and the proverbial heat of Gwalior, plus the exertions that the ceremonies demanded, put a heavy strain on his diminishing resources of stamina. It was clear that the function had given him some inner satisfaction, as of a vow fulfilled or a debt paid off. We went back to Bombay. The wayside fruit-stalls were a dazzle of yellow with their artistically arranged pyramids of Alphonso mangoes.

In May the schools closed for their summer holidays, and Bhaiya joined us in Bombay; except for Akka, the family was complete, and so it seemed, was my husband's happiness. He could not bear to have his children out of his sight.

We always celebrated family birthdays according to the Hindu calendar, and that year, 1961, my husband's fell on 9 June. He had been in such low spirits that he did not want any of the customary celebrations to be held. Nonetheless, courteous as ever, he forced himself to receive some of his old officials who had come long distances to offer him greetings. One of them was Baburao Pawar, who had reitred many years earlier and was now a very old man. One of the first things he said to my husband was: 'I'm so glad to see Your Highness up and about, for there was a rumour in Gwalior that you had died. They even stopped the clocks.'

That particular news, blurted out by Mr Pawar no doubt in order to express his relief at seeing my husband in better health than he had feared, had a terrible effect on Jivajirao's state of mind.

That same day he took to his bed, and a week later he died, on the night of a wild monsoon thunderstorm and torrential rains. He was forty-five years old. The doctor, flown from England, had prepared us for the worst, but right until the end my husband was fully conscious of everything around him. I kept mumbling the name of Krishna, my private god, and somehow my husband too. Bal Angre was beside him when he breathed his last, and Bhaiya sobbed on his shoulder.

The subsequent happenings are a blur in my memory: streams of people, whom no one remembered seeing before, pouring into Samudra Mahal; the bed, the room and then the adjoining rooms filled with the garlands and wreaths that they had brought; a night of numbness and shock too terrible for grief, while others bustled about doing whatever was necessary; the long cortège of cars on its way to Bombay's airport, the trip to Gwalior and the packed crowds gathered on the runway, leaving barely enough room for the plane to land.

For a few hours only, my husband's body, decked in flowers on a platform in the veranda of Jaivilas Palace, lay in state. As the people of Gwalior filed past, it struck me how close he had been to their hearts and minds as a symbol and, I like to think, as a person also. It was as though the whole city was emptying itself and converging on the palace, the city and the adjoining villages. They were silent, they were bowed with grief, almost as though at the death of one of their family.

Tributes poured in from all sides, from Presidents and Prime Ministers, friends and acquaintances, from distant lands and from newspaper editorials, but they were as nothing compared with the tribute Jivajirao Scindia was given by his people, which had nothing artificial or conventional about it. It was as sincere as a sob.

I had no part in the actual cremation; it was an all-male ritual. It was the sixteen-year-old Bhaiya, now the Scindia, who had to steel his heart to set alight the great bed of sandalwood on which his father's body had been placed. For me, it was as though a blackness had engulfed the world. My gods had played me false. I did not even want to step into Usha-Kiran, in which I had begun life as a bride twenty years earlier. Where had those years gone?

*   *   *

The intensity of grief, like pain, cannot be properly understood by those who are not afflicted by it. My grief was like an explosion; it disoriented me. All my life, I had believed that I had been close to my God; indeed, at times, that I could actually converse with Him. Now the feeling came over me that there was no God at all, only images of metal or stone which we endowed with holiness. If there were a God, how could He have let this happen to me, who, for as long as I could remember, had never faltered in my devotion. For days, weeks, I lived without my God, a defiant heretic in a self-made darkness. And then I went back to Him, in repentance and humility, knowing that I could never fathom His higher purpose. Now I needed my God more than ever, so that from Him I could derive the necessary strength to face the remaining years.

This realization forced itself on me with the suddenness of one coming out of anaesthesia. I had responsibilities to fulfil: a son to be brought up to his heritage and duties, three daughters to be educated and found husbands for. They looked upon me as their source of strength. I could not fail them and the hundreds of others who were our dependants. Everything had stood still while I had given in to grief. From being a wife, I had become a widow; from being a Maharani, I had become a *Rajmata* or Queen Mother. But the change that called for the most immediate adjustment was that I had become the head of the Scindia family.

Hitherto, all major decisions that concerned the family had been made by my husband. Suddenly, it was I who had to make them. If the bitterness had evaporated, a numbness remained. I sought to assuage it by little personal sacrifices. I gave up wearing jewellery and dressed only in white saris – in India white is the colour of mourning. I gave up eating meat, fish and eggs, and then I added to the list the things my husband had especially relished, such as chewing paans after meals and mangoes. My *pujas* became more elaborate and acquired a discipline of their own, so that if I missed out on some part of the morning ritual I invariably made up for it at bedtime. I began to observe all the religious fasts that were normally required of widows and added a few others for good measure. I also resolved that for a whole year from the death of my husband I would remain confined to my house.

I had been brought up by my grandmother to believe that it is only through self-denial and prayer that one acquires strength. I was forty-one, and I desperately needed all the underpinning that my religious observances could give to enable me to carry out my responsibilities.

My husband had done his best to leave his affairs as tidily as possible. But in a country which fourteen years after independence had become the highest taxed in the world, with a host of laws seemingly designed to undo the work of the well meaning and honest tax-payer, this had been a futile exercise. So I found myself plunged into a long drawn-out and frustrating wrangle against the many-headed, many-armed machinery of the state.

The paperwork connected with my properties has ever since been a routine of life; in the early days of my widowhood it came in a floodtide, demanding precedence over everything else. The interminable sessions with tax experts and my own financial advisors left me feeling physically and mentally battered.

With all this work and my desire to be left alone, I had even less interest in my responsibilities as a parliamentarian. But the Government, both of our state and at the centre, had been in office for five years and another election loomed. Urgent messages began to arrive from the nerve centre of the Congress organization. This time they depended on me to offer myself as their candidate for Gwalior itself. They had changed my constituency from Guna to Gwalior as a concession to my resolve not to appear in public for a year.

I chose to ignore the signals. But the high command was persistent. A month or so before the elections were due, the aged Chief Minister of our state, Dr Kailasnath Katju, came to see me, bearing a personal message from Jawaharlal Nehru. The message told me how I must play my part in the cause of making our nation great. Mr Nehru had sent me a behest as from a father to his daughter that I must not shirk from this great duty. All I would be called upon to do would be to sign the nomination paper and need not even stir out of the palace; Mr Nehru would himself come and canvass for me.

I gave my consent. When the time came I signed the nomination paper, not caring whether I won or lost, yet knowing, of course, that there was no question of my losing. I had seen in what numbers the people of Gwalior had come to pay their last respects to my husband. In the event, their response was overwhelming, and my margin of victory created a new record.

Thus I allowed myself to be drafted as Congress Legislator in the nation's parliament for another five-year term. But this time there was a difference. I had, almost without knowing it or desiring it, acquired a substantial following. For five years Bal Angre had been busy building up a base of our own in the old Gwalior territories, and the wave of sympathy generated for me by my husband's death had not been lost on the Congress leaders.

PART IV

THE POLITICIAN

CHAPTER EIGHTEEN
The Tragedy of Bastar

IN THE SPRING of 1962 Bhaiya passed his senior Cambridge examination and was ready to go to college. My husband and I had been both particularly keen that Bhaiya should, as far as possible, be saved from the excessive flattery that the children of Indian princes grew up with in their own environments. I therefore decided to send him to an English university. That summer, after my year's self-imposed seclusion had ended, I took him to England and discovered that since Bhaiya had five A levels he was eligible to enter an English university. I got in touch with the Dean of New College, Oxford, and was able to clear the formalities for Bhaiya's admission.

So, with the satisfaction of seeing my son well installed, I returned to India towards the end of October, just in time for the shocks of November. The Indian army, with its reputation for being second to none in efficiency and valour, had suffered crushing defeats at the hands of the Chinese at every point of contact. It was then forced to accept the added indignity of a unilateral cease-fire imposed by the enemy.

An era had ended. Nehru's dream-castle had come tumbling down. It was sad to hear him admit in parliament: 'We have been living in a world of our own making.' Who were the 'we', I wondered, as I listened to the speech in the stunned silence of a normally noisy house. No one else could be held remotely responsible for what had happened. It was like a general blaming his officers and men for a defeat he had led his army into.

It is difficult to imagine the government of any country being able to take such a national humiliation in its stride. But that is what the Congress Party did. The only change Mr Nehru made in the Government was to dismiss his Defence Minister, Krishna Menon. That done, the juggernaut rolled on, without change of direction or pace, with Nehru, weary and demoralized, as firmly in the driver's seat as ever.

I suppose it happens in other countries too. In India it happens as surely as night follows day: a national crisis is quickly harnessed by the party in power to strengthen its own position. The whole gigantic machinery of the government is put into over-drive to generate a groundswell of national solidarity; a call for everyone to put his shoulder to the wheels of the juggernaut, demanding more and more sacrifices from a people, a third of whom live permanently below the starvation line.

* * *

One sacrifice the people of India were called upon to make in the service of the Government was to give up their gold. Morarji Desai, who was then our Finance Minister, was the progenitor not only of this abomination but also of prohibition, which he imposed with fanatical zeal wherever he found himself in a position to do so. In certain states the punishment for being found in possession of a bottle of brandy was heavier than for ordinary theft. Those who had to follow Mr Desai in enforcing these laws had to pay the price of his obsession, are still paying, and indeed are realizing that to undo its evils is impossible. For, unable to buy liquor, people took to making it in their houses and sold it cheaply. Soon illicit distillation, under unimaginably unhygienic conditions, burgeoned into the country's most widespread – and most profitable – cottage industry. Now it supports its own protection-racket, in which the police have come to have a vested interest, its own political lobby which can sway the results of elections, and above all an industry with a turnover that runs into billions of rupees, all of it in black money. And drunkenness is worse than ever before.

Gold control was a venomous sister of prohibition, smothered in the same aura of sanctity, nearly as unenforceable but equally handy as an instrument for the midnight raiding of houses or, as in my case, for penalizing politically inconvenient citizens for supposed infringements.

I neither drank nor, since my husband's death, wore any jewellery. But I had plenty of gold in my house, in the form of articles of daily use and especially of ceremonial use, such as eating plates, goblets and tea and coffee services. We even had elephant *howdahs* plated with beaten gold in which the Scindia and his family members rode during ceremonial processions. In the course of conforming to the bewilderingly complex tax laws of the country, all the gold objects I possessed, from elephant *howdahs* to the tiniest nose-ring, had already been weighed, listed and declared to the various authorities.

When Mr Desai brought in his gold control order, yet another set of authorities had to satisfy themselves as to the legitimacy or otherwise of a citizen's gold possessions. I remember that, in response to Mr Desai's appeal, I gave away a thousand tolas (25 lbs) of gold to the war effort. After that we went through the now familiar exercise of making dozens of copies of the lists of our gold objects, sending the lists to the various authorities.

* * *

In the summer of 1963, I went briefly to Kodaikanal, the beautiful and quiet hill resort in the deep south where two of my daughters were at school. Kodi, as it is called, is a small town, where small-town courtesies prevail. Visitors either go boating on the lake or take walks on the paths that circle the lake, and everyone gets to know everyone else.

On one of these walks I ran into Sheikh Abdulla of Kashmir, who was being held in Kodi under house arrest. After that we met once or twice in the dining room of the hotel where I had been staying. I had never seen eye-to-eye with many of Sheikh-saab's political views. Nonetheless, I believed that it was wrong of Mr Nehru to have had him arrested and held in custody without a trial.

On my next visit to Delhi I sought out Mr Nehru and pleaded the Sheikh's cause before him. What effect my intercession had on the Prime Minister I shall never know, but within a couple of weeks of our talk the Sheikh was released. He went back to Kashmir, was elected as its Chief Minister, and ruled Kashmir almost single-handed almost until the day of his death in 1982.

*   *   *

On 26 April 1969 my eldest daughter Akka died, leaving two small daughters.

Her marriage had gone wrong and I knew that she was intensely unhappy. My efforts to remind her that it was the duty of a good Hindu wife to be understanding and submissive and to make the marriage a success had only resulted in her estrangement from me. She died in circumstances that were mystifying, for she went to sleep after a party and never woke up. She was used to taking sleeping pills and the inference was that she had taken an overdose. As no mother can altogether separate herself from the lives of her children, the feeling that Akka might have died believing that I had denied her the sympathy and understanding that she had a right to expect has never quite left me. I know that her father, to whom she was the apple of his eye, would have given her what she most needed, love and comfort rather than advice.

She was only twenty-two years old. A firm believer in the continuing cycle of life, as I have said earlier, I have since been haunted by the thought that Akka had paid a debt that I, in some previous existence, had contracted to the ancient house of Tripura and on which I had defaulted by not going myself as the bride of one of its sons.

*   *   *

That same summer Jawaharlal Nehru died. In retrospect, he emerges as a man who had not only planted the sapling of democracy in the unsympathetic soil of India, but managed in spite of his own popularity, which could have so easily been harnessed to promote personal rule, to nurse that sapling and keep it alive. It was only after his death that the whole concept of rule by the will of the people was pulled out of shape by his daughter to such an extent that it is all but unrecognizable as an offshoot of the democracies which between them spawned our constitution, those of Britain and America.

In Nehru's place we elected Lal Shadur Shastri, a compromise candidate who looked the part. A small man with a face like a dried berry, unworldly, homespun and devoid of charisma, he was a complete contrast to the theatrical Nehru. It was easy to feel sorry for him that he should have been called upon to fill Nehru's shoes at a time when the country was in worse shape than it had been since independence.

India was in the midst of a raging famine. Almost Shastri's first move was to put out a frantic call for everyone to miss a meal a week. Then the nation, half-starved as it was, was plunged into the second of our wars against Pakistan. That war showed the mettle of the Prime Minister. Little he may have been, but he was a man of steel. In contrast to the inertia and indecision of Nehru's handling of the war against China, Shastri was tough, bold and in command; in the place of the rout, we came through with honours roughly equal so that both sides could claim a semblance of victory. And even as they were celebrating, Shastri died in Tashkent, where he had gone to sign the treaty for calling off hostilities, his death providing a touch of dramatic neatness to the climax.

So once again we got down to electing a new leader from among the ranks of the party. The two main contenders were Indira Gandhi and Morarji Desai. Mrs Gandhi's only asset was that she was Nehru's daughter; she had no experience of government. Mr Desai, in contrast, was steeped in it; he had been the Chief Minister of Bombay and, more recently, a minister in the Cabinet. But Desai, needless to say, lacked no enemies in the Party. The man who was principally responsible for defeating him was Dr D. P. Misra, who had been introduced to me soon after the 1962 elections by Bade-Angre-saab. Angre, who was now in his sixties, had mellowed and come to accept me as head of the Scindia household. He had thus once again taken his rightful place as a respected family elder.

After Mrs Gandhi's election, Dr Misra emerged as her staunchest supporter. And after that, predictably, he could do no wrong: his position as the Chief Minister of Madhya Pradesh became virtually unassailable. Scholar he certainly was, and perhaps a man of God, but as the head of a state, he proved to be a real despot. Complaints about his arrogance, his oppression and his severities against all dissent became more and more frequent.

Unfortunately, his style of running the state was soon to become the standard operating procedure in most of the Congress-run states.

* * *

I had sent Bhaiya to Oxford, but I was keen that he should not lose touch with his roots. I went to England every summer and saw as much of him as possible, and I encouraged him to come back to India every winter holiday. In 1966 he was going to be twenty-one, and it had been decided that he should take a year off from his studies so that he could perform the ceremony of ascending the *gadi* or throne of his ancestors; for, even though there was no state to rule, he still bore the title of Maharaja and, above all, he was the Scindia. I felt that it was essential for him to familiarize himself with this part of his heritage and I was also anxious that he should get married, and was trying to select a bride for him.

Towards the middle of February, as I was just getting ready to go to the airport to catch a flight from Delhi to Bombay, I was brought a somewhat garbled message that the Maharaja of Bastar, Pravirchandra Bhanjdeo, was in town and wanted to see me. I asked Bal Angre to find out what he wanted to see me about and to assure him that I would see him as soon as I returned in a couple of days' time. But when Bal went to the hotel where the Maharaja was staying he discovered that he had already left.

A month later while Bhaiya and Bal were driving along Delhi's Hardinge Avenue, Bhaiya suddenly said: 'Look, Uncle!' Their car was passing a newspaper hoarding which proclaimed:

BASTAR RULER KILLED IN POLICE FIRING

At least eleven of the Maharaja's followers too had died, all within the premises of his palace. Perhaps fifty or so others had been wounded.

It was horrifying, a mindless terrorist killing. Bastar was a part of India out of the pages of a Victorian romance, a land of mysterious rites and superstitions with a reigning goddess, who was Danteshwari-Ma, and her priests, who were the hereditary rulers or Maharajas. To his tribal subjects the Maharaja was both God and King. It was a little world whose primitiveness the British had taken especial care to preserve intact as a relic of some lost medieval culture. Now Dr Misra was dragging Bastar into the embrace of his democracy, screaming and wounded.

The Maharaja had formed his own party to contest the 1962 elections. In the event, he lost his seat, but most of his nominees defeated their Congress opponents. Between them they formed a fairly vociferous lobby in the local legislature and, almost as a sop to them, and in an effort to defuse a volatile situation, the Government restored Pravirchandra's estates to him. But having previously taken the hasty and quite irreversible step of declaring his brother to be the Maharaja, they had sown the seeds of a family feud. For the elder brother was now only the temple-priest, while the younger enjoyed the prestige and titles of a Maharaja.

It was to seek redress against these outrages that Pravirchandra had gone to Delhi to see Mrs Gandhi, and afterwards come to my house. He returned to his capital, Jagdalpur, in an obvious state of despair, and shut himself in his palace. Outside the tribesmen and the state's police were on collision course; the former intent on reaching the palace to see the Maharaja, the police just as determined to prevent them from entering.

What actually happened on 25 March 1966 no one will ever know. But one thing seems clear, Pravirchandra was killed *inside* his palace, which means that his killers had entered the premises. So there was no question of his having died during the firing resorted to by the authorities to subdue a threatening mob, or still less of someone having killed him in self-defence.

Thus democracy and civilization penetrated a sunless world of voodoo and ignorance. But if what happened in Bastar shocked me, the indifference of my Party's leadership shocked me even more. There were subtle pressures to sweep the whole mess under the carpet, to make out that it was an act wholly justified by the circumstances. Indeed, the supporters of Dr Misra spoke about it as something commendable, for he had put down with promptness and despatch what might have developed into a far more widespread agitation.

I made no secret of my disgust. But, of course, one does not quit lightly a political party of which one has been a member for nearly ten years. I wanted no office either in its ministries or in its organization. Nonetheless, I had come to have a good deal of influence in it, as much through my close contacts with its decision-makers as through my reliable voting block in the Madhya Pradesh assembly, and I still nursed visions of using that influence for good.

CHAPTER NINETEEN
Toppling

ON 9 MAY 1966 Bhaiya was married to a girl from one of the Rana families of Nepal. Upon marriage he was given the new name of Madhavi. The wedding took place in our house in Delhi, and Mrs Indira Gandhi was present to bless the couple.

A couple of weeks later I was to see Mrs Gandhi again, at the hill resort of Pachmari, in our state. She had come to preside over the annual rally of the youth wing of the Congress. Since another election was in the offing, it was widely believed that this rally was going to be used as a sounding board to determine election strategy. All the Party big-wigs were there. Dr Misra made a long speech full of self-admiring allusions to his contributions to the freedom struggle.

I had resigned myself to the standard flow of platitudes when I suddenly realized that the speaker had turned his artillery on the ex-princes. Since I was the most prominent, if not the only, person present who belonged to a princely family, it was clear to me, as it must have been to those present, that I was the target of the attack. So Dr Misra was hitting back at me for my widely expressed horror and disgust at his handling of the Bastar situation. I saw heads turning in my direction and distinctly heard him say: 'These Rajas and Maharajas can never give their hearts to democracy. It is just that in a democracy we cannot debar anyone from joining our party. We have to admit them. But we can definitely render them ineffective. They are not to be trusted.'

I was angry at thus being put on the spot by a man whose vanity had become the subject of jokes, and who was far more despotic than any Maharaja would have been. I was determined not to let his remarks pass, and, as soon as the meeting was over, I tackled him about it. But he retreated into soothing words and ingratiating smiles and tried to convince me that I had heard him wrong.

*　　*　　*

In the summer I went to England. These annual excursions to the saner democracies of the world have tended to serve as my therapy for the tensions generated by the irritations of daily life and the murk of politics in India. In London, New York, Paris or Chicago, I can go about in the streets in total anonymity, and even though I lead just as busy a life as in India, I invariably return from these trips refreshed to face my problems with renewed vigour. It is, of course, possible that foreign trips have this tonic effect because I am uninvolved in the problems of the lands I visit; and my European or American friends tell me that they, for their part, feel just as rejuvenated after a few weeks in our country.

When I returned to Bombay in September 1966, I had no idea that I was soon to be provoked into a hard and bitter confrontation with Dr Misra and, by projection, with my own party. I had been looking forward to the ceremony connected with the re-installation of an idol of the Sun-God, Suryanarayana, in Kalia Deh. For the ceremony of consecration, I had invited Y. B. Chavan, who was our Defence Minister. Chavan was a Maratha, and thus of my husband's clan; he was also a family friend.

Alas, other priorities were to elbow out both the Sun-God and Mr Chavan.

*　　*　　*

On 17 September I was in Bombay, making preparations to proceed to Ujjain, when someone rang from Gwalior. I was informed that, on the previous day, there had been a clash between students and police. The police had resorted to a baton-charge, and one student had died and several had been wounded.

My reaction to the news was the same as when I heard, twenty years earlier, that the police had killed a striking millhand. At that time I was the Maharani of Gwalior, and I had made sure that there would be at least no further bloodshed by the threat of a hunger strike. Now I was the MP for Gwalior, chosen by its people, and thus even more responsible to them. I cancelled plans for Ujjain and hurried to Gwalior.

The moment they heard of my arrival, a deputation of students came to see me. Behind them trailed others, whose bodies were bruised and swollen with the marks of beatings. The students were mere teenagers; if they had grievances, surely it was up to the person responsible to find out what they were and to do something about them. How could anyone bring himself to beat a defenceless youngster, I kept asking myself.

But the students needed more than my sympathy, so I advised their leaders to go and see the Chief Minister and put their complaints before him. Dr Misra refused to see them. He had already given them his answer on the floor of the assembly: unless the students apologized for their unruly behaviour, he would not hesitate to order the closing of schools and colleges in Gwalior for an indefinite period. Then he sent me a verbal message that I had better not involve myself in the student agitation but leave him to deal with it in his own manner.

I recognized the authentic language of ultimatum. Dr Misra wanted to feel free to deal with the students as he had dealt with the people of Bastar. I was not prepared to advise the students to kowtow. The agitation caught on. It spread to other areas of our state. College students in places hundreds of miles away from Gwalior held meetings to denounce the stand taken by the Chief Minister. Dr Misra's response was to crack down on them with his police, and to impose curfews upon entire towns.

One of these towns was Ujjain. The university campus had been a gift of the Scindias. In the face of the curfew, there was no question of my going on with the ceremony I had planned for re-installing the Sun-God in his ancient temple. Mr Chavan had to cancel his visit, which was perhaps just as well because I was determined not to leave Gwalior at this juncture. The students had come to look upon me as their guide and mentor. They derived their strength from my presence in their midst; I could not let them down. Privately, I had made up my mind already to let Bhaiya receive Mr Chavan and do the honours on my behalf. I knew that the Sun-God would understand.

*   *   *

I had an awful feeling that I had placed myself in the identical position to the Maharaja of Bastar. Even though I had warned the student leaders that their protest must be peaceful, I knew that the police had their own methods of turning non-violent agitations into violent ones. But by and large the students remained passive. As their agitation caught on, it found echoes in cities well beyond the borders of our state. All Dr Misra had to do to stop it was to offer to set up an inquiry into police excesses. Instead, he ordered the closing of yet more schools and colleges and his police cracked down on the students with undiminished ferocity.

I took the student leaders to Delhi and arranged for them to see the Prime Minister and her senior Cabinet colleagues. Mrs Gandhi made sympathetic noises; she issued a statement to the effect that she deplored the use of force against students. The Education Minister, M. C. Chagla, was more forthright. He called on the police to respect the sanctity of institutions of learning and not to treat students as though they were criminals. None of this had the slightest effect on Dr Misra. When G. L. Nanda, the Home Minister, called on him to do something about the agitation, Dr Misra as good as told him to mind his own business.

By now the conscience of the people had been aroused. However desperate they were for the schools to reopen, not even parents wanted the students to back down. Then one of the last of the original Gandhian veterans, Acharya Kripalani, lent his support to the students. If the authorities were not prepared to listen to their legitimate grievances, he told the press, the only way open to them was to take them to the people. The student body announced that a hundred thousand of them would march to Delhi and demonstrate before the House of Parliament.

At last good sense prevailed. Who turned the right key never became clear – nor did it matter. One by one, the schools and colleges began to open and the students went back to their classes without anyone insisting that they should atone for their sins. The agitation had gone on for nearly two months, and that much teaching time had been lost to the students. They would have to make it up by giving up their winter vacations. Dr Misra had only lost face; he no doubt had already made up his mind how he was going to retrieve his loss.

And for me, too, there had been an accounting of sorts. I had made up my mind to leave the Congress Party. The experience had been sadly disillusioning. If, even while I was a supposedly influential member, I was not able to prevent the Bastar tragedy and had to engage in a trial of strength against a Party colleague to secure justice for the students, my place was not in the ranks of the Party.

I had seen for myself what immense capacity for good there was in the right kind of politics. Now was certainly no time to walk away. Congress had become synonymous with the country's government; all the more reason, therefore, to remain in politics and work for principles. I could do this better and more effectively in the company of people who broadly shared my beliefs, and, even more, whose ranks had not been corrupted, if only because they had not so far tasted the heady wine of power.

*   *   *

But which opposition? The choice was wide; there were certainly a dozen or so national parties, and many more regional ones. I looked upon all parties with suspicion. Since the 1967 general elections were almost upon us, I had to make up my mind in a hurry as to which party's symbol I would adopt. In India these party symbols have an importance that is not readily appreciated in the West. A large proportion of the voters are illiterate and cannot read a candidate's name on the voting slip, so they identify a candidate by symbol.

In the end, still unable to decide between the Janasangh and the Swatantra, the two parties with those programmes I was broadly in agreement, I decided to contest the elections as representing both, but having made it clear to them that I had joined neither. I put in my name as the Janasangh candidate for the legislative assembly of Madhya Pradesh from the Karera constituency, and as the Swatantra candidate for parliament from the Guna constituency.

Then followed a hectic month of canvassing. Bhaiya and Usha, my second daughter, threw themselves into the effort with all the gusto of youth, and were cheered wherever they went as though they were film stars. Within a week, I could see that we had set up a wave; it was as though the people of the old Gwalior state were rejoicing in my return to the fold.

Our cavalcade merely had to pass near a village for that village to empty itself and form a procession behind us. Once when my car passed an election meeting held by the Congress at which Dr Misra was the main speaker, the bulk of his audience left the meeting as at some signal and ran after my car. At another meeting a young man sliced off the tip of a finger with his knife and placed a bloodmark on my son's forehead, pronouncing undying devotion to him.

I won landslide victories in both my contests, and my Congress opponents had to suffer the indignity of having their deposits forfeited. I won the parliamentary seat in Guna by 200,000 votes over my Congress rival, incidentally breaking the Maharani of Jaipur's record by 50,000 votes.

*   *   *

Thus we ended the winter on a note of contentment and thanksgiving. In the Madhya Pradesh assembly, the Janasangh had 74 seats. With our associates who sat with us, we totalled 130 in a house of 300; the Congress had 162. Of course, that still left the Congress as the ruling party in our state, but its position was far less secure than before.

The opposition parties implored me to become their leader in the state's assembly instead of going to the parliament. So I resigned my parliamentary seat and began to spend a good deal of time in Bhopal, the state's capital. And here late one evening a Congress stalwart, Govind Narayan Singh, came to see me with a couple of his senior colleagues. They had come to discuss a secret deal. They were so fed up with Dr Misra's style of governing that they were thinking of coming over to the opposition along with around thirty of their colleagues. Which, of course, would bring the Congress government in Madhya Pradesh crashing down.

In most parliamentary systems such a proposal would be

regarded with horror, as being unethical. Elected representatives have no business to defect. If, for some reason, they
wanted to change their affiliations after their election, the right
thing for them to do would be to resign their seats and face the
electorate all over again.

But not in India. Here the Congress Party had made
something of a speciality of 'toppling' governments run by
opposition parties; to lure a sufficient number of its dis-
gruntled members with bribes or offers of ministerial positions
had become accepted as a clever trick of political gamesmanship.

If toppling offended one's sense of decency, the ground rules
had at least made it an acceptable hazard. But a hazard it was,
and a dangerous one. Defectors were not people to be relied
upon. But in the bare-knuckled politics of India, you could not
afford to be squeamish. Besides, here it was all in a good cause.
At least we might be able to rid the state of Dr Misra.

Late into the night, in my hotel room in Bhopal, I listened to
Govind Narayan and his adjutants expounding their scheme.
While I showed no great enthusiasm for it, I did not discourage
them either.

*   *   *

That summer the famine was even worse. I visited some of the
stricken areas, and saw children with bloated bellies, rickety
limbs and listless staring eyes, and their elders searching the
fields for edible roots or berries. The wells had dried up and
drinking water had to be strictly rationed. Many people died
of starvation.

Although the Congress Government obviously had not
created the famine, I felt that it was not doing enough to
alleviate the people's suffering. Its propaganda machine was
trying to prove how not a single death could be 'directly'
attributed to starvation, thus reducing the realities of hunger
to an exercise in semantics.

I did what little I could in the way of temporary relief from
my own diminishing resources and went to Delhi to seek Mrs
Gandhi's help in shaking up the state's lethargy. I showed her
the roots, bark and berries I had brought as a sample of the
subsistence diet of some of the people in Rewa and Sarguja.

My efforts at least had the effect of forcing the local government to abolish the restrictions on the movement of food grains. Now, those who were willing and able to take food to the needy could do so without being stopped at the numerous barriers and without fear of being penalized for their troubles.

I returned to Gwalior in the midst of the raging summer, and prepared for yet another election campaign. My new-found zest for politics did not permit the luxury of an annual holiday in Europe.

*　　*　　*

By giving up my seat in parliament in preference to my assembly membership I had caused a parliamentary vacancy and a by-election. I requested Acharya Kripalani, who had supported the students earlier, to contest the seat as an independent candidate supported by my party.

J. B. Kripalani, known as Acharya or 'spiritual guide', was a 'lean and hungry' man who, like Cassius, thought too much. Since thinking men of proven character who were also outspoken did not fit well in the Congress organization as reshaped by Mr Nehru, he had tended to drift in and out of parliament as an opposition member. He had failed to win an election since 1962. Being chosen as our candidate was therefore a direct challenge to Congress. They rose to the bait. They poured in money and brought all their heavy guns into play. Their front-rankers virtually camped on location and used the full machinery of the Government as though it was a department of the Party. They even tried to make out that an accident suffered by their candidate was due to sabotage on my part. The papers dubbed the election as a 'prestige' contest.

None of this made the slightest difference to our voters. The Acharya won even more votes than I had. It shook the Congress. Within a week, at a party meeting called to analyse the cause of the election reverse, some of the members made angry references to the ex-rulers, demanding that the privileges, titles and privy purses that they still enjoyed should be abolished.

*　　*　　*

At the end of June 1967 my second daughter, Usharaje, was married to Rana Pashupati Samsher Jung Bahadur of Nepal from our palace in Gwalior. Usha had been more or less my constant companion of late; young as she was, she had worked in both my election campaigns with the involvement and dedication of a veteran party zealot. I knew I was going to miss her greatly.

She and her husband left Gwalior on the night of 2 July, and within a few hours of saying goodbye to them, I too had to rush to keep station at Bhopal, where the assembly was to start its budget session in the morning. Exciting things were about to happen; for the first time ever, we were going to turn the tables against the Congress. Govind Narayan Singh had been busily engineering the necessary number of defections, and Bal Angre, who was keeping in close touch with him on my behalf, had reported to me that he was ready to strike.

For the next two weeks, nothing happened, but there were distinct signs of restlessness among the Congress ranks. On 16 July the balloon went up. The first broadside was fired by Dr Misra's side. One of his supporters got up and charged that my aides had 'kidnapped' one of their members and were holding him captive. This accusation led to angry rebuttals from our party, and while the question was still being debated, another Congress member rose to address the speaker:

'Sir, myself along with thirty-five other members of this house who now represent the Congress Party, have decided to renounce our affiliation to the Congress and join the opposition. We request that we should be allotted seats in the ranks of the opposition.'

There was a stunned silence and then an abrupt explosion of sounds reminiscent of a football crowd. Members rushed at one another, tried to drag each other to their corners, as in some kind of children's game, shouted slogans, yelled abuse, thumped tables and all but came to blows. At the end of the day's session, the Congress MLAs walked out, leaving the rest of us to take a head count in peace. We were 155, a majority of five. In triumph we marched through pelting rain to the Governor's residence to establish our majority and the right to form the government.

Meanwhile, Dr Misra too had rushed to the Governor,

complaining that the opposition had intimidated several Congress members and was holding them in custody, and demanding that the house should be dissolved.

Under our constitution, one of the principal functions of a Governor is to act as umpire in precisely the sort of situation that had arisen that day in Bhopal. Governors rarely gave decisions that might offend the ruling party. Luckily, K. C. Reddy turned out to be hearteningly independent-minded. He flatly told Dr Misra that he could not act upon his advice, since he could see for himself that he had lost his majority. As the constitution did not permit him to accord us recognition as the party in power, he advised us to take our problems to the President in Delhi. In the meantime, he adjourned the house *sine die*.

That was how the opening round ended. We had Dr Misra on the run, but that did not mean we had won. Now we were halted before an uncharted area of our constitution, there being no rules or even guidelines for Presidents to deal with such crises other than by their own sense of fairness and conscience.

And so followed two weeks of frenzied activity. Logic, truth and the civilities of life were thrown to the winds in an unceasing barrage of accusation and slander. It was like being involved in a tug of war in knee-deep mud.

* * *

Over the next couple of days five more Congress legislators defected to our side, raising our number to 160. I hired a dozen or so buses and took all of them to New Delhi. Here, our party workers had arranged that they should stay in a *dharamsala* or charitable rest-house. When I went to see them there, I found that they were living like refugees, crammed in rooms without enough beds or such amenities as fans, mosquito nets or functioning toilets. It was not easy to find accommodation for the entire group, so I told Bal Angre to hire as many rooms as he could get in one of Delhi's most prestigious hotels.

In Maiden's Hotel we were able to create a real 'camp' atmosphere. Dispersal, we knew, was fraught with dangers. Congress touts lurked in the vicinity, waiting to lure back the waverers into the fold with offers of cash or of ministerial posts, and our volunteers had to be vigilant to keep them at a distance. We even feared attempts at kidnapping or attacks by professional hooligans.

On 20 July I paraded our legislators before the President, Dr Zakir Hussain. After a careful head-count, he was satisfied that we represented the majority. But even that did not mean that the issue had been finally resolved. We still had to contend with Dr Misra's wiles and clout. Desperate to save face, he had mounted a vigorous campaign to have the house dissolved.

Goliath was being attacked. The spectacle was so rare that it galvanized the opposition parties into a semblance of unity. The press scented blood. The tempo of criticism mounted as we held daily press conferences and public meetings, at which the most prominent leaders from all parts of India joined in a chorus of denunciation of the Congress.

At that time the Congress leadership was a little less thick-skinned than it was soon to become, and it was shamed into accepting the inevitable. On 22 July an edict was issued from the Party's headquarters saying that the Madhya Pradesh government would convene the assembly on 28 July in order to test whether it still enjoyed a majority.

We drove back to Bhopal as though we were a convoy passing through hostile territory. We avoided the main roads and sent scouts ahead to find out if road blocks had been put up or if gangs had assembled in our path to pick fights and delay the arrival of our supporters. We knew that if we reached Bhopal too soon, some of our people would be arrested on charges of kidnapping, intimidation or just breaking the peace in order to reduce our numbers at the count. When we heard that a hostile crowd had collected at Beora, we rushed a lot of our volunteers there in jeeps to augment our numbers. I remember that Bhaiya and Bal Angre were enthusiastic members of this force. Luckily, this show of strength deterred the hooligans from molesting our caravan.

When the test came, on 31 July, we proved our majority: 153 against Dr Misra's 136. But for three more days Dr Misra did not give in. He made another dash to New Delhi to rally the support of his party's hierarchy. But by now they had realized that he was no longer the 'Iron Man' of his heyday, but a loser, someone expendable. They told him that there was no question of the assembly being dissolved merely because he was no longer the head of the government.

We had won. I still remember the spontaneous rejoicing that Dr Misra's ousting provoked. Even in the remoter villages the people distributed sweets, set off fire-crackers and lighted up their huts as though they had been given a bonus *dewali*, which is our festival of light.

*   *   *

It was a heady feeling, and yet a time to keep one's head. The victory, I knew, would have to be paid for. I had offended those who had come to think of themselves as the ruling élite, indeed its monuments. I had not only abandoned their ranks, in which I had been a privileged insider, but had also opposed their Party openly and routed it at the polls. And now I had helped to bundle out its government from our state.

The punishment was already being debated in the innermost Party conclaves, in the form of a threat dangling over the heads of the ex-princes. It acquired both momentum and a sharper edge. Originally, the idea had been to divest us only of our titles and privileges, as being a violation of the 'concept of democracy'. Now they decided to take away everything that had been left to the princes by their predecessors and which had been solemnly enshrined in the guarantees of the nation's constitution.

*   *   *

Politicians who profess to be disinterested in accepting ministerial office are seldom believed. Nor was I. Everyone had assumed that I had taken a prominent lead in toppling our state's government because I wanted to be its Chief Minister. My protests that all I wanted to do was to bring into office a reasonably efficient, responsible and clean government had been put down as the rhetoric of campaigning. Now the office was mine for the taking, and there was a move to draft me to head the government. I stood firm.

By general agreement, we set up a coalition of the opposition parties which we called *Sanyukta Vidhayak Dal* or the SVD, and elected Govind Narayan Singh, the principal architect of the defection, to be our Chief Minister. I became the leader of the house. We formed a body to keep a close watch on the performance of ministers and to ensure that there were no excesses or malpractices. I toured the state and was heartened by the public response. They rejoiced at our coming into office; it was up to us to live up to their expectations.

There can be little doubt that we gave our state a far better administration than the Congress's. But good governments are not necessarily stable governments, particularly when they have been stitched together from whatever material is at hand. In retrospect, it is something of a wonder to me and to my Janasangh colleagues that our SVD experiment lasted as long as it did: for the next twenty months.

The Congress members, who were now in the opposition, registered shock and dismay at being let down by their leaders in New Delhi: the state's government had been allowed to slip out of their grasp when it could so easily have been saved by the timely dismissal of Dr Misra. Their clamour found echoes in New Delhi. The leadership was aghast at the reverse and desperate to make amends.

Efforts were begun to put the clock back and the signals went out: come back Govind Narayan Singh – all is forgiven!

After waiting only long enough to make sure that he would still be retained as the Chief Minister, Mr Singh defected back to the Congress, taking with him the same bunch of followers. He tried in an offhand way to take me along too, but when he found that I had no wish to return to the Congress fold, he hastily dropped the subject.

We accepted our defeat without fuss and made a quick descent from the heights to our familiar position as the opposition. At the swearing in of the new ministry I was asked what our role would be in future. I pointed to the sentry standing near the porch and said: 'The role he plays. We will continue to guard our democracy.' It was about this time that I formally joined the Janasangh, which seemed to be more closely in accord with my political convictions than any of the other parties.

CHAPTER TWENTY

De-recognition of the Princes

NINETEEN SIXTY-NINE was the year in which Indira Gandhi achieved absolute control over the Party machine and thus, by projection, over the nation as well. In May the President, Dr Zakir Hussain, died. In his place, the Congress Party decided to put up Dr Sanjiva Reddy as its candidate. Mrs Gandhi, who earlier had herself proposed Dr Reddy at the Party's meeting, then defied all procedural norms, as well as the Party's mandate, to back a rival candidate, V. V. Giri. In the voting, Mr Giri squeezed through by a narrow majority. Thus, in this crucial test of strength, Mrs Gandhi proved that she had a bigger following among her Party's legislators than her indefatigable adversary, Morarji Desai.

This victory was, in fact, made possible by the fifty or so ex-princes, together with their supporters in the Congress Party, who put their weight behind Mr Giri. Why they did so is difficult to say. In the proposal that had been simmering for some time to cut back the princes' pensions and privileges, it was Mr Desai who had been their unwavering supporter. Perhaps the princes believed that if they helped Mrs Gandhi in her hour of need, she would in turn do something to temper the ferocity of their deprivations. In this they were to be sadly disillusioned.

But I gave neither my nor my party's vote to Mr Giri, who thereafter showed exemplary loyalty to Mrs Gandhi. In being ever ready to bend over backwards to do her bidding, he set the pattern of 'rubber-stamp President' for at least two of his successors. On the occasion of my fiftieth birthday, which fell a month later, he sent the following greeting: 'The President sends his best wishes to the Rajmata for many years of health and happiness in the service of the nation.'

That message came with a gratifying number of others, from friends, ex-rulers and religious and political leaders. The Warden of New College, Sir William Hayter, wrote, as did Lord Mountbatten, recalling his visit to us when he was Viceroy and mentioning his claim to friendship with the Scindia family for three generations. Sir Paul Gore-Booth also made kind allusions to a holiday he had spent as our guest in Gwalior.

Some of my friends, who had formed a committee for organizing the celebrations and religious ceremonies that are customary on such occasions, had these messages printed in the form of a commemorative volume for private circulation. Occasionally I glance through this volume. Some of the messages cause a glow of warmth as they conjure up images of the friends who sent them and some, inevitably, provoke sad and sobering thoughts because their writers are no more. But the one with the unfailing capacity to churn up my innermost feelings is an article that Bhaiya contributed. His thoughts were precise echoes of mine towards him, and recognized that in those days we were a mother-and-son team. What might we have achieved if only the team had remained unbroken!

*   *   *

In September 1970, the Government's bill to deprive the ex-princes of their pensions and privileges was rushed through parliament in an exercise that gave the impression that logic itself was made to stand on its head. Mrs Gandhi told the legislators that she was going to 'strengthen' the ex-rulers by taking away their pensions and privileges. History, she told them, was 'replete with instances where, what was sacrosanct in one age was considered inhuman in another', thereby categorizing these leftovers of princely heritages as an outrage against humanity itself. Then her Finance Minister Y. B. Chavan, a staunch yes-man, took up his cue and told us that 'history had ordained whatever they were about to do'. I could not help being reminded of how Lord Dalhousie had justified his annexation of the kingdom of Oudh, because not to have done so would have been wrong in the eyes of God.

What they were about to do, was to divest the princes of everything that had been left to them by their predecessors, and that process necessitated a change in the Constitution. This in turn could not be effected without a two-thirds majority in parliament, as well as in the *rajya sabha* or upper house.

With history and, more practically, every communist and socialist member in the house on its side, the Government moved in for the kill. The ex-princes numbered less than one in every million of the country's vast multitudes; it was like a sledgehammer being brought down on a peanut. The motion was carried by 336 votes to 155.

Triumphantly, they took the bill to the upper house. Both sides had done their best to muster their maximum strength. One of our Janasangh MPs was so determined to register his dissent that he had to be taken in on a stretcher (he died within a week). Of the total 250 members, 224 were present. This meant that the bill needed 149 and one-third votes for its passage. It got 149 votes and was thrown out. What history had 'ordained' had been torpedoed by the third portion of some non-existent supporter of the motion.

The consequences were explosive. Gone were the orotund flourishes of speech, the allusions to a high and holy purpose, the dictates of a historical decree; instead it was Mrs Gandhi who ordained a decree of her own to bring about instant 'de-recognition' of the princes by a single presidential order dutifully signed by President Giri. The princes reacted with a yelp of dismay and challenged the President's order in the nation's highest court. Three months later, a full bench of the Supreme Court ruled that the Presidential order was illegal, and that the princes were entitled to all their 'pre-existing rights and privileges, including the right to privy purses, as though the order had not been made.' In parliament Mrs Gandhi's supporters greeted this judgement with cries of 'Shame! Shame!' Her own way of showing her displeasure was to dissolve the house and order mid-term elections.

She won with a convincing majority and returned to the fray, now claiming that her programmes had received a 'clear mandate' from the people. The princes made conciliatory gestures. But they were left in no doubt that they had been guilty of gross insubordination and were not going to be forgiven. The sweeping amendments to the nation's constitution that were necessary to place the proposed act beyond the sphere of the law courts were swiftly made, and finally on 27 December the axe fell. In a pointed gesture the announcement that the President's assent had been given was withheld for three days so that it should coincide with New Year's Day.

The main loss to me was the title of Her Highness. Bhaiya was deprived of his privy purse, the title of Maharaja, the courtesy title of His Highness, immunity from being prosecuted in a court of law, the twenty-one gun salute, entitlement to a free police escort wherever he went, the right to have his own shooting preserves, and exemption from the Arms Act and custom duties, most of which had either fallen into disuse or become unusable.

What hit both of us hard was the withdrawal of tax exemptions. These had been conceded to us not so much to set us apart as a cushioned species, but out of a realistic appreciation that our principal assets – our palaces – were loss-making assets. They had been built almost as monuments, with full-dress levees and Viceregal visits in mind; they were stuffed with chandeliers, carpets, carved furniture and decorative statuary bought without thought of cost. They were about as impracticable as family residences as elephants were as a means of transport; and these too we happened to possess in embarrassingly large numbers. When was I or my son ever going to give a party that could fill our durbar hall, or host a sit-down dinner for over a hundred guests and dazzle them with our special silver plate and crystal?

We could neither put down our elephants nor demolish our palaces. The only thing to do was let the poor beasts live out their days in diminishing comfort and watch the palaces sag and crumble and their exotic gardens wither and become dustbowls. It was no longer possible to maintain the hundreds of servants that were needed for their routine upkeep. Today even a painting job is out of the question, let alone major repairs. What money we are able to save by economies or to realize by selling valuables or bits of land is invariably eaten up in tax payments.

The possessions of the ex-princely families are not only

arrestingly visible but minutely documented. They seem to serve equally well as practice targets on which new and eager tax men can cut their teeth and their seniors show off their expertise. The struggle to keep up with their unceasing inquiries and, even more, to find the money for their insatiable demands is a continuing war of nerves. None of us is quite free of it.

Both Bhaiya and I lost our entitlement to diplomatic passports. But even before we had lost them, as it were, we regained them by becoming members of parliament. In the mid-term poll of 1971, the 'Indira Wave' that had swept over the rest of the country had not made much of a dent in our traditional sphere of influence. Bhaiya, who was now over twenty-five and thus eligible to become a candidate, had contested my old Guna constituency and won with a resounding majority.

I did something else during that mid-term election of 1971 of which I feel proud, or at least thankful. I have always believed that our legislatures should not be filled only with professional politicians, but possess a sprinkling of men of stature and integrity who have already made their mark in other walks of life. Ramnath Goenka was the owner of India's largest, most influential and, as was soon to be amply proved, most fiercely independent chain of newspapers, the Express Group. Ramnathji, as his friends call him, was a close and valued friend, someone I had got into the habit of consulting on the more difficult problems that one or other of the numerous governmental agencies kept throwing at me, just to push me off balance. He himself had gone through the same mill and survived, and I had come to look upon him almost as a family elder, ready with sound advice, practical help and words of cheer.

I approached Ramnathji to stand for parliament as an independent candidate for the Vidisha constituency with my party's support. Since it had once formed part of the Gwalior domain, it was, for a candidate of my choice, a fairly 'safe' seat. At first Ramnathji was reluctant. He pleaded that he was (in his late sixties) far too old to become an MP and that, in any case, he was too busy to do any intensive canvassing. But I assured him that he would not be called upon to do much canvassing and that I and my party colleagues would see that he was elected. In the end, seeing how keen I was to get him and, I am sure, only because he did not want to disappoint me, he gave his consent. He was duly elected.

It was almost as though some sixth sense had guided me not to take 'no' for an answer from this kind and courageous man. When the Emergency of 1975 came, Ramnathji was an MP and thus entitled to the immunities and special privileges that membership of the nation's parliament confers on a citizen. Otherwise I shudder to think what additional indignities, deprivations and harassment might not have been visited on him during those nineteen months of what the *Times of India* was to describe as 'hell', for his dogged refusal to applaud the Emergency or tolerate the excesses that were perpetrated in its name.

* * *

If the Congress leadership had turned against the princes because they had not given it their unquestioning loyalty, it had a deeper grievance against me. This found an outlet in a particularly spiteful display of venomousness when Mr S. C. Shukla, the new Chief Minister who had been foisted on our state by Mrs Gandhi, proceeded to deprive me of an honour that had come to me neither by heredity nor marriage, but by the concensus of so august a body of intellectuals as the senate and governing board of Sagar University.

This university owes its existence to an eminent son of the soil, Sir Harisingh Gaur, and he somehow contrived to obtain for it a privilege which few if any of the other universities in the country enjoyed: that of electing its own Chancellor – in most other universities in India, the governor of the state is also automatically their chancellor. So when in 1969 the Board of the University elected me its Chancellor for the ensuing five-year term, I accepted with a boundless feeling of gratitude, for Sagar, my home town, has always had a special place in my heart.

But in order to deprive me of my Chancellorship, Mr Shukla had also to deprive the university of its cherished privilege of electing its own chancellor. Undaunted, he went at this task with exemplary despatch. Almost as though he feared that to keep me in office even for the few weeks that would be taken up in enacting the necessary legislation would be to do the university some irreparable harm, he proceeded to clip the university's wings by resorting to the passing of an ordinance, one of the most savagely arbitrary devices that the Indian Parliament has armed its satraps with.

*   *   *

So our titles were taken away. Or were they? Honourifics have always been a part of the very fabric of life in India, and nowhere else are people more particular about the civilities of social intercourse. Almost no one with any claim to breeding or recognition can go through life without acquiring a handle to his name. Our singers are 'Pandits' or, if they happen to be Muslims, 'Ustads'. Our holy men are 'Sants' which means saints, and even 'Maharajas' which is how they are referred to on the state-controlled radio network. And, paradoxically, even the Congress government which set itself up as the champion of a classless society, has created an aristocracy of its own by doling out titles which are no less a mark of an elevated status than those periodically bestowed by the British monarchs on their citizens. Under this dispensation, Jawaharlal Nehru, already a 'Pandit' to the public at large, was also declared a 'Bharat Ratna'.

In a land as steeped in tradition as ours, you cannot divest people of their titles by legislative acts. As it happens, I don't set much store by them anyhow, as I demonstrated when our party became a major component of a coalition government. I cheerfully voted for the scrapping of the 'Socialist Order of Nobility' that the Congress had set up. But no matter what my private feelings on the subject might be, I would never think of addressing a Sikh gentleman as anything other than a Sardar, nor a Muslim lady as other than a Begam, because I have always done so.

And my own feelings on the subject seem to mirror those of the average Indian. By and large it is the government servant, and then only in an official communication, who addresses an ex-prince as 'Shri', or Mister. And even he is aware of doing something not sanctioned by custom, so that if he happens to meet the same Maharaja, he would be careful to call him Your

Highness. To fail to use a lost or even a pretended title is regarded as a social error. And this is especially true of people who have lived in the *riyasats* or princely domains which, after all, once formed a third of the country's area.

Within our own circles, of course, things have hardly changed. Here the whole range of courtesies are scrupulously observed because they are held to be inviolable, so that even in the most informal gatherings there is always a discernible pattern, a semblance to a court. The Marathas still do *mujras*, the Muslims their *salaams* and when Rajput nobles meet, the air hums with a reciprocal chorus of *khamma ghani*.

These are not pretensions so much as a subconscious effort to close ranks, to retain a class identity, to defer – by keeping its manners and customs alive, by observing its rituals, by making the proper tribal signals or responding to them – its inevitable disintegration. And intricately woven in this tapestry of our orthodoxies were our concepts of marital alliances – perhaps, too, part of a subconscious desire to keep our identity barricaded. The most sought after mates for our offspring were the sons and daughters of other ex-princes. In this our attitudes resembled those of Britain's nobility in the days of Queen Victoria.

* * *

By 1971 Bhaiya, now in his mid-twenties and the father of a son and daughter, had settled down comfortably in his role as the *karta*, or head, of the Scindia family. He had kept his father's racing establishments going but on a much reduced scale, he was an MP, and the paperwork connected with the management of the family's possessions kept him fully occupied. And while in his activities connected with the turf he had begun to act more and more on his own initiative, in almost everything else, and particularly in his role as the head of the family, he still relied heavily on his uncle Bal Angre as a confidant, guide and mentor, and the two had become all but inseparable companions.

Which is the background to the engagement and marriage of my third daughter, Vasundhara.

I have mentioned how traditions die hard in India. But die they do, otherwise an alliance such as the one we were contemplating would have been altogether unthinkable a hundred or even fifty years earlier.

The prospective bridegroom was the Maharana of Dholpur, Hemant Singh, and the rulers of Dholpur and the Scindias were traditional enemies. The history of the eighteenth century was full of their relentless efforts to destroy each other in battle or by making common cause with their enemies of the moment.

It was only after the British had taken over India and put the princes behind their 'Ring Fence', that my husband's grandfather, Jayajirao Scindia, put an end to the feud by embracing the then Maharana of Dholpur, Nihal Singh, at a public durbar. Later still, my husband and Dholpur's Maharana, Udaibhan, became close friends. Nonetheless, even in their days, it was difficult to imagine that the two families would so far forget their historical feud as to think of a marital alliance between their offspring.

When the proposal came, as is customary almost tossed into conversation with studied casualness by a mutual friend, my reaction was one of pleasurable excitement, and so was Bhaiya's. The alliance seemed to us not only dynastically perfect, but also historically appropriate, the dénouement of a process which had been set in motion by Bhaiya's great-grandfather ninety years earlier. In retrospect, I can see that our unreserved and spontaneous enthusiasm may have swayed my daughter, then aged eighteen, into believing that something wonderful was being planned for her future happiness and that all she had to do to make it come true was fall in line with our wishes.

Bhaiya and I had the horoscopes of the prospective pair scanned by family priests as well as by some of the astrologers in whose infallibility we had faith, and when they were pronounced to be complementary, we arranged for Vasu, as we called my daughter, and the young Maharana to meet at a family party. Both of them seemed instantly to take to each other.

It was at this stage that reports reached us that Hemant Singh's mother was keen for him to marry the daughter of one of her close relatives, and we made up our minds not to pursue the negotiations. However, a couple of weeks later, while we were staying in Delhi, Hemant Singh himself came to see Bhaiya and me. He was rather upset about his mother's interference in his affairs. He admitted that she was not in favour of his marrying Vasu, but he assured us that he himself was not to be swayed from his resolve to marry her. He pleaded that it was up to us to help him out of his predicament.

For our part, it was all we needed to hear to set our minds at rest. After all, it is not unusual for mothers to disapprove of their son's choice of a spouse; my mother-in-law had not approved of me either, but that had not deterred my husband from marrying me, and after a while she had taken it all in good grace. So, as much to help young Hemant Singh as because we too were eager for the alliance, we went on with the arrangements for the marriage.

The wedding took place in our Poona house, Padma Vilas, on 24 November 1972, and Vasu became the Maharani of Dholpur. She and her husband divided their time between their New Delhi house and their palace in Dholpur. A pile of rose-pink stone surrounded by a moat, the palace was straight out of *The Far Pavilions*. In its echoing halls pigeons fluttered near the recesses of the ceiling, ornate rooms with marble floors were packed with carved furniture, old silver, statuary and a collection of priceless clocks. It had secret entrances and narrow twisting staircases suddenly opening out on to bright terraces. Beyond were a walled garden, a deer park, and an aviary of extravagant proportions with innumerable artificial nests and pools of water designed to entice the birds to roost there, the thick foliage of the creepers that formed its roof giving it an eerie submarine light. From another palace, not far off, you could look out on herds of deer roaming below or even a pack of leopards that had been trained to appear on call.

A year passed. Vasu gave birth to a boy, whom they named Dushyant Singh. A few months later her husband left Dholpur in circumstances that were very mystifying, as well as ominous. He had taken away with him as much of his moveable possessions as he could cram into a fleet of lorries — the carpets, the silver, the clocks and much of the statuary and wall decorations of Chinese porcelain — leaving behind his wife, his new-born heir, and his hauntingly beautiful palace.

When an arranged marriage breaks up, the arranger can

never escape a sense of guilt. And so it has been with me ever since I heard the first garbled reports of the story. Initially, we tried to comfort ourselves with the hope that whatever had happened was no more than a histrionic tantrum, that sober reflection and the counsel of friends would soon prevail. But as the months passed we became reconciled to the finality of the separation. Attitudes hardened on both sides, releasing a storm of recriminations and accusations. All I could do was to keep reminding myself that such adversities are visited on us to test our inner strength and to prepare us for a purer and nobler way of life, and also that it was as though history itself had rejected our puny efforts to span the breach between the two families.

But, of course, these convenient generalizations could never assuage the mental laceration that my daughter has suffered, and still less make amends to her little boy for the deprivations that his father has caused him.

CHAPTER TWENTY-ONE

A State of Emergency

THE INDIRA WAVE, which had swept the Congress Party to its dominance in the country's parliament, had not quite spent itself before it got another boost. India's intoxicating victory in the short and swift Bangladesh war and the literal 'cutting down to size' of its traditional enemy Pakistan whipped it back to life just in time for the elections to the state assemblies in March 1972.

No politician could have failed to make capital of such a windfall. 'We have won one of the decisive wars of history,' Mrs Gandhi told the crowds that flocked for her *darshan* or sight wherever she went. Just as the applause subsided, she would add: 'Why, we've even won the cricket test match series against England.' As the architect of at least the first victory, President Giri accorded her the title of Bharat Ratna. I wonder how much irony she read in the messages of congratulations that many of the ex-rulers, whom she had divested of their titles, sent her.

The Bharat Ratna is rather like the British Order of Merit, the highest honour that the Queen can bestow. In this case, it was as though the Queen was bestowing it on herself, or at least letting the President bestow it on her. For the trend of voting in both elections had clearly shown that the people had not voted for the party so much as for Mrs Gandhi herself.

No one could have been more conscious of her fantastic personal appeal, or fitted herself more easily into the image of queen, than Mrs Gandhi herself. She began to rule her lieutenants with a rod of iron, making it clear that unquestioning obedience was the only qualification for ministerial office.

The Chief Ministers of states whose support had hitherto been regarded as being indispensable, were now left in no doubt that they were themselves dependent on Mrs Gandhi's goodwill to remain in office.

Thus, democracy in India took on many of the aspects of a Mughal court, with the Cabinet Ministers serving as courtiers, and the Chief Ministers of the states as the Subahdars of the provinces. Except that the Mughals never possessed as obedient and as vast a crop of bureaucrats as India had managed to build up since independence.

With a regiment of grateful legislators eager to prove their devotion, Mrs Gandhi proceeded to hack away at such bastions of the nation's constitution as stood in the way of the radical reforms she had set her heart on: for instance, the nationalization of the country's banks. In the process, the safeguards to the citizens' 'fundamental rights' – to own property, of free assembly, free speech, a free press and the due process of law – were to be undermined. Parliament even gave itself the blanket right to 'amend any part of the constitution, including the fundamental rights'. It was as though an American President had managed to give himself the power to do away with the Bill of Rights.

When the press set up a concerted howl against this assault on the constitution, its wings were severely clipped. It became the subject of a host of restrictive measures, such as the rationing of newsprint to recalcitrant papers or the withholding of Government advertisements. After that, the same disciplines were imposed on the judiciary. Judges who gave verdicts that were unpalatable to the Party found themselves transferred to other posts, and those who toed the line were promoted out of turn. In the 'newspeak' of the Party, a 'committed' judge was to be preferred over a fair, independent and efficient judge. The promotion of one such 'committed' judge to the post of Chief Justice over the heads of three uncommitted senior judges resulted in their prompt resignation and effectively changed the character of the Supreme Court.

And that was when, with Mrs Gandhi in absolute command and the opposition reeling against the ropes, the petition filed four years earlier by Raj Narain limped along to its final hearing before Mr Justice Jagmohanlal Sinha of the Allahabad High Court. Mr Narain had been Mrs Gandhi's election opponent, and he wanted her election nullified on the grounds that she had made use of official machinery. Judges, by the very nature of their calling, have to show themselves to be upright and fearless, but few of them can have had to contend with the sort of pressures brought to bear upon Justice Sinha, or come out with so shining a reputation. An offer of half a million rupees was dangled before him, as was the prospect of elevation to the Supreme Court. And when he spurned both, he was requested at least to put off the delivery of his judgement by a few weeks. In indignation, he advanced it.

On 12 June 1975 Justice Sinha ruled that Mrs Gandhi had been guilty of electioneering malpractices. He unseated her membership of parliament and disqualified her from standing for elections for a period of six years. Then, at her counsel's earnest pleading that the Party would need a little time to elect a new leader, he gave Mrs Gandhi twenty days in which to give effect to his verdict.

As it was, thirteen days was all the time she needed to show Justice Sinha and the Indian public that courts of law have no power over absolute queens – or dictators.

The normal course for anyone debarred from public office by a court order would have been to file an appeal against that order in a higher court, and to step down from office pending its hearing. Mrs Gandhi did, indeed, file the appeal, but at the same time she made it abundantly clear that she had no intention of resigning. She called a meeting of her 500-strong parliamentary board; which was like inviting the heads of all her fan-clubs to give a concerted and orchestrated performance of their allegiance. Fan after fan rose to say how they must stand by their leader because, as Y. B. Chavan expressed it: 'What happens to her happens to India; what happens to India happens to her.' D. K. Barooah, the Congress Party's President, went one further: 'India is Indira and Indira is India.'

So, instead of abiding by the High Court's verdict, Mrs Gandhi proceeded to put herself beyond the jurisdiction of the courts by resorting to what can most fittingly be termed a 'coup' against the constitution itself. She declared a state of

'Internal Emergency' and assumed totalitarian powers.

In the proper tradition of such coups, it was executed at midnight, on 25 June 1975. An emissary called on the President, Fakhruddin Ali Ahmed, and placed before him an order that said: 'A grave emergency exists whereby the security of India is threatened.' It included measures to invest the Government with sweeping powers including censorship, the suspension of court proceedings and the imprisonment without trial of any citizen, ostensibly to deal with the crisis.

When the President of India obligingly signed the order, he plunged his country into an Orwellian nightmare, nine years ahead of its fictional advent.

*　　*　　*

That night I had given a party at our house in Rajpur Road in Delhi. Four days earlier my youngest daughter, Yeshodhara, whom we called Yesho, had passed her twenty-first birthday. But, for some reason, we had chosen to celebrate on the twenty-fifth. Dinner had been late, and I was about to leave Yesho and her friends to pop music and games and go to my rooms for my end-of-the-day *puja* when I was called to the telephone.

'They're arresting all the opposition leaders tonight. About five hundred in Delhi itself,' my caller told me. He was a party worker who was well known to me. He had been given the tip by the party secretary, Madan Lal Khurana, and told to pass on messages of warning to as many of our leaders as possible.

The plotters had guarded their secret well. The several Deputy Commissioners in charge of different localities had been told to keep their forces ready, but nothing more. It was not till 10.30 p.m. that they were called to police headquarters, where their Inspector General, Banwari Lal, told them that they were to arrest all the important leaders of the opposition parties before dawn. A list was handed round. 'Get cracking,' the Inspector General told his subordinates.

Similar late-night conferences were being held in the score or so state capitals, where the procedure was just as mechanical, the orders just as stunning. By the next morning, no opposition politician was to remain free. This was only the first wave of the assault: soon these tactics would be extended to the common man, so that nobody could feel that he or she was immune from arrest. After all, the purpose of the Emergency was to silence all dissent by terror. Overnight, India was transformed into a police state in which any petty official could settle a private grudge by having his adversary thrown into jail. After all, the example was set by Mrs Gandhi, who ensured that Raj Narain was one of the first to be put behind bars.

*   *   *

I did not want to break up my daughter's party. In any case, I had serious doubts about the correctness of the message. I woke up one of my maids and told her to pack some clothes in a suitcase as for a long journey, but this was just a precaution. And then I went to my prayer room, performed my usual *puja* and retired for the night.

This was not Idi Amin's Uganda or Papa Duvalier's Haiti, I kept telling myself. This was India, where, however much we decried our subjugation to the British, we still cherished the institutions that they had left behind. We looked to the awesome power of the courts to redress wrongs; the law courts were the citizen's arms against the excesses of the state, his ombudsman. Like the police officers, I went to sleep asking myself: 'Under what law can they make these arrests?'

I did not know it then, but the Inspector General's efforts to find the answer to the question from the Prime Minister's house had earned him a curt rebuff, which he had promptly passed on to his subordinates: 'Just pick them up wherever they're found. No need to tell them under what law you're doing it. Now get on with it.'

*   *   *

On the morning of the twenty-sixth, Bal Angre was in Calcutta, where he had arranged to meet Ramnath Goenka. He had been unable to find any newspapers, but had thought little of it. Ramnathji could hardly believe his eyes when he saw him being ushered into his room. 'What on earth are you doing here!' he gasped. 'How have you escaped arrest?'

Which was how Bal Angre heard of the Emergency. Ramnathji, who because of the numerous news services at his disposal was more fully informed of the previous night's events than anyone else, told Bal that, to the best of his knowledge but much to his disbelief, I was still free. Most of the other opposition leaders had been arrested.

Bal has this quality of imperturbability in the face of calamities that makes him an ideal associate in moments of stress. Instead of being bowled over by events, he seeks relief in action. He borrowed a car from his host and had himself driven to the Indian Airlines office, where he managed to get himself a seat on the first plane leaving for New Delhi. He then arranged for a friend to ring me, giving his arrival time as 6 p.m. As he drove to Dum Dum airport everyone was talking about the Emergency, but no one had a precise idea of what was happening. In the plane, too, everyone seemed to be suffering from shock and outrage. A group of a dozen or so Congressmen, who were obviously rushing to the capital to be counted among the cheerleaders, were chattering like excited birds, slapping each other's backs and laughing uproariously. They looked surprised to see Bal Angre still a free man, and one or two of them who knew him waved their arms in exaggerated greetings.

*　　*　　*

I am an irrepressible scanner of newspapers. I have made it a rule in all my houses, and indeed wherever I go, that all the available local and national newspapers in English and Hindi are sent up to my room as soon as they arrive. Thus, by the time I have finished my morning *puja*, there is usually a stack of them on a special table in my bedroom. That morning there was not one. At 1 a.m. the previous night, just as the morning's editions had been 'put to bed', the electricity supply of Bahadurshah Zaffar Marg, New Delhi's Fleet Street, had been cut off at the mains. It remained cut off for the next three days.

The first reports of the Emergency came over the BBC's morning broadcast; the All India Radio news bulletins made no mention of it. The telephones in our party's Delhi offices, as well as those of the officials, had gone dead, and my efforts to ring Gwalior to find out what was happening there were futile. At 8 a.m. someone triumphantly brought in a copy of a paper called *Motherland*, and there it all was in screaming headlines: MIDNIGHT SWOOP ON OPPOSITION

> Shrimati Indira Gandhi today invoked the hated Maintenance of
> Internal Security Act, MISA, to put behind bars in a pre-dawn
> swoop Jayaprakash Narayan ... (and) other leaders of the
> democratic opposition.

The front page was splashed with photographs of the
victims. Prominent among them was Jayaprakash Narayan,
whom the nation knew merely as JP. A thinker and philos-
opher more than a politician, he, above all, was qualified to be
the nation's conscience and to bear Gandhi's mantle. Now he
had been made national enemy number one.

At what stage I became aware of a sense of loss of reality I
cannot recall; with the evidence of *Motherland* that life had
suddenly become transformed into a horror movie, I could not
believe that I was still free. But the riddle was solved when,
towards noon, a messenger arrived from Gwalior with the
news that they were looking for me and for Bal Angre. So we
had to thank bureaucratic procedure for the respite we had
been given. Since we were residents of Gwalior, the responsi-
bility for our arrests had been passed on to the Madhya
Pradesh police. Only after they had failed to find me in
Gwalior would they send out radio alerts to see if I was at any
of my other houses. How many hours did that give us?

Among the guests at our previous night's party were Mr and
Mrs Surinderlal Dewan. Mr Dewan's father had left his home
in Lahore, in the Punjab, during the partition and had brought
his family to Shivpuri, where he had set up a factory. My
husband had given his son all the help he could, and the
business had prospered. Over the years, our friendship with
the family had continued to grow.

As proof of that friendship, Mr Dewan, who was staying
with relatives in New Delhi, came to my house that morning
with no other thought than to give me whatever help he could.
It was he who suggested that I should go underground, at least
for a time, and see how things developed. He took it upon
himself to find a place for me to hide.

I now forget who suggested that I should not dress in the
all-white garb that had come to be associated with me.
Anyhow, for the first time in thirteen years I put on a coloured

sari. My three daughters and Bal's wife, whom we called Munoo, between them brought out armloads of their coloured saris and accessories for me to take away. Mr Dewan whisked me off within the hour. Munoo and my girls stood on the steps, rigid with anxiety, but waving wildly and trying not to cry.

Behind us the trees closed up and hid the house, and suddenly I was struck by the extravagant display of colour they had put on in the burning summer heat. Every single tree was bowed down with the weight of blossoms – pinks, yellows, magentas, blues and vermilions. They had never looked so lush or flowered so profusely. It was almost as though they were making some sort of a farewell gesture, knowing what I did not: that I was never going to set foot in that house again.

*   *   *

Bal Angre's plane from Calcutta landed in the evening. I had sent a car to meet him at the airport, with a message carried by a trusted official of my Delhi establishment that I had fled and was staying with 'friends', to whom he was to be brought. But, fearing that he might be followed, he chose to go to Rajpur Road, which he did not reach till well after 8 p.m. He had an early dinner and went to sleep. He was woken up a little after 4 a.m. by Dr Ragini Jain. She and her husband, Dr J. K. Jain, one of the capital's most brilliant surgeons, formed a young and fearless team and plunged into our party's affairs to the hilt of their capacities and convictions. Ragini had been delivered of her first baby only three days earlier, but she had driven all the way to Old Delhi in the small hours of the morning because she was on a mission that she could not trust to anyone else. She had been charged by one of our party's most ardent and respected torch-bearers, Nanaji Deshmukh, who had also gone underground, to bring Bal Angre to his hiding place. Bal got up, pulled on some clothes and got into her car.

Within minutes after they had driven off, a police party came to arrest me. My daughters later told me that they even searched the overhead cisterns of the house in case I was hiding there.

*   *   *

I was hiding elsewhere. At first Mr Dewan had taken me to the house of a close relative of his, a senior government official. But the next day, tipped off by a friend that the police had traced my whereabouts, he shifted me to the house of another relative. From here too we had to leave in a hurry, only an hour or so ahead of the police.

What risks they took, these kind people who gave me shelter. They might have been sent to jail under that dreaded catch-all device, MISA, or have been subjected to an income-tax raid or to some other refinement of spitefulness, such as their children failing to make the grades in examinations or finding themselves mysteriously debarred from jobs.

My next host, Sardar Amarjeet Singh, a recently retired brigadier, had never met me and indeed did not know who he was being asked to put up until I arrived on his doorstep. He had gamely agreed to accommodate 'a high-born lady from Jodhpur who needed protection from her enemies' merely because Major Jaswant Singh had requested him to do so. Jaswant Singh, who is related by marriage to Bal and known in our household as Jasoo, is one of our party's most industrious workers. He has brought to his career in politics not only the ethics of his earlier profession as an officer in one of India's crack tank regiments, the Central India Horse, but its cavalier disdain for occupational hazards. And it was heartening for me to see, in a world that cowered in the face of despotism, these secure islands sustained only by strands of personal relationships and gentlemanly instincts. Brigadier Amarjeet Singh registered neither shock nor dismay when he realized who it was he was giving shelter to, but quickly ushered me into a room and went about his business as though nothing had happened.

Usha, Vasu and Yesho paid me visits and from them I learned that Bhaiya, who had been staying in Bombay when the Emergency was declared, had managed to escape to Nepal. A couple of days later a messenger Bhaiya had sent from Katmandu came to see me. He reported that my son was absolutely disconsolate that I and his young sisters should be living in India, which, he was convinced, had come under a dictatorship bent on crushing the opposition with ruthless determination; for us to stay on was to invite the fate that had befallen the Russian aristocracy after the Bolshevik revolution. He had charged his messenger to implore me to bring Vasu and Yesho to Nepal, and to say that he had made all the necessary arrangements for our safe passage. 'Please tell Amma,' Bhaiya had told his emissary, 'that my heart bleeds for her. That if she does not want to remain in Nepal, we can go somewhere else from there and make a new life in some civilized country. Luckily, we have enough to live on wherever we might decide to emigrate.'

It was a touching message, and I was so overcome by it that I could have cried. And yet I had made up my mind to stay on and see things through, no matter what lay in store for me. I told the messenger to thank my son, but that I had no intention of coming to Nepal; he should look after himself and the rest of the family and I would do my best to look after myself. I sent him my love and blessings.

But Bal Angre, who had been listening with obvious displeasure to our dialogue, had his own message for his nephew: 'Tell our Maharaja that we and those who were his father's subjects look upon him as the Scindia; that it is not proper for him to think of his own safety and show fear of the sort of people that have taken over the running of the country.' Bal believed that Bhaiya's only course was to remain on Indian soil and to fight them out as his ancestors had. The worst they could do to him was to send him to jail. Well, let the Scindia's erstwhile subjects say that their Maharaja chose to go to jail, but did not abandon them in their hour of need. 'Tell him from me,' Bal continued, 'that it is his duty to come back here; not to take away his mother too. Show these people that he is not afraid of them, as she is doing.'

In Hindi, Bal's words sounded much more stern and reproachful than they do in an English rendering. It was not the sort of message that my son, who had done his best to rescue me from certain imprisonment, would have relished. But I must confess that I could not bring myself to find fault with its import.

By now police vigilance had increased and my houses were kept under constant watch. There was no possibility that Vasu and Yesho, both barely out of their teens, would be able to escape. How could I myself run away and leave them to fend for themselves and, in addition, be victimized for whatever crimes I was supposed to have been guilty of? But against this, I had to weigh the risks to which I was putting my hosts. It was not possible to remain in one place for more than a couple of days. Far too many people knew that I was in town. I was even sounded out to lead a protest march that my party had planned to start from Chandni Chowk, the very heart of Mughal Delhi. Thinking that to court arrest openly was a good way of dealing with my indecision, I agreed; but our local leaders had second thoughts about the usefulness of such a march and gave up the idea.

On 27 June Brigadier Singh gave a dinner party. While the party was in full swing, Bal Angre, who had to pass an urgent message to me, had to be ushered past the guests, two of whom were ex-princes. As they both knew him well and knew that he was my principal advisor, they must have realized that I was hiding in the house. It was this incident as much as anything else that made up my mind for me. It was far too nerve-racking for me and far too dangerous for my hosts for me to remain in New Delhi.

Once again, Surinderlal Dewan took matters in hand. He and his wife had stayed on in the capital just in case they could be of service to me. He now appeared, exuding quiet confidence and an air of rocklike dependability, ready with a solution. He had, he revealed, lined up a couple of other houses for me in Delhi, in case the need arose for another quick change of address. But since I now wanted to leave he had the ideal hiding place for me: a solitary farm that his wife's family owned deep in the Terais, the foothills of the Himalayas which are almost next-door to the Nepal border.

'Your Highness can stay on the farm in complete anonymity,' he assured me, 'or go from there across to Nepal.' He must have been as aware as I was that, in offering to help me to escape and, indeed, by remaining in my company, he was putting on the line not only his family business, which had taken him a whole lifetime to build up, but his personal freedom as well. His brother-in-law who ran the farm was also being exposed to all kinds of risks. But over the years we had fallen into the sort of relationship that does not permit conventional expressions of gratitude, and as soon as I had agreed to his plan, he began to arrange our departure.

The suitcases were quickly packed. A last-minute anxiety, presented by the fact that the numbers and descriptions of my cars must have been circulated to all the police stations along the roads leading out of the capital, was resolved when a friend lent me his car. It was brought to the side entrance and we piled in.

* * *

There were four of us in the car: Surinderlal, his wife, Bal Angre and myself. We drove for hours without pause. It was difficult not to ruminate about the effect of faith on actions, of the conflict between principles and conformity. What had I done that I should be running away as though I were a criminal dodging the forces of law, except that I had tried to remain true to my principles?

The long summer day wore itself out. The darkness brought its own wave of depression. I had left behind the people I loved, the things I loved; what else was there that was worthwhile? Towards midnight we reached our destination. From here the Nepal border was only forty miles away. Once across, I would be safe. That was the answer then to the question of what else was worthwhile – freedom. Then again, was I mixing up freedom with safety?

We spent the next seven days on the farm. I confined myself to my room, even though I was quite sure that all the servants in the house had discovered who I was. The others occupied themselves making sure that we would not be stopped by the border checkpost.

The spell of Nepal became increasingly irresistible. There I had roots: there they spoke the language that I had learnt as my mother tongue; there I had plenty of friends and my daughter, Usharaje, was married to one of the most influential of the Ranas. My daughter-in-law too came from Nepal. There my son Bhaiya waited for me.

On the morning of 6 July 1975 we set out again, this time in the direction of Nepal. Once again there were only the four of us in the car. The road wound through prosperous farms, which had replaced the famous Terai jungles, and there was very little traffic. Within a couple of hours we would come to the frontier.

I don't know how far away the frontier was when I requested Surinderlal to stop the car. I had been wrestling with the problem ever since leaving New Delhi. The other three had made it clear that this was something I had to decide for myself, and that they were not going to influence me. Now I had made the decision. I could not bring myself to run away, seeking safety and leaving others to face the music – I, who called myself a leader and who had been accepted as such by a large number of people. Leaders did not run away.

Only the previous night we had heard reports that the Government had decided that those who fled the country to avoid arrest would be treated as enemies and their possessions expropriated. There was no escape; every move was blocked off. Like a cat playing with mice, the Government was showing off the power of its muscles, the reach of its paws.

In the bright late afternoon sunshine on the lonely road, the confusions of the past few days were shed. Faith and principles had won. I told Surinderlal to turn around. As we faced south once again, everything fell into perspective. 'I'm going to give myself up,' I announced.

Bal Angre behaved as though he had known all along that I would renounce the plan to escape. Even before we had returned to the farm, we were discussing practicalities. We would go straight back to Gwalior, and there give ourselves up. In view of that decision, it seemed unreasonable that Mr and Mrs Dewan should expose themselves to any further risk by being in our company. We tried to persuade them to detach themselves as soon as possible, but they would not hear of it. 'We're going the same way in any case,' was Mr Dewan's argument. It was only in Jhansi, almost next-door to Gwalior, that we parted company, the Dewans going off to Shivpuri and Bal and I back to the centre of the vortex.

It was as though I had passed some crisis in an illness. I could sit back and think of other things besides my immediate problems. In the long, long journey back from the very edge of India, I even had moments during which I could look at things as an outsider. For the first time I was assailed by the external aspects of the Emergency, the crude portraits of Mrs Gandhi going up on hoardings, her vituperative pronouncements about foreign hands and forces of disintegration drummed up into patriotic slogans.

What I saw of my land in that journey towards my moment of truth convinced me that India itself had become a vast prison, held in stricter bondage than at any time during the Raj's tenure; that somehow the prisons had become the pockets of freedom, for here at least I would be among people like myself who had defied the ideological strictures of totalitarianism.

I kept thinking of the torments my children would suffer at the thought of their mother, who never went anywhere without half a dozen attendants, a follow-up car in case of breakdowns, and even her own special linen, being thrown into a jail. It was important not to let my mind wander. I had made my decision and I knew that, if I wavered now, I would never forgive myself. Now my one desire was to go and offer a prayer to the family gods in the palace in Gwalior. We took a detour because I wanted to give myself up with formality and dignity, not to let them have the satisfaction of having caught me like a thief.

We made halt at an obscure hotel in Agra, from where I sent a messenger to Gwalior. It was reported that the palace was not actually surrounded by a police force, even though it was suspected that all the entrances were being kept under watch. Like a mouse on its final dash towards the trap, we drove on, waiting for darkness to fall so that I could sneak into Jaivilas Palace without being observed. I took a bath to wash off the grime of the journey and went to the family shrine to say a farewell prayer to the gleaming idols that had looked after the Scindias over two and a half centuries. I did not know when I was going to see them again, but my faith was strong enough not to doubt.

It was nearly 8 p.m. when I finished my prayers. I told Bal Angre to ring up the police. They took six hours to turn up. I later discovered that the delay was due to P. C. Sethi, the Chief Minister of our state, being bothered by his conscience. He sought a clarification of the orders from his superiors, or at least a re-affirmation. It was clear that whoever he contacted suffered no such qualms.

CHAPTER TWENTY-TWO

A Guest of the Government

A DEPUTY INSPECTOR GENERAL of police had brought a large party of his men to arrest us. Dozens of functionaries, who held offices in various Scindia trusts, and a hundred or so servants stood around with shocked expressions. Bal Angre took his time trying to impress upon the DIG and his men that I must be treated with respect and not denied civilized comforts. He reminded them that, even if they had orders to arrest us, we were entitled to certain privileges since we were both members of parliament. They, for their part, could hardly have been more accommodating. On Bal's plea that I was not in good health – which, God knows, I wasn't – they even agreed to issue a special warrant for my young step-brother, Dhyanendra Singh, whom I had recently taken on my secretarial staff, so that he could accompany me into prison. I was also allowed to take my own maid.

It was characteristic of Bal Angre that, even though he too was going to be arrested and taken away from his wife, children and aged parents, his principal concern should be for me. As one of my husband's closest relatives and his closest friend, he had over the years since my husband's death made himself indispensable to my family. There was a very close affinity between my political beliefs and his, as well as in our concern for the Hindu religion. Our interests had become his interests to such an extent that he had become a financial advisor of unquestionable integrity, trusted confidant, guide and trouble-shooter. I don't believe his position in our household can have many parallels among non-feudal families, for no decision is made without consulting him, and yet he has never presumed to make decisions on my behalf.

They took Bal away first, in a couple of cars and a jeep crammed with policemen armed to the teeth. It was not till after 2 p.m. that my own convoy set off. The night was breathless and sultry, with dark heavy clouds obscuring the outlines of the fort. But it was one of those days when nothing seemed capable of depressing me. I kept thinking how ironical it was that I had arrived in Gwalior in a special train to become its Maharani, had lived in it in regal splendour, played hostess to kings, viceroys and fellow-princes, and was being taken away from it under arrest. And so we left the well-remembered environs of the city, which my husband's forbears had created on land they had ruled as kings; through villages peopled by my husband's subjects, who used to line the roads for hours just to be able to offer him their greetings or to try to catch a glimpse of their Maharani.

After we had been on the road for a couple of hours, the hill fort of Datia with the ornate facade of the Maharaja's palace edging its contours loomed against the pre-dawn sky. Almost without thinking, I said to my escorting officer who seemed to be sitting at attention on the front seat: 'Do you think we could stop here for a short while, so I can seek the blessings of Guru-Maharaj?'

Without hesitation he brought the convoy to a halt and gave the necessary orders. When we arrived at the gate of the cloistered precincts, he told me: 'Please take your time.'

I had been brought up to treat holy men with the utmost respect. Before I found Swamiji of the Pitambar Peeth of Datia, my search for a guru or spiritual guide had been ceaseless, wide-ranging and deliberate. When I had found him, so close to Gwalior, I was convinced that here was someone who had acquired a touch of divinity through a lifetime of prayer, penance, renunciation and, above all, profound scholarship. For the past ten years or so, he had been an unfailing source of spiritual strength, courage and solace. That the road to wherever they were taking me should go past Datia, that my escorting officer should prove so cooperative, seemed to be good omens.

So, at four in the morning, I walked into the silent ashram. I requested one of the disciples to wake up Guru-Maharaj and when he came out, I announced: 'I've come to say goodbye; I'm being taken to be a guest of the government.'

It was like any other time; our interview was a reiteration of my faith in him and somehow his confidence in me. For a few minutes I sat at my Guru-Maharaj's feet and then rose to go. He blessed me as usual and told me: 'Don't ever veer from truth, *satyam*. Make that your watchword.' I walked into the night, feeling rejuvenated and inwardly fortified.

We set off again, and I might have even dozed off for an hour or so. A new day dawned and the sun shone pitilessly. Towards noon, we were climbing the familiar hills around my birthplace, Sagar. At the outskirts of the town, other police cars joined our convoy and we were led in an impressive procession into what I recognized as the Officers' Mess of the Police Training School. As we drove into its porch, I was taken aback to see Bal Angre flanked by a couple of policemen waiting on the steps as though to receive me. It seemed that his escort too had decided to use the Mess for a wayside halt, and that they were already on the point of leaving. But now, as prisoners, we were not permitted to talk or even say goodbye. As I peeped out of the window of the room they had given me, I saw his convoy move off.

I was not to see Bal Angre again for twenty months. The first nineteen months of the Emergency he spent in the District Jail at Jabalpur, initially in solitary confinement, but after a few weeks, much to his delight, he was joined by a friend and fellow party member, the ex-Maharaja of Panna, Narendra Singh Judev. It would be difficult to wish for a better companion, for Panna-Maharaj is as full of high spirits as a child, and in many ways innocent as a child too, one of those rare individuals of whom one can say with conviction that they are not even capable of harbouring an evil thought.

*   *   *

My jail was no jail. It was a pleasant little bungalow called Bison Lodge, and almost a landmark of the hill resort of Panchmadhi, a plateau 3,500 feet above sea level, with heavily forested country all around. Once it had been a sort of mini-Simla of the Raj, its club with a long veranda overlooking a golf course, winding red roads leading to viewpoints and picnic spots, of which Bee Dam, the name of a small lake, was the most popular. The British, who called the place Pachmari, used to transport the whole machinery of the government of the Central Provinces there for the summer months. The place and, even more, Bison Lodge still bore a flavour of the Raj.

No Chambal dacoit could have been more heavily guarded. In the room that adjoined mine camped half-a-dozen police-women, and at the gate and at the back of the house were armed sentries. I was provided with a maid, whose name, I remember, was Divya-Kumari and who also doubled as my cook; I had a doctor all to myself. My jailer was a gentle and god-fearing man with rigid notions of duty. He allowed his two schoolgirl daughters to keep me company whenever I felt like sending for them, but nevertheless pleaded that he had no authority to let me go and visit a nearby shrine, even under police escort. I then and there made a vow that I would visit the temple as soon as I was free to do so. I had to wait for more than a year before I could fulfil that promise.

There was nothing to do. My step-brother, Dhyanu, and I played cards interminably but after a couple of weeks, as I got used to the routine of my incarceration, I sent him away. I saw no point in keeping him as a fellow prisoner just so that I should have someone to play cards with. I was allowed to receive newspapers, but they contained little real news. But since the enemy of censorship is the irrepressible human urge to pass on bad news, and since most of the news during the Emergency was bad, even in my isolation I was fairly well-informed of the happenings outside.

The arrests had gone on apace. It seemed that any citizen could be arrested without his being told what he had done wrong; even the judiciary had been deprived of the right to know why an arrest had been made. People who had been released by verdicts of the High Courts could be, and were, re-arrested the moment they came out of the court's premises. The institution of bail had been all but abrogated by the magistrates, who were cowed down by the Party's arm-twisters into refusing it to detainees or demanding outrageous securities.

Even Bal's father, Bade-Angre-saab, the archetype of orthodox conservatism and now turned eighty, had been made out to be a 'danger to national security'. He was running a temperature at the time, but was nevertheless imprisoned in the Gwalior jail as a common felon. It was at the height of summer, when deaths by heat-stroke are common, but he was not allowed a fan. He too remained in jail for the full term of the Emergency.

For those already in jails, they devised further forms of harassment. I was informed that they had 'frozen' all my bank accounts. All of a sudden, my various establishments had to be maintained on money raised by the sale of assets or borrowed from friends, which was by no means easy because those who lent money to the victims of the Emergency themselves risked arrest, or at least an income tax raid.

The tax raid had been forged into a weapon of torment. Not a week, not a day, seemed to pass without the tax-men swooping down on some unfortunate person who had offended against the disciplines of the regime, had not paid enough money to the Party funds, or had merely failed to pay proper homage to its reigning family. They worked on the theory that even a modestly affluent citizen was bound to have something that could be blown up into an illegal possession. The young Maharaja of Jaipur, Bhawani Singh, was found to have a few dollars left over from a foreign trip – he was thrown into jail. Others who had not toed the line were jailed for possessing a couple of bottles of Scotch whisky. Such offences appeared in the censored newspapers as being in possession of 'foreign currency', or 'foreign liquor', and there was almost no raid that did not yield its haul of supposedly 'incriminating documents'.

From my private prison in the rain-soaked hills I thought about what was happening with a sense of unreality, as something remembered from a dream from which one had mercifully woken, shaken and perspiring. And even as I was agonizing about how my daughters were managing to find the money to keep things going, I was told that the income tax raiders had descended on all the Scindia properties, in Delhi, Poona, Bombay and Gwalior.

I had nothing to conceal from them, but I knew that the real purpose of such raids was not so much to discover undeclared wealth as to cause maximum harassment. I kept thinking of young Yesho, now in sole charge of a vast palace crammed full of a bewildering accumulation of bric-à-brac gathered by generations of her forbears. Even my maids knew more about my possessions than my daughters. Everything had been documented, accounted for and declared, but Yesho knew nothing about it. I imagined her being grilled by professionals who prided themselves on being able to extract confessions from hardened criminals. My heart bled for her.

I knew I could magic away the ordeals that my family was being subjected to merely by the despatch of a telegram to the right people saying the proper things. Indeed, a senior High Court judge even sent me a message through a relative that I should give up my obduracy and make peace with those whom I had offended. I did not. Instead I dashed off a telegram to Yesho, enjoining her to cooperate with the tax authorities and to answer all questions fully and truthfully.

*   *   *

The raiders came early. Yesho was barely awake before her nightmare began. She pulled on a shirt and jeans and rushed down to the entrance hall where they were gathered, eight or nine stern-faced men and a couple of women. The head of the team introduced himself and told her that they were carrying out an income tax raid. Then they proceeded to seal off every room in the east wing of Jaivilas Palace.

When the telephones began to ring, the raiding party did not permit anyone in the house to go near them. But when they discovered that the calls were from their opposite numbers in Delhi, Bombay and Poona, where our other houses were being simultaneously raided, they let my daughter take the calls. All she could do was to promise the callers that she would come and see them as soon as she was able to.

They wanted the *jamdarkhana* or strong-room opened. Yesho told them that she did not have the keys and did not even know who had them. They put a guard on the strong-room door and sought orders from their central office in New Delhi. That office sent someone of a much higher rank who threatened Yesho that, if she persisted in making things difficult for them, he would have her sent to jail. At this stage, my principal maid called Yesho aside and told her that she had

had the keys in her possession all along, but had loyally pretended otherwise. Yesho promptly got her to hand them over. When they threw open the door and were about to march in in triumph, she was able to get a bit of her own back: 'Don't you know that a *jamdarkhana* in a house like this is actually a shrine?' she chided them. 'We all remove our shoes before going in.' Sheepishly they removed their shoes.

In the strong-room they found nothing that had not been listed in the returns either I or Bhaiya had filed, copies of which they had brought with them. By now my daughter too must have begun to realize that we had nothing to conceal. That was when she thought she would leave the raiders to go on at their own pace and make a quick visit to Bombay and Poona to see what was happening there.

It was at this stage, with the tax-men feeling a little cheated because they had failed to make the sensational discoveries that would have pleased their superior, that my telegram arrived. As is customary in such situations, the officials read it first. To minds trained to be suspicious, my message must have seemed charged with sinister import. Here was some family code that their central office would break in no time. Meanwhile, they redoubled their vigilance, and went about their business with renewed zest.

Every room was gone through as though it was a smuggler's storehouse, and anything that the tax-men thought should not be in the house was seized. Part of the gold, from which I had earlier given the Government 25 lbs, was pronounced to be 'smuggled' and confiscated. (It took them nine years to decide that it was not after all smuggled.) A gold coin of the reign of Shah Jehan, which we had always thought of as a curio, disappeared. Weighing nearly a pound, it was one of the sort that figures in the *Guinness Book of Records* as the biggest ever minted. Mahadji Scindia had brought these coins back in camel-loads, but in my time only one remained. It went, as did the notation of the *raga* that Alla-ud-din Khan had composed and named after me. Old records and mementoes of no value to anyone outside the family also went, and must even now be mouldering in some high-security storehouse.

Knowing that they would make difficulties if she told them she was going to Bombay, Yesho had kept her plans to herself.

But as she was being driven to the airport, a police car following made frantic signals for her to stop. She ordered the driver to ignore the signals. When they finally caught up with her in the airport building and told her that she could not leave Gwalior, she did something that someone of a more mature age would not have dared to do. She made a scene. In the hearing of the passengers and airport officials, she turned on the officer who had come to detain her: 'You know perfectly well that your own department has raided all the Scindia houses in Delhi, Bombay and Poona, and your colleagues are demanding my presence in all three places and threatening dire consequences if I don't show up. And here, just because I happen to be in Gwalior, you people are preventing me from going. I cannot be in all four places at the same time.'

The officer who had come to detain Yesho must have realized how idiotic his prohibition was, and he agreed to let her go provided that she returned within forty-eight hours. Luckily, the Bombay and Poona raiders made no difficulties about Yesho returning to base in the given time.

The Gwalior team pressed on with determination. They sent for experts to look for buried treasure. Men with mysterious boxes equipped with shining dials and joined by rubberized wires to telescopic arms went about like figures in a science fiction film, probing and taking soundings. Their detectors emitted alarming beeps at the oddest places which, when dug up, were found to conceal nothing more sensational than waterpipes or rusted iron braces, which had been planted by the architect to support wall fixtures. Yesho's frantic protests that the floors were made of irreplaceable matched Carrara marble fell on deaf ears, leaving her convinced that they would just as diligently hack away the Ajanta paintings, if they were given the order.

But after a couple of weeks of fruitless digging, with many of the rooms and the yards littered with debris and damaged pipes spouting water, their zeal began to lose its edge. By now Yesho had come to know every member of the raiding team by name, and the servants had taken to exchanging gossip with them. From being regarded as a menacing presence, they had been reduced to the status of squatters, unwanted but tolerated. And as though conscious of their diminished capacity to instil fear, they began to go about their business with no more than minimum application, working to a leisurely schedule and taking all the official holidays. This loss of dedication must have been reported to their New Delhi superiors, because another set of storm-troopers was pressed into service to augment the first team.

The new arrivals belonged to the customs department, and they were presumably charged with the task of finding out what items there were in our house on which we had somehow managed to evade duty. They marched in as though they owned the place, swaggered, struck attitudes, shouted at the servants and made themselves thoroughly odious to everyone, including their fellow-raiders. Accustomed to dealing with hardened smugglers, they lacked the ordinary refinements of social intercourse that the tax-men, for their part, had been scrupulous about observing. They spoke with cigarettes dangling from their mouths and while chewing *paans*, and sprawled on sofas with their feet propped up before them, so that Yesho had to remind them to mend their manners.

The first thing the customs men did was to put their seals on all the rooms, irrespective of whether they already bore those of the tax-men. Thus they pre-empted the right of the tax-men to continue their searches. A glorious interdepartmental row ensued, involving questions of jurisdiction, priority and the seniority of the functionaries on the spot. Yesho joined in spiritedly on the side of the first arrivals.

Each team went about as though trying to down the importance and efficacy of the other. Yesho did her best to keep the feud simmering by making tender inquiries as to their progress and giving the impression that they would have fared so much better if it had not been for the obstructive tactics of their rivals. It was at this point that Dhyanendra Singh, whom I had sent back from Pachmari, returned to Gwalior. A mimic and practical joker, he planted in Yesho's mind the thought of livening up the proceedings a bit. For a couple of days he and Yesho went about as though racked with anxiety about what would happen if either of the teams were to discover the real secret of Jaivilas Palace. And then, almost as though making an inadvertent slip, they revealed the presence of an underground passage.

This transformed the nightmare into sheer farce. At first, both teams staked priority to the tunnel. But when Dhyanu told them that, while he would show them its entrance, he would only do so from a distance because it was believed to harbour a nest of cobras, their zeal receded and they generously offered it to one another. As a compromise, they decided to call in the police. But the policemen were not keen to go in either. Finally, wearing helmet, gumboots and voluminous protective clothing and carrying a rifle, one made his way down the steps. Within seconds, he had shot back out of the hole, swearing that he had heard a cobra's hiss.

For a day or two, they left the tunnel alone. Then one morning my daughter heard what she thought was *sehnai* music. Since it had been the custom in the palace to have *sehnais* playing on someone's birthday, she asked whose birthday it was. It turned out that the tax-men had sent for a snake-charmer from Agra, and he was playing his *pungi* or gourd-flute from the entrance of the tunnel for all he was worth. He too had refused to enter the tunnel unless the raiding parties guaranteed that his family would be indemnified in case he died of snakebite. This they had no authority to agree to.

So the raid fizzled out to the wail of a snake-charmer's flute. Thereafter they seemed to lose interest, not only in the underground passage (which, in fact, was one of several Mukhel Sahib had provided for sweepers to carry away toilet receptacles from bathrooms before the days of flush), but also in the remaining rooms of the main house. One morning they were gone. Yesho was so overjoyed that she could barely wait to pass on the good news to friends. She rang up the Dewans in Shivpuri and breathlessly announced: 'They've gone! Gone!'

'I know,' Surinderlal Dewan answered. 'They're here.'

*   *   *

None of my houses had yielded anything worth making a fuss about, but that did not mean that the raiders turned away from their objective so much as that they changed tactics. They went back and 'opened up' my accounts; the hundreds of returns that had been sent up to the various tax authorities on my behalf for fifteen years were gone over with the sole purpose of

finding fault with them. The very threat of having accounts
'opened up' is enough to make even the most scrupulous
taxpayer break out into a cold sweat. And, predictably, it was
discovered that some return or other of my gold holdings
which had been submitted to one department was not on the
file of the other. They magnified this lapse, if indeed it was one,
into a wilful default, and sought to impose a staggering fine.

As a shattering footnote to the tax-raid on my Gwalior
house, I shall recount the story of a close family friend,
Yuwaraj Pratap Singh, the eldest son of the Maharaja of
Alwar. A deeply religious and feudal man, he lived with his
pretty wife in a walled-off mansion that had once been his
grandfather's shooting lodge. He lived in self-imposed
seclusion, surrounded by the animals which he and his wife
adored: dogs, horses, elephants, deer, and even a couple of
tigers and leopards. Having dropped in on Yesho, he professed
to be greatly incensed at the way the tax-men had all but taken
possession of Jaivilas Palace. 'How could you bear to let such
people enter the Scindia palace?' he kept asking Yesho. 'Why
didn't you shut the doors, order your guards to stop them, set
your dogs on them?'

When Yesho protested that it would have been quite futile
to do so, he told her that that was what he would do if they ever
dared to search his palace. 'No matter what the consequences!'
A few days later, when his own house was raided, that was
precisely what Pratap Singh did do: he let loose his dogs,
elephants and leopards and put them to flight. In retaliation,
the tax-men ordered his water and electricity supply to be cut
off, and waited for his surrender. His house became a place of
siege. For a week or so he held on grimly, and he could have
gone on for much longer had it not been for the howls of his
animals. And yet the thought of surrender did not even enter
his mind. His solution was a horrifying amalgam of the Rajput
code of honour, Rajput obstinacy and, dare one say it, heroism
– something torn from the pages of Tod's *Annals of
Rajasthan*. He and his ADC, who was also a close friend,
repaired to the family shrine as though for prayers. The report
of a shot was heard – at least, it sounded like one shot, even
though two were obviously fired. When they ran into the
prayer-room, his servants found both the Yuwaraj and his

ADC lying dead, each with a bullet hole in the head. Who killed whom first and what sort of death-pact they had made will never be known.

Heroic or perverse, nevertheless they remained true to their private values, however contorted, however out of date they might seem to us.

*   *   *

The makers of the Emergency meanwhile had struck another blow against me. Towards noon one day in August, Yesho was called to the telephone. The distracted manager of our Delhi house told her that 37 Rajpur Road had been requisitioned.

I, who nurse quirks of mind that lie buried deep in the subconscious, perhaps have more in common with Yuwaraj Pratap Singh than with my own children. The pragmatism shown by my youngest daughter, bred to a culture of riches, rank and the fetishes of feudal orthodoxies yet pitchforked into the combat zone of the Emergency, has never ceased to surprise me. This time her reaction was equally sensible. Knowing that 'requisitioned', in the context of the times, meant that the takeover team must have moved in and thrown out of the house whatever they did not want to use, she hired a couple of lorries and sent them, along with a few servants, to the capital with instructions to retrieve whatever they could and to have it stored in the sheds of our ceramic factory.

As it happened, a family friend, Major General Ajit Guraiya, had also acted with extraordinary promptness and used his formidable contacts to get us a couple of days' respite. It is wholly due to Yesho's and Ajit Guraiya's combined action that I still possess some decent furniture and other household articles in my smaller house in New Delhi.

My own response to this outrage was neither practical nor rational. For me it was a particularly cruel blow. Ever since my husband's death, the Delhi house had become our second home. As the two bungalows belonging to the potteries were in occupation by pottery officials, we now had no place to live in Delhi. What made me livid was the purpose for which the house had been taken over: the Twenty-Point Programme, a particularly unimaginative list of points for public behaviour, such as might have been drawn up by a high-school debating society, blown up into a mantra for solving all the nation's ills. And it was to house the functionaries of this Orwellian apparatus that they had taken over my lovely house. It was as though they had deliberately polluted something I held to be sacrosanct. Even though I was in prison, I made a resolve that I would never enter that house again.

But I suppose that my anguish at having exposed my daughters to the punitive measures of the Emergency had to manifest itself somehow, and it may have been the real cause of the request I made to be moved to some other place of confinement. What actually triggered this request was something quite different. It was my growing feeling that, by remaining in my bungalow in Pachmari, I was somehow allowing myself to be made an accomplice in a propaganda drive launched by the Government to give the outside world the impression that the thousands of 'detenues', as the victims of the Emergency were called in its newspeak, were being treated like pampered guests. I knew that, in actual fact, the conditions prevailing in the jails, into which they had been crammed like cattle, were horrifying.

I don't remember now when it was that our High Commissioner in London, B. K. Nehru, wrote in a letter to *The Times* that 'the care and concern showered upon the detainees (was) . . . almost maternal.' But that letter was all of a piece with the Government's propaganda. I did not then know that such claims were already washed away by events: that *The Times*' own man in New Delhi, as well as most other foreign newspapermen, had been bundled out of the country and that the British public was more likely to believe Amnesty International than Mrs Gandhi's accredited spokesman. What irked me was that I could be shown up as an example of a privileged detainee. I certainly did not want to be made a prop of their perversion of truth.

The grounds I gave for my request were that solitary confinement was having a deleterious effect on my health. It worked, and with the sort of speed that made me think that they were just waiting for some such representation to demonstrate to me how much more distasteful life could be made than my confinement in Bison Lodge. Before a week had passed, orders were received for transferring me.

CHAPTER TWENTY-THREE
Prisoner No. 2265

WHATEVER CURIOSITY AND excitement I had built up about my place of transfer evaporated long before we reached the environs of New Delhi. In their place came mounting horror. Surely they were not taking me to Tihar? They were.

Tihar. Most Indians react to the mention of the word as to a piece of terrible news, for as a place of incarceration it can have few equivalents in other countries. I needed all my reserves of faith to maintain a measure of equanimity as I was led through its portals.

I still have in my possession a yellow printed form which purports to be my 'history sheet' while I was an inmate of Tihar. It is dated 3 September 1975 and shows that the 'crime' for which I had been admitted came under MISA, 'The Maintenance of Internal Security Act', although the Government later attempted to make out that I had been jailed for a smuggling or foreign exchange offence. My offence was that I had opposed the ruling party. My prison number was 2265.

The formalities of registration over, I was taken to the women's section of the jail. Swarms of unkempt women, some with suckling infants stuck to their bodies like limpets, others holding squealing toddlers by the hand, gawked and giggled nervously as I passed. At the entrance to the section set apart for condemned prisoners stood Rajmata Gayatri Devi, the ex-Maharani of Jaipur. We bowed to each other and folded our hands as we would have at a social occasion, but the greeting she came out with was one of agonized concern: 'Whatever made you come here? This is a horrible place!'

Gayatri Devi had been given an old office room with a

veranda, but we shared the bathroom which adjoined my cell. The bathroom had no tap, and a hole in the ground served as its toilet facility. The prison sweeper came twice a day to clean it and brought water in buckets to flush it. In this respect we were privileged, because the rest of the women's prison seemed to have no toilet facilities at all. The few common latrines did not function; the prisoners and their children squatted all along the open drains of the yard.

The condemned cells were at the very edge of the women's section and adjoined one of the male wards. My cell was a long and narrow room with a small grilled window high in the wall. The toilet hole had been covered with a plank. I had two dealwood chairs and a string bed. There was a single electric light with a naked bulb.

Except during the hours of darkness when they were locked up in their wards, we could see the other women going about their prison routines. Between them they formed a cross-section of degraded humanity such as I had not known even existed; no vice, no obscenity, no depravity was unrepresented. It was a sub-culture of warped minds, of instincts bred to aberrations. Born in vagrancy, these women had lived by scavenging, thievery and prostitution, and most of them could not have had a kind word said to them throughout their lives.

Gayatri Devi and I may have been ex-Maharanis, but Tihar had its own 'Queen', an under-trial prisoner who had twenty-seven registered offences against her, including as many as four murders. She went about with a razor-blade concealed in her blouse, threatening to 'carve up the face' of anyone who dared to cross her path. She could scramble over walls with the agility of a monkey, and every so often would post herself on the roof of my cell, which overlooked the men's prison. There she would engage in long and intimate talks with one of its inmates, who was her lover, and make elaborate arrangements as to how and where they would meet. Her vocabulary of abuse was horrifyingly inventive and her laughter brought on goose-pimples. The other convicts obeyed her slightest wish, and even the wardresses invariably looked the other way whenever she happened to be around. She stole food or whatever else took her fancy with impunity. When we complained to the jail superintendent about her intrusions into our part of the prison, he promptly had our cells surrounded by a barbed-wire fence. She climbed over it as though the barbs did not exist, shouted at me that she was not coming to our cells, and then shinned up the drain-pipe that led to the roof to have her usual chat with her lover. What a commando she would have made!

*   *   *

A stench that was as thick as a vapour, flies which we had to ward off with one hand to be able to eat our meals with the other, and a cacaphony of noise that may have been especially designed as some kind of torture – can hell be much different? When the flies went to sleep at night, the mosquitoes and other insects came in their place; the noise and the stench seemed to remain constant. Sandwiched as we were between the men's and women's wards, we were subjected to a dual set of barked orders, of hobnailed boots slithering on the flagstones, of hawking and spitting and the howling of children, of slanging bouts and political slogans, midnight bursts of songs, screams or maniacal laughter.

It was depressing beyond words. Gayatri Devi, who was ill and in need of major surgery, had convinced herself that she was going to die in Tihar. 'Only my body will be taken out,' she used to say, and she had given her family instructions about where and in what manner she wanted to be cremated. In an effort to soothe her, I would pretend to second sight and give her a date some weeks in advance before which she would be released. But when that day passed, she would never fail to point out that my prophesy had not come true. Sheepishly I would confess to a miscalculation and give her another date.

Her stepson, Bhavani Singh, the Maharaja of Jaipur, was also a prisoner in Tihar, and he had been permitted by the jail authorities to come and see her once a day. His visits were a real tonic for her. He had always been the 'happy warrior' type, immersed in his profession, which was soldiering, and the sport of his family, which was polo, and he was not at all interested in politics. What could he have done to have qualified as an enemy of the nation, particularly in view of his decoration for valour in the latest war against Pakistan?

Gayatri Devi had already been in Tihar for two months, and

was thus allowed the customary privilege of having a weekly visitor. Through these visitors, she had managed to have brought in a badminton and ring-tennis set, a couple of small cricket bats and several dozen balls. After that, she had busied herself teaching the children in the jail to play games. It was wonderful to see the amount of cheer she brought to their lives and to hear their laughter; there was nothing that those children would not have done for her.

*   *   *

For my first month in Tihar I was allowed no visitors. In fact, my daughters did not even know where I had been taken from Pachmari. They were frantic with anxiety about me; and I was equally frantic about how they were coping. My son was in Nepal, but Usha left her husband in Nepal to come to India and join forces with Vasu and Yesho, all three bent on securing my release. Their concern for my welfare fills me with pride; nonetheless, while I was in Tihar, it was the main cause of my sleepless nights.

Of necessity, they divided forces. Usha, the eldest, took overall charge of the campaign. She stayed on in New Delhi and tried to make friends with people known to be close to the throne. Upon the youngest fell the role of looking after the home front, Gwalior. That left Vasu, who had to put aside her own worsening marital problems and leave her little son in the care of maids, to shuttle between these two bases and also dash off to other places where some VIP of the regime who might be of help happened to be.

Usha, by sheer doggedness, was able to wear down the resistance of R. K. Dhavan, Mrs Gandhi's righthand man, to get an interview with her. She was subjected to a metal-detection test and a search before being admitted to the presence. Mrs Gandhi was stern and self-righteous. 'You know, of course, that your mother has not been imprisoned for political activities but for a smuggling offence,' she pronounced.

Usha didn't know. What she knew was that the tax raiders had done their best to make out that some of the gold in the palace was not 'Indian'. But she did not allow herself to be put off by the charge or to admit defeat. Even after the interview, she kept pegging away at anyone she could think of who might, in some way, advance her cause.

Vasu's experiences were different. In normal times, her many friends in the capital would have gone out of their way to do her a favour. Indeed, she was especially friendly with Rajiv and Sonia Gandhi, both of whom frequently dropped in to see her – and one could hardly get closer to the throne than that. But during the Emergency such connections were all but useless. Ministers and officials were scared even to show common courtesy to those who sought their intervention on behalf of its victims. Several swashbuckling musketeers had found the abnormalities and immunities of the Emergency to be their element, and had become insufferably tyrannical and despotic. One such person, with a particularly unsavoury reputation in his dealings with women, insisted on making appointments to see Vasu in the luxurious suites he seemed to have permanently at his disposal in the capital's two most prestigous and expensive hotels, where tables for two, in the authentic style of Hollywood assignations, seemed to be laid just as permanently. Exasperated by Vasu, who made a point of never showing up at these rendezvous without a servant trailing behind her, he took her aside: 'Tell me, what sacrifices will you be prepared to make to have your mother set free?' Then, to show that he was privy to the highest secrets of the regime, he revealed to her my new place of captivity with all its capacity to induce shock: 'Your mother has been sent to Tihar.'

Which was how they came to know where I was and how, when the month of special segregation had passed, all my three daughters were waiting outside the prison gates. I was allowed to see them only one at a time, for perhaps ten minutes, in the presence and hearing of a prison official. I had spent the previous day in trembling anticipation, wondering how I was going to prevent myself from dissolving into tears when I saw them and, even more, how to keep them from doing so. I solved the problem in my own way. When each one was let into the enclosure for visitors, I bombarded her with a long and elaborate list of things I wanted when she or her sister next came to see me in two weeks' time. It was a list of children's clothes of sizes varying from infants to ten-year-olds, and shawls, bottles of cough-syrup, vitamins and boiled sweets. For while the women prisoners were supplied with clothes under prison regulations, the children they had of necessity brought with them did not qualify for the prison's permissible handouts. Most of them went about in rags.

The device worked. By the time my daughters had finished taking down their lists, to which I kept adding items to fill the time, their allotted time for the visit was over. They went back shaking their heads and feeling cheated out of whatever they had wanted to say to me. Yesho later told her friends that when I had been led back out of the interview room and into the bowels of Tihar, it was the squeaks made by my rubber sandals over the stone flooring that brought home to her the state of deprivation I had been reduced to. I have nowadays taken to wearing rubber sandals quite frequently, but before I went to prison I certainly don't remember wearing them. Yesho, of course, only knew how fussy I had always been about shoes and other accessories, buying them mainly on shopping sprees in London and Paris. It was my rubber *chaplis* that broke the defences built up by my lists of children's needs.

* * *

Until I got the things on my shopping list, I had nothing to give my unfortunate fellow-prisoners apart from kind words. It was amazing to see how they responded to kindness; so unused were they to the normal civilities of life that at first they would shy away suspiciously, like wild animals at the approach of a human being. But within a couple of weeks they were telling me the stories of their lives and seeking my advice. It was sad to see their degeneration, to realize that Tihar was somehow their natural condition of existence, that here they were just a shade more secure from the iniquities and insults with which they had to contend in the outside world.

One, who was being held on a murder charge, pulled strings to have herself allotted to me as my personal maid. Seldom have I come across so willing and so devoted a servant. The food prepared in the prison kitchen was all but unfit for human consumption (I saw prisoners using the *rotis* they were given as fuel to brew the tea which they were allowed to make in their own yards). I was given the privilege of having my rations cooked in my own rooms. It was Satya who did the cooking and conjured up out of prison rations fairly palatable meals.

After the little garments were distributed and the children had lapped up the cough syrup as though it were honey, the prisoners' anxiety to do things for me became almost an embarrassment. One day a group of them came to entertain me with a 'cabaret', which was their name for the latest film songs sung in chorus with the sort of gestures and innuendoes which must have won applause from their male acquaintances. When I suggested to them that I would infinitely prefer it if they sang *bhajans* or religious songs for me, they practised a few and the evening sing-song became a feature of prison life. And yet they could never understand why anyone should prefer *bhajans* to cabaret, and would try to make conditions: 'All right, *bhajans* too, but cabaret first, right?'

'Right.'

By this time I was allowed visitors once a week. My daughters came bearing whatever I had asked for and went back with more lists for my prison disbursements; it was getting colder every day and the children needed warm clothes. The prison authorities were becoming less fussy about letting me have things brought in. It was only later that my daughters protested: 'You kept giving us lists, and we were at our wits' ends to find the money. Even ten rupees meant a lot.'

But prison life was having a peculiar effect on my health, manifested in a multitude of persistent nagging aches and pains. A letter I managed to sneak out to my daughters at this time survives. It is written on graph-paper, which Satya must have procured from somewhere, and contains so many erasures and interpolations that it is almost indecipherable; and these, more than its contents, represent an accurate chart of the state of my mind:

My darling ones,
I am touched by your anxieties for me, but please do not make yourselves miserable because of me. To tell you the truth, it is really this thought which makes me unhappy. After all, I have chosen this path with open eyes, so I should not (bemoan) its adverse consequences. We must be ready to face such adversities bravely in order that our future generations will learn to live with *swabhiman* (pride). I am afraid it is going to be a long, long

struggle, and will demand many sacrifices. I know you are all quite capable of acting as circumstances demand and of looking after the family's interests . . . I am not at all worried. We have nothing to fear and have a clean slate. I have no regrets whatever . . . because I was not playing with politics . . . but fighting against injustices. I shall consider myself most fortunate indeed if I can be one of the *sacrificial* offerings at the feet of mother India.

Meanwhile, Usha's perseverence was beginning to make a dent in the Government's intractability. The fact that Usha's husband, Pashupati, was recognized as a powerful influence in Nepal's politics (he is now the Minister for Power and Irrigation in Nepal) no doubt helped, for the policy-makers in India have always been careful not to tread too heavily on the toes of the hierarchy of Nepal.

I doubt if Usha's campaign by itself would have had much effect on – or even penetrated to – the principal decision-makers of the Emergency, Mrs Gandhi and her younger son, Sanjay, had not something happened to bring home to them that my release would be politically expedient. It was Bhaiya's decision to throw in the towel. Through Usha, he had put out feelers to Mrs Gandhi that he was prepared to give up his allegiance to the Janasangh and give up politics. From her response, it seems clear that Mrs Gandhi regarded this as a singularly welcome development. Bhaiya was forgiven his sins and allowed to return.

In my cell I was not aware of these developments. Tihar's news-blackout was virtually watertight. Such news that filtered through the approved newspapers had convinced me that the organs of democracy had been reshaped to make India a dictatorship like Cuba or Pakistan.

Winter had set in. One day of darkness at noon, when the sky was a roof-high blanket of clouds that dribbled moisture but not raindrops and I was feeling particularly empty of purpose, a prison official on his rounds told me that, if I were to ask for a month's parole on health grounds, he was sure that the application would be favourably considered. 'After that, all you have to do to keep out of jail is to renew the application every month.'

Initially, my mind recoiled at the thought of seeking a favour. But on the next visiting day my daughters, who seemed to know all about the offer, looked quite shocked at my inaction. 'But Amma, you don't know how hard we've all been trying to get this to go through,' they protested. 'After all, it's for your health, remember – even if the anguish of your daughters doesn't mean anything to you.'

I withstood their accusing stares; I had long ago hardened my heart to that particular vulnerability. Almost as though they had read my mind, they brought out their trump card. 'We've talked it over with Swami-Maharaj at Datia. He too has advised that you should ask for parole.'

That was the clinch. In any case, I argued with myself, it was not irrevocable. All I had to do to get back into jail was to fail to renew my application at the end of the trial month.

There were formalities. For them to prove that I was ill I had to be sent to a hospital. But everyone, including the prisoners, seemed to know I was not coming back. The day before my departure, the prison chorus came to treat me to their last 'cabaret' and sang all my favourite *bhajans*. Poor Satya cried her heart out as she packed my belongings. And when I left, women stood in two lines as far as the inner gate and strewed flowers in my path.

I never thought I would feel close to tears at leaving Tihar!

*   *   *

I was admitted to the All India Institute of Medical Sciences, for observation and treatment. I was put in a private room with a night-and-day guard at the door and permitted no visitors. A visitor barged in nonetheless. He was Sheikh Abdulla of Kashmir, the Lion of Kashmir, who was himself undergoing treatment at the Institute. It was an ironic reversal of our roles of twelve years before, when it was he who was the prisoner and I his unpermitted visitor.

What the doctors who examined me made of my ailments was never revealed to me; indeed, they did not even return my medical file, which I had handed over to them. One morning I was told that I was being released on parole because of my deteriorated health. Suddenly, after six months, I was no longer a prison number, but restored to my own name. I dressed and went past the sentry thinking he was going to prevent me, but he didn't. Outside, at the other end of the corridor, stood my three girls, smiling and crying at the same time.

CHAPTER TWENTY-FOUR

The Parting of the Ways

I HAD GONE to jail for political reasons; I came out for domestic reasons. Yesho was twenty-one. As her mother, I should have found a husband for her earlier. Now she had fallen in love with someone whom I did not think was at all suitable. Which meant that I had not only to try to make her change her mind, but also to find someone else whom she would agree to marry.

Moreover, I wanted to do something to safeguard our property. My experience of the past few months had taught me how vulnerable my position was. If I had gone to Nepal, everything I possessed might have been already taken away as 'evacuee property'. It was imperative that I should attend to these matters. After that I could revoke my parole.

* * *

Bhaiya, after making sure through Usha's contacts that there was no warrant out for his arrest, returned to India, shaken and anxious to please the rulers. Our family was once again united, this time in the capital, where I had to spend most of my time because of my parole. Since we no longer possessed a house where all of us could live in comfort, we were reduced to making do with the annexe of the manager's bungalow of our ceramic factory. The girls, who between them had arranged to see that I was not left alone for long, often had to share rooms.

Bhaiya's decision to quit politics did not upset me; indeed, it fitted neatly with my own increasing reluctance to resume political activities, for the simple reason that in a totalitarian regime there was no such thing as an opposition. The

Emergency was at its zenith. Those who were still out of jails had fallen into line with its constraints. The press had accepted its 'crawling order' and become used to minor officials re-writing or disallowing such items as might offend 'someone' of importance. To be kept under surveillance, to have your mail opened and your telephone tapped, was, for political outcasts like myself, the normal condition of life.

It was difficult not to brood, not to agonize about how the balance of things had slipped, how the loss of national manhood was being passed off as national discipline, the absence of dissent as peace.

I made a brief visit to Datia to see Guru-Maharaj. Here, in the cloistered recesses, I felt much more at home. Was an ashram from now on to be my natural element, as Tihar had been of its women prisoners? On an impulse, I ordered the building of a set of rooms for myself no different from the ashram's accommodation for its itinerant pilgrims. The thought of living the life of a pilgrim, with neither possessions nor desires, held me captive. I was in my mid-fifties, which I thought was not too early for taking *sanyas*, which means the renunciation of a worldly life for one of prayers and penance.

Sanyas became an obsession. Back in New Delhi, I sent for the family lawyer and told him to prepare the necessary documents to enable me to give away everything I possessed. He made detailed notes and went off to put them into legal phraseology. He did not show his face for three weeks. By then the fit had passed.

*   *   *

And so had the first month of my parole. I dutifully took steps to have it renewed and applied myself to the problems for which I had come out.

Yesho's young man, Siddharth, was the youngest son of one of Bombay's most eminent cardiologists, Dr Kirtilal Bahan-sali. He had just qualified as a doctor and was working as an intern at one of the city's major hospitals. Siddarth and my daugher had met in the exclusive members' enclosure of Bombay's race-course. He insists that the very first thing Yesho said to him was: 'There's no point in talking if you don't want to marry me.' This may well be apocryphal, but it brings out the essence of their mutual infatuation. He obviously found the appropriate rejoinder to so startling an ice-breaker, for after that first encounter they continued to meet at the race-course, the Willingdon Club or other similar Bombay haunts and fell desperately in love.

Here were the ingredients of an authentic Barbara Cartland romance: a princess, rich, young, beautiful, and in love with a handsome man of good family and good education. Most mothers of marriageable daughters would have crowed with delight.

Most mothers, but not myself. I was dismayed, and so was Bhaiya. We both kept haranguing her to come to her senses and forget Siddharth, and we set about trying to find her a husband who was from our own caste and background. From among a dozen or so eligible scions of princely families, we chose one whose credentials appeared to us to be such that no sensible girl could turn him down. When we tried to press Yesho at least to agree to a meeting with him, she threw a tantrum. 'I've made up my mind,' she told us flatly. 'I want to marry Siddharth.'

'And suppose we don't let you,' we asked her.

She did not, as she could have, remind us that she was already of age and could marry anyone she liked without our permission. Instead she announced: 'In that case I shall remain unmarried.'

After that the laughter went out of our rummy games. Yesho would sit with her face set into a mask, and the silences were long and charged with unspoken resentment, making me lose track of the cards and ponder over the gap between my mother and my daughter. How vastly unlike each other they were in their attitudes to wedlock and yet how infuriatingly alike in their determination. My mother had obstinately threatened to remain unmarried because she had been shown a photograph by her parents and considered herself mentally wedded to the man in it. And here was my daughter, equally obstinately refusing to so much as look at the photograph of the husband I had chosen for her because she had already made up her mind to marry someone of her choice.

Bhaiya and I believed that, given time and also persistent pressure, Yesho's infatuation would pass off. The question was: how much time? The months passed. Yesho retreated into her private world. Meanwhile, I turned my attention to more mundane affairs.

*   *   *

Our possessions were the targets on which the various tax authorities seemed to have declared a permanent open season. They were never quite free from the danger of confiscation resulting from political spitefulness.

A few years earlier all our possessions had been valued by experts and put into a company, whose shares my son and I held in equal numbers. But, even under this arrangement, all our immoveable properties were held to be jointly owned by both of us. Now the time had come to share them out between us.

This division was accomplished in the most amicable manner, both my son and I bending over backwards to give the other whatever either especially fancied. It was only after the details of the partition had been settled that we got down to the practical question of what to do with our main white elephant, Jaivilas Palace.

It is not easy for outsiders to grasp the dimensions of Jaivilas, which are something in the order of the British Museum doubled and redoubled, for there are perhaps fifty or so ancilliary structures dispersed over the compound and hidden among the trees.

A portion of Jaivilas had already been put to use as a public museum, to which we had passed on much of the Scindia collections either because we did not have much use for them or because they were so valuable that it was no longer prudent or seemly to keep them in the house as articles of decoration. We had set aside as the family's future residence an annexe of the palace with its own entrance. But that still left the bulk of the palace vacant, maybe fifty or so barnlike rooms and a dozen outbuildings, for which neither Bhaiya nor I could have any conceivable use.

I had always longed for Jaivilas to be associated with the cause that my husband had sought so hard to foster: education. I saw the palace as the nucleus of a new system of learning in which I had been taking increasing interest. It borrowed heavily from our ancient methods of imparting knowledge, but rejected much of what we had blindly adopted from the British. Bhaiya, while he was in general agreement with the appropriateness of my plans for Jaivilas, nonetheless felt that to donate the palace would be a disproportionate drain on his means. We got over this impasse by my buying the palace and its environs from him outright. I paid him by giving him shares in our joint company to its full value.

So Jaivilas, the home of the Scindias, became mine to do whatever I wanted with it, which was to make it the headquarters of my new university. I formed a separate trust for the management of this property and, so amicable were our relations at the time, appointed both my son and his wife on its board of trustees of five members, while I became its chairman.

*   *   *

All this had taken the best part of 1976. Meanwhile, Yesho had been waiting, or stamping her feet. Bhaiya and I had not been able to break her resolve, so we gave in and told Yesho that she could marry her young man, and the date for the wedding was settled: 9 March 1977.

I explained to Yesho that hers would have to be a quiet wedding; the fanfare that had marked her sisters' or her brother's nuptials would be out of keeping with the austerities of the Emergency and the low-key living that was now expected of us. My lukewarm attitude to her romance made not the slightest difference to Yesho's joy; she looked radiant and exuded good cheer.

So I had accomplished my objectives, if not quite in the way I had planned – and my health had greatly improved. Now I had no excuse to go on renewing my parole, particularly since I had learned that my imprisonment was being used as a bargaining point in the efforts to pull my son into the Congress fold. Bhaiya was now told that it was not enough to leave politics; he had to show his change of heart by joining the Congress Party. Unless he did so, I would have to remain in jail, or on parole.

I thought I would clear the decks for him by revoking my parole. It was a sort of gut-reaction, and I cannot explain its rationale. I told my children that I had made up my mind not to renew my parole application at the end of January, and privately hoped that I would be let out for Yesho's wedding.

But Mrs Gandhi had decided otherwise. Having made sure that the opposition had been reduced to a state of insensibility, she now decided to drag it out to face a trial of strength. On 18 January 1977 she announced that parliamentary elections would be held in the middle of March. She ordered the release of political prisoners so that they should make such preparations as they could for the contest that had been sprung upon them, and she even relaxed press censorship. That I was not let off my parole along with the others was added proof that my release had been made a condition of the package deal offered to my son.

Bal Angre came out of prison unsubdued, his resolution sharpened. He made no secret of his disapproval of Bhaiya's trying to strike a bargain with the perpetrators of the Emergency.

For my part, I had become convinced that India had ceased to be a democracy and would be run by Mrs Gandhi as a one-party state, so that any future involvement in the politics of principles would be meaningless. Bal believed that the Congress would be trounced in the forthcoming elections, and that Mrs Gandhi's decision to call them was going to bring about her downfall. Bhaiya, for his part, was equally convinced that the future lay with the Congress – or at least the Gandhi family.

It was painful for me that Bal, who had been so close to all of us for so long, and my son should hold such diametrically opposed views, and I was anxious that they should meet and talk things over. But even this, when we had proof that all of us were watched like hawks, was not easy to arrange.

They met in a bungalow I own on the clay mines near Delhi's airport. My son told Bal: 'Uncle, we've had enough. We can no longer go on as we've been. We'll be ruined.'

But Bal, for all his nineteen months in prison, his family affairs in disarray, and his business and farms in ruins, had obviously not had enough, and told Bhaiya so. He held out for the sanctity of principles over expediency, which Bhaiya could not have liked at all, and – what he must have found even more distasteful – his obligations as a Scindia to those who had once looked upon his forbears as their protectors and food-givers. He reminded his nephew, whom he also, until then, called his Master, that he bore the name of the great Mahadji, and that itself should ensure that there was no such thing as having enough of adversities. Then he proceeded to expound his belief that, in the coming elections, the Congress was going to be routed. And this my son must have found utterly beyond the bounds of possibility. The meeting ended abruptly; they had said what they wanted to say to each other, and each withdrew into his shell.

Nevertheless, Bhaiya knew enough of the minds of the voters in his area of influence to realize that they would reject even him if he were to offer himself as the Congress candidate – so unpopular was the Congress at the time. It was decided that he should stand as an independent candidate but sponsored by the Congress, who would not field an official candidate against him, and with that compromise-solution, the bargain was sealed. I was released from prison while still on parole. How well I remember Bhaiya's anguished remark: 'Amma, it was like giving with one hand to be able to take with the other. I just had to go along with them to be able to secure your release.'

*   *   *

The jolt that Mrs Gandhi had administered to the groggy opposition had the effect of shock therapy; it galvanized the various parties into coming together as nothing else could have done. Drawn together solely by their hostility against the party which had hounded them as though they were criminals, they were able to offer the voter an all-but-unrefusable alternative to their present state of slavery: freedom.

They called their alliance the Janata Party.

And the people of India, who had accepted the insults and injuries of the Emergency with lamblike meekness, now seemed resolved to demonstrate that the vengeance of sheep is a terrible thing. They did what neither Mrs Gandhi nor any of the leaders of the opposition had believed they were capable of doing: they turned upon the Congress in their multitudes and routed it at the polls.

What they did in my own state, Madhya Pradesh, was a fair

sample of what they did in the rest of the country. Out of a total of forty parliamentary seats, the Janata won thirty-eight and the Congress just one, and one seat went to an independent who, of course, was Bhaiya. And even he, a Scindia seeking the support of those who had been his father's subjects, had found the going so tough that he had come to me to support his candidature. I did not deny him that declaration.

Meanwhile, Yesho had been married. Her husband's family, the Bhansalis, had planned to give their wedding reception in Bombay on 20 March, which was also the day on which the election results were going to be announced.

By the time the guests began to arrive, it was becoming clear that the Janata Party was winning. People were celebrating in the streets and each victory was the cause for a fresh burst of fire-crackers. The party was still in full swing when we heard on the BBC that Mrs Gandhi herself had been defeated at the polls by the very man who had driven her to declare the Emergency, Raj Narain.

How could a party given on such an evening, when freedom had returned to India, be confined to the plans that the hosts had made for it? Somewhere along the line it took off on its own and burgeoned into what the society papers were later to describe as the most memorable wedding reception of the year.

With such blissful auguries to set it off on its course, Yesho's marriage has been a singularly happy one. Whatever reservations I might have entertained about Siddharth's eligibility melted soon after I met him and have long since become the subject of jokes between us. They live almost at the other end of the world from me, in New Orleans in America, where he, still in his early thirties, is one of the city's most successful cardiac surgeons. His speciality, a process called angioplasty, is believed to be far more effective than bypass surgery and much safer.

*   *   *

The next morning, a tearful Mrs Gandhi took steps to call off the Emergency. This, from someone so steeped in political gamesmanship, was an astoundingly artless move, for it gave proof, if proof were needed, that the whole edifice had been a device for clinging on to power. If there had been a genuine need for its imposition, how had that need now ended by Mrs Gandhi being thrown out of office? In other words, the very same thing that had provided Mrs Gandhi with the excuse for declaring the Emergency had somehow become the reason for its ending. Or again was she, as many people believed, worried that the instrument might be used against her and she herself bundled off to Tihar without much further ado?

The Janata Party, that hotch-potch of divers and mutually hostile elements which had come together merely for the purpose of the election, suddenly and much to its own astonishment found itself pitched into the driver's seat. I suppose only an incurable optimist would have gambled on its lasting out its full five-year term in office, for there was little to hold its super-stars together except the desire for office. That the show lasted even as long as it did, for nearly three years, was something of a miracle. If its rule was not the *ramjajya* or Utopia that those who had voted it into office had hoped for, it was certainly far far better than what they had experienced over any equal period since the advent of freedom. No government, however inefficient, could ever be as oppressive as Mrs Gandhi's during the Emergency, and few as bad as the increasingly monolithic rule she had practised before it. In contrast, this was a period of authority exercised with restraint and sobriety, of neither excesses nor acts of vengeful retaliation; even Mrs Gandhi, her son and the principal whip-wielders, for example, were not summarily flung into the now emptied jails. For the first two years it was an era of plenty. Prices dropped dramatically with the relaxation of controls that had crippled the economy, and the shops were full of consumer goods.

If Janata rule achieved anything, it restored sanity and sanctity to the legislative processes by removing the most pernicious of the provisions that had been grafted on to the constitution for the express purpose of making the Emergency analogous with unvarnished dictatorship. But they never formed a team. Their short and tempestuous tenure and their inglorious exit make a sad commentary on India's political maturity. One day they were conducting the affairs of the country with an unbeatable majority, and the very next they had collapsed like a house of cards in a breeze. In October 1979, the President called yet another parliamentary election.

*   *   *

The politics of the country had their miniature mirror-image in our own household.

I had taken no active part in the 1977 election, but had later been elected to the Rajyasahha by accepting a seat in that house which was in the gift of the Janata Party. My son, on the other hand, was somewhat in the doldrums. Having found, much to his chagrin, that he had backed the losing side, he was trying to retrace his steps, and this had put his hard-won friendship with Mrs Gandhi and Sanjay Gandhi in jeopardy. Now having realized how unpopular the Janata combine had become, he was once again trying desperately to prove himself a staunch Congress man.

I heard it announced in the course of a television news bulletin that I was going to oppose Mrs Gandhi in her constituency of Rae Barrielly.

I myself was surprized and dismayed. I tackled my party's President about the announcement, but he blandly assured me that it was merely an idea mooted by some of his colleagues. But obviously the idea had caught fire and revived sagging morale, and in its flare the Janata leaders saw me as the one person who just might be able to defeat Mrs Gandhi.

Almost certainly I could have done so in Gwalior, but not in Rae Barrielly, which was her home ground, as it had been her husband's before her, a constituency that between them they had nursed assiduously for more than twenty years.

I tried to reason with my party colleagues that they had made a blunder in taking me away from the place where I could have been useful and putting me against Mrs Gandhi in her own stronghold. But I could see that it was already too late for them to back down. The announcement had received the widest publicity, and for me to have refused to go along with it would have been to let my colleagues down with a resounding thump. I did not feel all that diffident about winning either, and was gratified to see that my being her opponent in Rae Barrielly must have caused a certain amount of worry in Mrs

Gandhi's camp, for she promptly announced that she was going to contest the elections from another constituency as well.

Bhaiya was horrified. It transpired that I had made him lose face and sabotaged his best-laid plans. He had decided to join the Congress, and indeed was anxious to be accepted into its inner circle. How could they go on counting him among the faithful now?

We had one of those strained interviews at which the only course open to both parties is to agree to disagree. I told Bhaiya that although this was not a decision that I had made myself, I was not the sort of person to refuse a contest because it was going to be a difficult one, or because of the inherent risks; that the phenomenal publicity which the announcement had attracted had made the contest a prestige issue, and that there was no way of backing out of it without causing incalculable harm to the party. Then I appealed to him to accept that although we were now in opposite camps politically, it did not mean that we should become estranged too.

My son did not see it that way. His reversionist zeal, his eagerness to prove that his loyalty to the hierarchy was beyond question, and, I suspect, his fear of retribution, gave his attitude a narrowness that I found hard to accept. 'But, Amma, you leave me no choice!' he protested. 'As far as I am concerned, this is the parting of the ways for us.'

*   *   *

And so I became Mrs Gandhi's opponent in what was recognized as a crucial contest. Most of my relatives and friends were appalled at the sheer audacity of the confront-ation, particularly since, for the first time, I was contesting an election outside the old Gwalior territory, where even people who were presumed to be opposed to my politics still held me in respect. And this aspect was brought home to me in a singularly dramatic manner, by an incident that occurred when I was on my way to my new constituency to begin canvassing. Our convoy had reached the borders of our erstwhile domain when we all but ran into an ambush set up by a well-known gang of highwaymen from among the Chambal decoits.

The road went down to a bridge across a river. Bal Angre was driving the car, and his wife and I sat at the back. The 'follow' car, which I always have behind me on long journeys in case of breakdowns, was perhaps fifty yards away, and in it rode Jaisingh, one of my aides who also doubles as a bodyguard and invariably carries a revolver whenever he accompanies me. What we saw of the ambush was a couple of buses halted nose-to-nose on the slope beyond the bridge, with their passengers squatting all around in orderly groups. We all thought they were pilgrims who had made a halt for a meal near the river. Bal slowed down the car, and then saw in his rearview mirror that Jaisingh was waving frantically for him to drive on. Then just as Jaisingh was getting out of his car, we heard the crack of bullets and saw the spurts of dust around. One of the shots smashed the car's front window and a splinter of glass penetrated Jaisingh's arm. But within a minute or so the firing stopped, and we saw half a dozen khaki-clad men arising from behind the bushes and standing in full view, gesturing for us to go past. It was clear that they had recognized my convoy, for as we sped past they folded their hands to me in greetings. The next day their leader sent word to Bal Angre offering profuse apologies for having 'mistakenly' opened fire against me.

*   *   *

Wherever I went I was greeted with the sort of enthusiasm that I had been accustomed to nearer home, and my meetings were well attended. Not everyone who came to listen to my speech or greeted me lustily as my car passed was going to vote for me too, but the signs looked good.

Aside from Mrs Gandhi and myself, there were twenty-four other candidates in the field. This meant that the ballot paper, usually the size of the page of a book, had to be a scroll three feet long; it had to have all our names one below the other in addition to – for the illiterate voter – our symbols. But the worst part of such a multitude of candidates was the over-crowding in the polling booths, which are normally small government offices or school rooms. In them, aside from the polling officer and his four assistants, room had also to be found for two representatives of each candidate, which meant that each booth had nearly sixty people in it.

It was only on the actual polling day that I discovered that most of the nuisance-candidates had been put up to facilitate the process of what is known as 'booth-capturing'. Their agents in the booths revealed themselves as strong-arm men hired for the purpose of throwing out my two agents and intimidating the polling officials into making sure that all the ballot papers were transformed into votes for the Congress. I received as many as seventy reports of booths in the vicinity of Rae Barrielly being captured, and I am convinced that hundreds of others in outlying areas were similarly taken over. No one took the slightest notice of the complaints lodged by our supporters, and even frantic telephone calls to the Election Officer only brought out the stock answer: 'If you want to complain about electioneering malpractices, you have to file an election petition in a court of law.'

I knew before the counting of the votes began that I had lost; the booth-capturing had seen to that. But the results over the rest of the country too showed that the Janata had been trounced at the polls. It was as though the pendulum had swung back. In the backlash of disillusionment with the Janata, the same public that had turned against Mrs Gandhi with such ferocity now turned against the Janata. Mrs Gandhi's Congress Indira, which was no more than a splinter of the old Congress Party, was returned to power with an overwhelming majority.

After that, the several components which had formed the Janata party fell apart. My own party, the Janasangh, which had remained almost intact and had managed to hold its own in our traditional areas of influence, took on a new name and a new flag. We called it the Bharatiya Janata Party, or the Indian People's Party. For the past two years, I have been its elected Vice-President.

*   *   *

Being on the losing side was nothing strange to me ever since I had left the Congress fold, but this time there was a difference; it was the painful realization that the disagreement between myself and Bhaiya was taking on the aspects of a fully fledged feud.

In his brief and jittery career in politics, my son had unfortunately acquired the image of a fair-weather ally if not a rank opportunist. In the latter days of the Emergency he had recanted his earlier affiliations in a desperate bid to ingratiate himself with the Congress leadership. Then things had gone awry. The Congress went out of power and the Janata came in. During the Janata regime, he had sought to woo its high priests, and it was only on the eve of the 1980 elections that he had made yet another switch and jumped on the Congress bandwagon.

He was thus, for the first time, on the winning side; but the winning side had ceased to trust him, and was so invincibly entrenched that it did not need his support. He, for his part, was desperate to prove his dedication, and it seems clear that he believed that the best way of doing so was by increasingly spiteful demonstrations of hostility towards his mother who, after all, had committed the ultimate sin of daring to oppose the very fountainhead of power, Mrs Gandhi.

Bhaiya began to see less and less of me and his sisters, but initially we put it down to his need to prove that his loyalty to Mrs Gandhi was total. It was only when I noticed that he had stopped sending his children to see me on special occasions such as their birthdays, that I realized that he really wanted to distance himself from us.

And it really hurt, as it was meant to, for my son knew me well. It was I who did not know him, or at least did not know the person he had now become. And this was very sad, for it left me wholly unprepared for the shocks that were soon to follow. Not content with renouncing me, Bhaiya wanted to make sure that I was left in no doubt of his hostility. Its virulence, its perversity, stunned me.

In the summer of 1982 Bhaiya, who was now living in New Delhi in a government bungalow to which he had become entitled as an MP, was involved in a road accident and fractured his leg. The moment I was given the news, I rushed to the hospital and was the very first of his near relatives to arrive there. After that, for a whole month while the fractured leg healed, I cancelled all my engagements to remain in Delhi on call as it were, and never failed to see my son every morning and evening. During these visits, I noticed that my arrival seemed to reduce my son and those who habitually congregated around him to a strained silence, so that the conversation was restricted to banalities, as though the others were privy to some secret which I was prevented from discovering.

And then one day the meaning of this conspiratorial behaviour became horrifyingly clear: one of my son's most trusted aides filed a criminal complaint alleging that a number of antiques, valuable vases and statuary in my Gwalior house had been stolen from my son. Returning home from one of these visits to my son's bedside, Munoo, Bal's wife, told me that the police had raided my Gwalior house, seized the articles which had been pointed out by my son's agent as having been stolen, and arrested her husband. That Bal Angre should have been the principal accused in the case was just as extraordinary as the rationale behind the authorities taking notice of such a fatuous complaint. As a magazine article put it: 'All three cases are filed by Madhavrao and though none actually names the Rajmata, it is obvious who the target is.'

This was followed by a sustained campaign to ease me out of the management of trusts that I myself had formed with a view to saving for Bhaiya and his sisters some of the more valuable among our landed properties from being swallowed up by the state under the Urban Land Ceiling Act. If these trusts had not been formed, I doubt if we would still have been able to call these properties ours. Even my ownership of Jaivilas, which I had actually bought from my son, has been challenged and become the subject of a bitter legal wrangle.

But a blow-by-blow account of this unedifying family quarrel has no place in the story of my life. It has become for me a constant source of unhappiness and disillusionment, and for both of us an exercise in self-immolation. But if only to bring out the savagery to which it has descended, I wish to relate an incident which has a tangential relevance to the story of my life as it appears in this book.

My work schedule gets increasingly more crowded, so that being on overdrive has become a routine of my life. I seldom average five hours' sleep a night, and I am rarely in the same place for two nights running. It is only when I make my annual pilgrimage to Europe that I am able to slow down the pace a little, and when I arranged with Mr Manohar Malgonkar that he should collaborate with me in the writing of this book, I thought it best that we should discuss the project during my European holiday. Accordingly in August 1983, he, Bal Angre and I flew to London, expecting to be there for about four weeks.

The very next day Hiranvan was raided.

Hiranvan had been lying vacant for years and it broke my heart to see such a fine building consigned to slow decay. Then Bal Angre suggested what a wonderful residence it would make for Bhaiya's son when he came of age and married, and needed a place of his own. As it happened, Bhaiya's son, Jyotiraditya, was then a mere toddler, but we were all taken with the idea and proceeded to have the necessary additions and alterations made to convert Hiranvan into the *Jyotirayan*, the new name we had settled upon for the house as indicative of its intended role.

The house was ready for occupation in 1974, but since its intended occupant was then only seven and not likely to move into it for at least another decade, we decided that Bal's family should occupy it in the interim. Indeed, in order that there should be no ambiguity about the terms of its occupation, I had formal documents drawn up and rented it to Bal's daughter, Chitralekha.

Bal and his family moved into the house in 1974, and at this time Bhaiya was still very much a part of the family and fully aware of the background. Since then he and Bal had fallen out, and he seems to have convinced himself that it is Bal's influence on me that has given my political beliefs their rigidity. Anyhow, he has taken special trouble to subject Bal to a host of major harassments, such as getting members of his staff to file criminal complaints against him and his family.

That summer of 1983 Bal's son, Tulajirao, who had been a tea planter in Assam, had returned home, and he and Bal were living in Hiranvan. Both are passionate dog lovers, and the son doted on the magnificent pair of Rotweillers which Bal had specially imported from Germany. That day, when Bal had gone off with me and Mr Malgonkar to London, and his son and wife were in Delhi bidding us goodbye, the house was empty except for the Rotweillers and an old maid-servant who lived in it with her four-year-old granddaughter.

In broad daylight, on 13 August 1983, Hiranvan was raided. According to one account, 'The raid was carried out in the presence of (a detachment of) the police. The dogs were shot, the old maid servant driven out at gun-point and her four-year-old grandaughter thrown out.' Then, like vandals gone berserk, they set about smashing furniture, glassware and pictures, till some of the horrified onlookers compelled the authorities to step in. That was when government officials took over Hiranvan and put their own seals on it.

I heard of this outrage in London, and I could not hold back my tears. I caught the first available flight back, and all the way to New Delhi my thoughts kept shuttling between the two men of my family who bore a common name: Madhavrao. The first of them, a legend in his own lifetime, had been so rigid an observer of his private code of honour that he had once refused to open an attack on the fortress of Chittore because legend said it had been built by the Gods. At the other end of the long, long line my own son, biding his time till the occupants had left their house and bringing off his attack by throwing out a frail old woman and shooting down chained dogs.

I was stunned by this fall in the scale of values; on one side the hallowed tower of Chittore, on the other the spectre of murdered dogs. And suddenly, like an icy wind, I was conscious of a sadness and humiliation brought on by the debasement of something which I had treasured all my life as a shining talisman: my good name.

Postscript

FOR ME THE five years after Indira Gandhi's miraculous return to power were like an unceasing election campaign. My party was anxious to build up a country-wide following and to establish dominance in the two states which we regarded as our strongholds, Madhya Pradesh and Rajasthan, and I threw myself into this work with gusto. As time passed and the next parliamentary election drew near, we began to scent success. In the spring of 1984, we won a heartening number of by-elections in widely separate areas of the country, in Uttar Pradesh, Madhya Pradesh and Maharashtra. Their trend clearly showed that Mrs Gandhi's party was fast losing ground and that there was little prospect of its being returned to power.

The signs of panic in the Congress Indira hierarchy began to manifest themselves in a number of ways. It contrived to capture power in Assam by what was virtually a mock-election, an exercise carried out in conditions of martial law and by methods so undemocratic that the sober and influential news magazine *India Today* dismissed it as an 'angry emotional and violent' rejection by the people of the state. After that, the Congress Indira's efforts to overthrow the democratically-elected, smoothly-running governments of two states in the south, Karnataka and Andhra, brought it into further disrepute. In Karnataka, its agents went about trying to buy up opposition assembly members. One of these agents was careless enough to make his offer in the proximity of a concealed microphone. His offer was tape-recorded and the tape given the widest publicity. In Andhra its machinations verged on the sinister. Andhra's Chief Minister, Mr N. T. Rama Rao, popularly known as NTR, had to go to America for a heart-by-pass operation. This was the time they chose to strike. They brought pressure to bear on the pliant governor of the state to accord recognition to a group of defectors from NTR's party as the real government of the state. The success of the plot depended on its manipulators being able to persuade a few more adherents of NTR to renounce him before he recovered from his heart surgery and resumed active politics. The plot ended up as an ignominious fiasco, because NTR's remaining colleagues refused to defect, and it was the governor who had to resign in a hurry.

Almost overshadowing these nefarious happenings in the south was the daily-worsening problem of the Punjab, where the machinations of the Congress Indira had got out of hand and flared up into an outrageous demand by Sikh extremists for a virtually separate state.

After such a dismal record for its years in power, the stock of Mrs Gandhi's party had plummeted very low indeed by the autumn of 1984 and not even its most loyal supporters believed that it would be returned to power at the centre in the coming elections. As to the states, at least six of the major ones were expected to reject Congress Indira's rule, and my party, the BJP, confidently expected to form the government in Madhya Pradesh and Rajasthan.

Then came 31 October. Two Sikh fanatics who were members of her own bodyguard gunned down Mrs Gandhi at point-blank range. In the process, they also made a gift of the parliamentary election to the party that their victim had named after herself, the Congress Indira.

Before the day was over, the entire electorate had undergone a transformation. A shocked and frightened people had only one thought in their minds: to be counted among those who deplored the murder. No other issue was even remotely relevant. It was like a science fiction fantasy come true, with mysterious emanations affecting the nation's faculty of reasoning flowing out of radio and television sets permanently tuned to just one scene, one commentary. The shrewd, hard-headed inheritors of the Congress Indira power machine worked feverishly to turn Mrs Gandhi's cremation into an instrument of propaganda. Barely had the flames died down when they announced the dates for the next parliamentary election.

Predictably enough, they made a clean sweep. The Congress Indira was returned to power at the centre with a majority variously acclaimed as being 'unprecedented', 'staggering', 'overwhelming' . . . and rightly so. Out of a total of 508 seats, it won 401. The opposition was virtually wiped out.

Yet these figures don't tell the full story. The Congress may have collared nearly eighty per cent of the seats in the nation's parliament, but its nationwide vote was neither staggering nor overwhelming — it was just under fifty per cent. What, however, was both staggering and overwhelming to me and my colleagues was that in my own state, where we had expected the Congress to lose, it managed to pull in as much as fifty-seven per cent of the popular vote, seven per cent higher than the national average. It eroded our overall votes in the state to a mere thirty per cent.

And our thirty per cent failed to win us thirty per cent of the parliamentary seats. In fact we did not win a single seat; the Congress Indira walked off with all forty of them.

If it is a travesty of justice that fifty-seven per cent wins all the prizes within sight and thirty per cent not one of them, it is no more than a professional hazard that people in politics have to take in their stride; for this is a quirk in the electoral system itself that we have blindly adopted from England. What distorted events in 1984 was the timing of the election. It took place while the average voter was still numb with shock, and his involvement with Mrs Gandhi's cremation at its peak. A few weeks later, we would not have made quite such a disastrous showing, and this was demonstrated in the elections for some of the state legislatures that followed. In these our party sprang right back into the scene, winning nearly as many seats as we had held in the outgoing assemblies of both Madhya Pradesh and Rajasthan. I have no doubt whatsoever that if the elections had been delayed by a few more weeks, we would have made an even better showing.

*   *   *

But in neither state did we win power as we had hoped to, and I personally was deeply hurt by this outright rejection by the electorate. It was maddening to think that a couple of crazy men with guns had wiped out what so many of us had worked so hard for. Alone in my shrine in the pre-dawn silence, I was conscious of a mist covering my eyes as I tried to find the answers to these riddles and to recall words of wisdom to comfort me. Someone had written, in connection with the inhuman segregation laws of South Africa, 'There are more reasons than victory for fighting any decent battle,' and the precise message that had been dinned into me ever since I first became conscious of being a Hindu was: 'Work alone is thy right, not the rewards of work.'

But to me as an activist, to me as a woman, these abstractions were the consolations of the defeated. What I had dreamed of were the rewards. Rewards not for myself, however, for there is nothing I can conceivably want for myself that is not really within my means. What I had longed for was to bring about a reversal of the galloping deterioration that had become synonymous with India under Congress rule.

My gods knew that my dream for my people was modest enough: it was to be in a position to give as many of them as possible a chance to live a life free from basic wants such as food, shelter and clothes, with as few man-made deprivations as are practicable in a well-regulated society. And I would not have been human if I was not aware, in moments of introspection, that for all my concern, dedication and hard work, even this modest dream remained as distant as ever.

But then it is some consolation that I am at least spared the shame and guilt of those whom the people chose to lead them and who must now live among the ruins of their promises. I fold my hands in gratitude that it was not I who broke faith. The degradation of the slum-dwellers in Bombay, the plight of the Sikhs in Delhi and the Hindus in the Punjab are not things I helped to make. It is not I who have to tell the millions who live below the starvation line that they are neither poor nor hungry because I have managed to magic away their squalor with a fine-sounding slogan, or face the accusing stares of the long processions of widows whose menfolk were massacred in Delhi while the policemen looked on, or, above all, share the sin of transforming the fabled land of the five rivers into a land of hatred and terror.

The mist clears. The flames in the butter-lamps become brighter. The idols gleam. I get up from the *puja* feeling cleansed of doubts and uncertainties and ready for the day, knowing that outside tearful widows and half-alive children wait. True, I may not ever be able to do anything for them. But that does not mean I must not go on trying.

Index